Strategic Himalayas
Republican Nepal and External Powers

Strategic Himalayas

Republican Nepal and External Powers

NIHAR R. NAYAK

idsa
INSTITUTE FOR DEFENCE STUDIES & ANALYSES
NEW DELHI

PENTAGON PRESS

Strategic Himalayas: Republican Nepal and External Powers / *Nihar R. Nayak*

First Published in 2014

ISBN 978-81-8274-761-6

Published by
PENTAGON PRESS
206, Peacock Lane, Shahpur Jat,
New Delhi-110049
Phones: 011-64706243, 26491568
Telefax: 011-26490600
email: rajan@pentagonpress.in
website: www.pentagonpress.in

Branch:
Prime Arcade
Office #11
1154 Saifee Street
Opp. M.G.Road, Camp
Pune-411001
Email: pentagonpresspune@gmail.com

In association with
Institute for Defence Studies and Analyses
No. 1, Development Enclave,
New Delhi-110010
Phone: +91-11-26717983
Website: www.idsa.in

The cover shows Machapuchare (*Fish Tail* in Nepali) in the Annapurna range of the Himalayas located in north-central Nepal. The photograph was taken from Dhulikhel by Dr Ashok K. Behuria in November 2013.

Printed at Aegean Offset Printers, Greater Noida, U.P.

Dedicated

To my loving wife, Swetalina

Contents

Foreword

Articulating India's strategic interests in Nepal, Jawaharlal Nehru had stated in the Indian Parliament in December 1950: "From time immemorial, the Himalayas have provided us with a magnificent frontier....We cannot allow that barrier to be penetrated because it is also the principal barrier to India." Historically, India and Nepal have recognised their mutual security interests and acted closely with each other. The agreements that Nepal has had with British Indian authorities and also with independent India attest to this fact.

Nepal is well-known for its strategic location in the Himalayas. It is situated at the meeting point of East Asia and South Asia, and between two big and powerful countries—India and China—who have gone to war with each other in the past. During the cold war years, because of its proximity to both these countries, Nepal also attracted the attention of world powers. It borders the restive Tibetan region of China and has a significant number of refugees from Tibet. Because of its open borders with India, Nepal has been used as an easy access point for subversive forces working against Indian interests.

In spite of having a comprehensive agreement with India, Nepal has its own sense of insecurity vis-à-vis India. In the classic realist tradition, it has often used external powers to balance India to minimise its sense of insecurity. This has often led to mutual misunderstanding between India and Nepal.

It is natural for external powers—both because of its strategic relevance, and its susceptibilities—to develop an abiding interest in Nepal. Over the years, through developmental interventions as well as diplomatic engagements, extra-regional powers have assumed importance in Nepal's foreign policy. They have had influence on domestic politics as well.

Since 2006, internal political dynamics have changed significantly. Nepal has become a republic and is in the process of drafting its Constitution. However, internal power struggles and political differences have made it difficult for the country to finalise its Constitution and stabilise as a normal state. It is visited by chronic political instability which has made it further vulnerable to external manipulations. In this context, the present book by Dr Nihar R Nayak seeks to examine the role external powers play in Nepal's domestic and external policies, and assess its impact on India-Nepal relations.

The present study is based on information collected both from primary and secondary sources. Government documents, foreign policy reports, statements of senior leaders and interviews have been used as primary sources. Secondary research inputs involve constant monitoring of day-to-day developments and events from open sources, viz. books, research articles, commentaries in the print and electronic media and reports of private research institutes. Dr Nayak's views are also informed by close interactions with a wide cross section of people during his fieldtrips to Nepal.

So far, limited work has been done to analyse and understand the role of external powers, as well as their influence on Nepalese politics and foreign policy, especially in post-monarchy period. Therefore, the attempt made in the book to understand the strategic interests of China, the US, India, the EU & major European countries and Pakistan is certainly welcome. I hope, this comprehensive study by Dr Nayak will add to overall understanding of the internal and external political dynamics of Nepal.

New Delhi

Dr Arvind Gupta
Director General, IDSA

Acknowledgements

This book would not have been completed without constant support and encouragement of well wishers. I am deeply indebted to many people, who supported me during the various stages of the writing of this book.

First and foremost, I am deeply grateful to Dr Arvind Gupta, Director General, Institute for Defence Studies and Analyses (IDSA), for his constant encouragement and support in bringing out this volume. He very generously extended the deadlines whenever I approached him. Without his personal interest and support, this book could not have been completed. I would also like to express my sincere thanks to Brigadier (Retd) Rumel Dahiya, Deputy Director General, IDSA, for his help in bringing this volume in time. I thank Prof. S.D. Muni, Visiting Research Professor at the Institute of South Asian Studies, National University of Singapore, for his selfless guidance in the formative stages.

The book would not have seen the light of day without the constant supervision and support of Dr Ashok K. Behuria, Coordinator, South Asia Centre, IDSA, and Dr Smruti S. Pattanaik, both of whom painstakingly edited the initial draft and offered valuable suggestions on it.

Mr Post Bahadur Basnet, Visiting Fellow at IDSA (March-November 2013) also offered valuable suggestions during various stages of the writing of the book.

My colleagues in the South Asia Centre and Vivek Kaushik, Associate Editor, IDSA, deserve thanks for their timely and valuable support. I would like to express my special gratitude to all the scholars, policymakers and journalists, who shared valuable insights with me during my interactions with them, and helped me in formulating my thoughts and ideas.

My deepest appreciation to Prof. Lok Raj Baral, Prof. Bishwambher Pyakuryal, Ambassador Dinesh Bhattarai, Trailokyaa Aryal, Josy Joseph, Dr Nishchalnath Pandey, Prashant Jha, Dr Uddhab Pyakurel, Akanshya Shah, Mahesh Acharya, Pramod Jaiswal and the anonymous referees for their valuable comments and suggestions. I must thank Shri Rajan Arya of Pentagon Press and his staff for their support in publishing the volume.

A special note of thanks to IDSA library staff and the many others who have contributed to this volume at various levels.

It would be unfair not to acknowledge the sacrifice and support extended by my wife Swetalina (Jolly) and daughter Jenny during the writing of this book.

I hope this volume will benefit all stakeholders and will provoke a healthy debate on the role of external forces in ensuring peace and stability in Nepal. Any oversights in the book are mine.

Nihar R. Nayak

List of Tables and Figures

List of Abbreviations

ACFIC	All-China Federation of Industry and Commerce
ADB	Asian Development Bank
AF	Air Force
APECF	Asia Pacific Exchange and Cooperation Foundation
APF	Armed Police Force
BIMSTEC	Bay of Bengal Initiative for Multi-Sectoral Technical and Economic Cooperation
BIPPA	Bilateral Investment Promotion and Protection Agreement
BOG	Basic Operating Guidelines
CA	Constituent Assembly
CCOMPOSA	Coordination Committee of Maoist Parties and Organisations of South Asia
CDO	Chief District Officer
CDP	Commission on Disappeared Persons
CHD	Centre for Humanitarian Dialogue
CIA	Central Intelligence Agency
CIAA	Commission for Investigation of Abuse of Authority
CIDP	Commission on Investigation of Disappeared Persons
CPA	Comprehensive Peace Agreement
CPC	Communist Party of China
CPN-UML	Communist Party of Nepal (Unified Marxist Leninist)
CRS	Congressional Research Service
CTGC	China Three Gorges Corporation
DFID	Department for International Development
EC	European Commission
ECAFE	Economic Commission for Asia and the Far East
EIDHR	European Instrument for Democracy and Human Rights
EP	European Parliament

EXIM	Export-Import Bank of China
FDI	Foreign Direct Investment
FICCI	Federation of Indian Chambers of Commerce and Industry
FMF	Foreign Military Financing
FNCCI	Federation of Nepalese Chambers of Commerce and Industry
FOSS	Forum of Small States
FTA	Free Trade Agreement
GEFONT	General Federation of Nepalese Trade Unions
GMR	Grandhi Mallikarjun Rao (Bangalore headquartered infrastructural company)
GNP	Gross National Product
GTZ	German Organisation for Technical Cooperation (GTZ)
HLPC	High Level Political Committee
ICBM	Inter-Continental Ballistic Missiles
ICWA	Indian Council for World Affairs
IM	Indian Mujahideen
IMET	International Military Education and Training
IMF	International Monetary Fund
INGO	International Non-Governmental Organisation
INR	Indian Rupee
ISI	Inter-Services Intelligence
ITC	Imperial Tobacco Company of India (Kolkata headquartered company)
ITEC	Indian Technical and Economic Co-operation
JEC	Joint Economic Commission
JKLF	Jammu Kashmir Liberation Front
JTMM	Janatantrik Terai Mukti Morcha
LCCI	Lahore Chamber of Commerce and Industry
LDC	Least Developed Countries
LeT	Lashkar-e-Taiba
LLDC	Landlocked Developing Countries
MCC	Millennium Challenge Corporation
MCC	Maoist Communist Centre
MoU	Memorandum of Understanding
MPRF	Madhesi People's Rights Forum
MRP	Machine-readable Passport

MW	megawatt
NA	Nepalese Army
NAM	Non-Aligned Movement
NC	Nepali Congress
NCDR	Nepal Council for Development Research
NCHFS	Nepal China Himalayan Friendship Society
NDC	National Defence Course
NDFB	National Democratic Front of Boroland
NMSP	National Madhes Socialist Party
NPTF	Nepal Peace Trust Fund
NPR	Nepalese Rupee
ODA	Official Development Assistance
OHCHR	Office of the High Commissioner for Human Rights
PIA	Pakistan International Airlines
PoK	Pakistan occupied Kashmir
PW	People's War
RMB	Renminbi (Chinese currency)
RNA	Royal Nepal Army
RoO	Rules of Origin
RPP	Rashtriya Prajatantra Party
SAARC	South Asian Association for Regional Cooperation
SPA	Seven Party Alliance
TAR	Tibet Autonomous Region
TEL	Terrorist Exclusion List
TIFA	Trade and Investment Framework Agreement
TRC	Truth and Reconciliation Commission
UCPN(Maoist)	Unified Communist Party of Nepal (Maoist)
ULFA	United Liberation Front of Asom
UN	United Nations
UNCTAD	United Nations Conference on Trade and Development
UNMIN	United Nations Mission in Nepal
UNPFN	United Nations Peace Fund for Nepal
UPA	United Progressive Alliance
USAID	United States Agency for International Development
WTO	World Trade Organisation
ZoP	Zone of Peace

CHAPTER 1

Introduction

International relations are driven by the politics of powerful[1] nations who perennially strive to maximise their power to achieve their national interests. Power maximisation involves a combination of economic growth, military modernisation and diplomacy. During periods of momentous change, it is often noticed that the status-quoist powers try to prevent others from advancing to a higher level while aspiring powers seek to counter these efforts with all the resources at their disposal. Ever since the end of the Cold War, the world has been passing through a period of power transition and the centre of gravity of international politics has shifted to Asia because of the economic and military prowess of the two aspiring powers—China and India. In this context, the US, as a status quo power, is perceived to be pursuing a twin policy of diplomacy of cooperation and containment to deal with them. China and India, on the other hand, given their geographic constraints, have been trying to sustain their rise by developing cooperative and friendly relations with their neighbours, as well as cooperating with each other at the global level. But as they are located in the same region, there is also competition between the two for resources and strategic influence.

This race for power maximisation among nations has implications for the world in general and the Himalayan states—Nepal and Bhutan—in particular, as they are situated at the meeting point of East Asia and South Asia. The Himalayas have long been a natural barrier between the two great Asian civilizations—Indian and Chinese. Both the civilizations have treated it as their protector against external and mutual threats. However, the myth of Himalayas as the natural protector proved wrong when China and India fought a war in October 1962. The invention and application of modern technology brought about a new but peculiar scenario that led to significant change in the nature of warfare. And thus the concept of security was redefined with the changing needs and demands of global politics.

Following the success of anti-colonial movement in China and independence of India, the Himalayan region drew the attention of major powers from other continent(s), who were involved in ideological rivalry. This caused concern for both China and India. Given their geographical proximity, both the countries integrated their part/portion of the Himalayas as their natural frontier. This resulted in competition for extension of influence in the proximate neighbourhoods for strategic advantage. Even after 60 years, both the countries while looking for solutions on the disputed borders, make unilateral claims on certain parts as their exclusive zone of influence. A sense of competition and mutual suspicion has intensified further to control the Himalayan water due to rapid urbanisation and industrialisation in both the countries and military infrastructure developments in Tibet. Since India is the only major power located in the south of Tibet, it can be implied that the military build-up in Tibet is possibly targeted at India.

In addition, the Himalayas are strategically important for countries like Nepal and Bhutan. These small states act as partial geographical buffers between India and China separated by hundreds of miles and they are also more dependent on their southern neighbour—India—for easy access to sea for trade with other countries. Between these two states, Nepal has attracted the greater attention of the external powers.[2] Historically, Nepal has remained a strategic location for big powers since the Cold War. It has also always figured prominently in the regional power politics centered around the Himalayan region. In return, Nepal took advantage of major/external powers' presence on its territory to counter balance the influences of its two neighbours and also to secure its territorial integrity. Despite that Nepal's foreign policy has mostly focused on maintaining balance between its two bigger neighbours.

From the Nepalese standpoint, engaging both China and the US is important because it can counter-balance India's influence in Nepal. Both are permanent members of the United Nations (UN). Being a small state, Nepal believes that these two countries can preserve and protect Nepalese interests (sovereignty and territorial integrity) in case of any external intervention, by exerting pressure through the UN. In case of any aggression from India, which Nepal has occasionally and indirectly hinted as a possibility, these countries can support Nepal in the UN and other international forums. The fact of the matter for Nepal is that the perception of India's aggression and territorial ambition was fostered by the monarchy to ensure its survival in the face of the pro-democracy movement. The Nepalese believe that China could be a much more powerful and influential neighbour than India. The periodic US references, especially in the initial years of the Obama administration, to that effect, have further enhanced its value in Nepal. Both countries supported the Nepalese establishment in its fight against the Maoist insurgents. Despite this, the Maoists still view China as a benign power that does not interfere in the internal affairs of Nepal. The Nepalese elites believe that the presence of China makes their economy more competitive and reduces the country's dependence on India. Referring to the West Seti project which was allotted to China, some Nepalese officials argue that "[t]here are Indian companies and individuals [who] control [projects of] around 10,000 MW directly or indirectly, and the cost of opportunities and deadlines missed has been huge for Nepal".[3] In reality, Nepal has been responsible for these projects not being able to take off.

As regards the US; it has never been a direct threat to Nepal, but Nepal expects it not to pressurise Kathmandu over the Tibet issue. Ever since the beginning of diplomatic relations between Nepal and the US, the latter has been mostly considered as protector of the former in case of any kind of military threat and political interference from China and India. The Nepalese elites are aware that the US will never be able to ignore Nepal because of the China and India factors. China also cannot neglect Nepal as long as the Tibet issue and its border disputes with India are alive.

From India's point of view, given the topographical similarities and contiguity, Nepal is part of its northern security system. It feels vulnerable in case of external powers presence on Nepalese territory beyond the normal diplomatic activity. It, therefore, expects Nepal to remain sensitive to its security concerns. This expectation of India has been misinterpreted in Nepal as an attack on Nepal's sovereignty and independence. On the other hand, Nepal understands that India could take care of both its economic development and security concerns more effectively than any other country. This feeling of interdependency has been reflected in the 1950 Treaty and also during official visits. The Treaty worked as deterrent to Chinese territorial interests in the Himalayan region. Despite historical and strong people-to-people contacts, open border and the Treaty(ies), the insecurity of Nepal against India continues. This sense of insecurity on many occasions has been responsible for uncomfortable bilateral relations between both the countries.

In the post-Cold War period, Nepal attracted the attention of the US because of the rise of the Maoist[4] movement since 1996, and the rise of China and India as economic powers. In 2001, the Maoists came on the US radar of the 'Global War on Terrorism'. Despite being aware that the Maoists did not pose any global threat and they could not harm US interests beyond Nepal, the US sought to firm up its presence in Nepal by extending military and technical support.[5] The US presence was viewed with relative discomfort by China—and also to some extent by India. However, China did not react to it openly, perhaps because it was confident that the US presence would not affect its strategic interests in Tibet, so long as the monarchy, with its express commitment to 'one-China policy', was well-entrenched in Nepal. China also perhaps left it to India to countervail the US influence in the southern Himalayan region because India considered it to be its natural sphere of influence and wanted no external interference there. This was acknowledged by China during Rajiv Gandhi's visit to Beijing in 1988 when India positively responded Tibet Autonomous Region (TAR) as part of China.[6]

However, this understanding between India and China was to some extent shaken by Chinese misapprehensions that followed India's negotiations with the US on the civil nuclear deal and India's bid in 2005 to support the demand of the democratic forces and the Maoists for a republican setup in Nepal, which eventually led to the popular uprising against the monarchy in 2006. India was also instrumental in bringing the seven political parties and the Maoists together. China viewed the US-India civil nuclear deal with suspicion and regarded it as a strategy to contain China. While earlier China had expected India to contain any external influence in Nepal, in the changed circumstances, it viewed the increased US presence in Nepal with suspicion, which added to its concerns about Tibet. Consequently, while the US and India refused to supply arms and ammunition to the then Royal Nepal Army (RNA)—now known as the Nepalese Army (NA) under the Army Act, 2006—after the king took over in February 2005, China continued to oblige the royal administration. Interestingly, the king also requested Pakistan for arms and ammunition and the latter assured him of support. Such bonhomie continued when both Nepal and Pakistan played a major role in inviting China to be an observer at the South Asian Association for Regional Cooperation (SAARC) summit at Dhaka in 2005, perhaps as a response to India's move to bring in Afghanistan as a member. This triangular alliance—Nepal, Pakistan and China —in India's backyard made India quite uncomfortable given its open border with Nepal.

India's decision to invite the US as an observer in the SAARC after the 2005 Dhaka SAARC summit may have further fuelled the Chinese anxieties over a possible strategic relationship developing between India and the US vis-à-vis China. In view of the changing relationship between the US and India since 2000, the US, to some extent, supported India's Nepal policy, although scholars differ on this issue. However, by 2005 differences between the two arose over India's decision to engage with the Maoists who had sent feelers for joining the mainstream politics by then. The US took an independent view on the situation rather than following India's policy towards Nepal.[7] This was further confirmed when President Obama during his visit to Beijing in November 2009 remarked that China should play a greater role in resolving disputes in South Asia.[8] Although some believe that the remark was made in the context of India and Pakistan, Scott H. DeLisi, the then US Ambassador to Nepal, while deposing before the Senate Foreign Relations Subcommittee, echoed Obama's views in the Nepal-China context.[9]

The post-conflict political transition in Nepal coincided with large-scale anti-China protests between March and August 2008 by Tibetan refugees living in Nepal—the most organised demonstrations in the past 50 years. In 2008 Tibetan separatists in fact tried to cross the border into the TAR to disrupt the journey of the Olympic torch to the Mount Everest and the summer Olympic Games in Beijing. This forced China to redraft its Nepal policy that year. Several reasons might have contributed for this shift in the Chinese policy. For China, Nepal is important because of its strategic location and the presence of a large number of Tibetan refugees; there is also a fear that these anti-China elements may take advantage of the prolonged instability in that country. Since Nepal is a major transit point for the Tibetans coming to India, China's particular concern is its (Nepal's) open border with India and the Tibetan refugees living in Dharamshala in India. The abolition of monarchy, which was the most reliable ally of China in Nepal over time, may have increased China's anxieties. Therefore, China considered it necessary to re-affirm its presence in Nepal to secure its interests, which, it felt, were threatened because of its encirclement by the big powers. From the Chinese point of view, both Tibet and Nepal are part of its integrated 'peripheral policy'. Because of its geographical location and as a minority area, the TAR has remained a vulnerable periphery for China since the Qing dynasty. Therefore, "China's Tibet policy is essentially driven by strategic considerations and periphery security."[10] Nepal's northern border being an easy gateway to TAR, increases China's worries that political instability in Nepal could lead to enhanced anti-China activities in Nepal. This also increases the possibility of the Tibetan separatists entering the TAR using Nepal's northern border. Moreover, the restoration of Parliament in June 2006 with a Nepali Congress-led interim government and the electoral victory of the CPN (Maoist) in April 2008 were other influencing factors for the change. China adopted a wait and watch policy towards political developments in Nepal and Beijing sent a number of delegations to Kathmandu to assess the situation and discuss matters of mutual concern.[11] Subsequently, by end of 2008 it revised its position in favour of a more pragmatic stand towards the Maoists.

There is a perception in Nepal that the delay in the peace and Constitution-making process in that country has both external and internal implications. Nepal being a Landlocked Developing Country (LLDC) with endemic poverty and a fragile political system, the donor countries can influence major political decisions. The political transition in Nepal since the Jana Andolan-II (People's Movement) in 2006 has increased the presence of external forces in Nepal given the strategic location of that country. While there may be a perception that the two big neighbours of Nepal—India and China—are only interested in addressing their strategic concerns, Western countries' interests in Nepal are also dominated by both humanitarian and strategic issues. Therefore, increasing external interventions and conflicting political interests of international community in Nepal have further exacerbated the prevailing uncertainty in the country.

The implications of this power play are already visible in Nepal; more will become apparent in the future, given the divergent interests of these powers. There has been political instability in Nepal since 2008. The Nepalese leadership, which has primarily been preoccupied with the peace process and Constitution drafting since 2006, has sought to maintain a balance between its two immediate neighbours and the US. On the other hand however, its internal political processes have been influenced by these external powers. For example, negotiations between the Maoists and the major political parties were delayed due to US reservations.[12] Similarly; India's concerns about integration of the Maoist combatants too delayed the process of reconciliation in Nepal. Moreover, the debate on federalism which delayed the Constitution-drafting process (2008-2013) was considerably impacted by China's reservations regarding the issue of ethnicity-based federalism. It is well-known that China did not support the demand for the formation of a Sherpa autonomous province and the Jadan province in Nepal. China apprehended that ethnicity-based federalism would provide space for the Western forces to instigate Tibetan nationalism against Chinese interests in Nepal.[13]

Despite some remarkable improvement in Indo-US relations since 2000, both countries still differ in their approaches to Nepal. Those differences surfaced in 2005 when India wanted to mainstream the Maoists and again over the continuation of the United Nations Mission in Nepal (UNMIN) after completion of the 2008 Constituent Assembly (CA) elections and formation of the Special Committee for supervision, integration and rehabilitation of the Maoist combatants in 2010. The US later softened its position, perhaps, because of the better strategic understanding between India and the US over the region and the world. The Indo-US strategic cooperation reached its zenith with signing of the civil nuclear agreement in 2008. Both the countries further enhanced their cooperation by agreeing on an annual strategic dialogue from July 2009. But in case of Nepal, even after removing the Maoists from the terrorist list, the US continues to be wary of them. It also feels marginalised because of unilateral initiatives in the conflict resolution and Constitution-drafting processes by India, especially after the UNMIN's departure from Nepal. There are perceptions in India that the US-led Western donors' support to the *Janajatis* on single ethnicity-based federalism might have been responsible for the dissolution of the first CA without framing a new Constitution. Moreover, responding to some Nepalese perceptions about US dependence on India for its Nepal policy, the then US Ambassador to Kathmandu, Scott H. DeLisi clarified that United States does not view its policy on Nepal through India's prism. Its policy is determined by national interest.[14] Therefore, the US reluctance to acknowledge India as an influential player in Nepal and its efforts to play a leadership role in the sub-Himalayan region could hamper policy coordination between the two countries on Nepal in the future.

Historically, India played major role in political transitions in Nepal. In all those changes, India had adhered to 'two pillar' theory which to some extent did not make other major powers insecure. But the differences between India, China and the US widened in 2006 as India restored democracy in Nepal by bringing the Maoists on board. The differences between these major powers on some global issues had an impact in this region too. This policy shift of India made China uncomfortable due to the abolition of monarchy and the US for mainstreaming the Maoists. This also brought divisions amongst Indian policy makers. There was a dominant section in the Indian establishment that considered the monarchy as being a stable political power centre. As a result, India continued its official twin pillar policy of multi-party democracy and constitutional monarchy until the restoration of Parliament by King Gyanendra on 24 April 2006. Even after prolonged negotiations the king did not accept the legitimacy of the constitutional and agreed to transfer power back to the elected government, as a result, India was forced to change track.[15] However, there are some in India who argue that the monarchy had neglected India's security concerns emanating from across the border on several occasions in the past. Earlier, Nepal also tried to undermine the alleged India's leverage when the then King Birendra declared Nepal as a

Zone of Peace (ZoP). His successor King Gyanendra purchased weapons from China and Pakistan, proposed China candidature as an observer member of SAARC, played the 'China card' against India and last, but not the least, turned a blind eye to active operations of the Inter-Services Intelligence (ISI), Pakistan's external intelligence agency, operations in Nepal. Nepal's apathy towards India's obvious security concerns changed its view towards monarchy. At the same time political parties remained divided and that made king powerful. Rather than resolving the crisis through negotiation; king's strong hand tactics exacerbated the political crisis in Nepal and resulted in widespread violence. Continuing violence threatened the stability of Nepal with whom India shared an open border. India facilitated the 12-point agreement between the Maoists and the Seven-Party Alliance (SPA) in November 2005. An interim constitution was agreed and the Maoists came to power after the Constituent Assembly elections and among the first things they did was the abolition of constitutional monarchy. In absence of monarchy and shifting of power center to political parties, major powers also developed their constituency within the parties. That brought dilution in India's sphere of influence. India's further shift in its foreign policy towards Nepal from active support to the democratic transitions (until 2008) to encouraging indigenous approach of generating consensus to draft a new Constitution created space for other countries to have major say in the domestic politics of Nepal.

Significance of the Study

This book was conceptualised when there was an intense debate among Nepalese scholars regarding both the internal and external factors responsible for the political instability since 2006. Most recent studies on major-power engagements in South Asia have generally focused on India-Pakistan-China relations and have neglected the external power dynamics in other South Asian nations. There is no in-depth scholarly work so far which seeks to analyse strategic interactions of external powers in Nepal and their impact on Nepalese politics and the region. This study seeks to fill the gap and analyse the nature of Indian, Chinese, the US, the EU[16] and European countries (the UK, Norway, Switzerland and Germany-hereinafter referred to as 'major European countries'), and Pakistani presence in Nepal, and its impact on the region. Even if Pakistan does not measure up as a major power, its strategic competition with India in the region and its partnership with China make it a significant player in the regional power politics. The external powers have been selected keeping in view the nature and intensity of engagement, influence and interests in Nepal.

The study also analyses Nepal's foreign policy towards these powers. It traces the involvement of India, China, the US, the major European countries and Pakistan in Nepal since 2006; the interests of external powers in Nepal and their stakes in its political transformation. It seeks to answer the following questions: Is Nepal going to face a new round of strategic competition in the Himalayas? Does the policy of equidistance reintroduced by the Maoist government (2008-09) impact China's Nepal policy in any manner? What will be China's policy towards the radical faction within the Maoists in Nepal? Has there been any visible change in China's relationship with Nepal after the abolition of the monarchy? Given the geographic barriers, can China play a decisive role in Nepal? Will the renewed Chinese interest in Nepal affect India's relationship with Nepal in the future? How does the US look at the political transition in Nepal? Does the US look at Nepal as a possible partner in its long-term strategy to tackle a rising China? What is the strategic relevance of Nepal for major European countries? Do major European countries synchronise their Nepal policy with the US policy towards sub-Himalayan region? How will China and India manage their economic interdependence and strategic competition in the region? How will India balance the Chinese and US presence in Nepal? What is the role of Pakistan in Nepal in post-conflict period? Does Nepal figure in Pakistan's look east policy to counter-balance India's look west policy? How will Nepal deal with the competing strategies of the major powers—regional and extra-regional?

The topic was identified after a diligent monitoring of political developments in Nepal over a considerable length of time. The present study is based on information collected both from primary and secondary sources. Government documents, foreign policy reports, statements of senior leaders and interviews have been used as primary sources. Secondary research inputs have involved constant monitoring of day-to-day developments and events from open sources. Books, research articles, commentaries, reports of private research institutes and relevant websites have also been referred to.

Chapter 1 introduces the volume and lays down the broad parameters and the research questions, which the study has attempted to grapple with. The scope of the study is focused on the ever-increasing influence of the external powers in Nepal's contemporary politics. The study also emphasises that the role of the external power is not limited to politics alone but also has a bearing on the country's society and economy. The active involvement of the external powers in Nepal not only influences its domestic policy but also regional political dynamics as a whole.

Chapter 2 examines the relationship between small and big powers and analyses the foreign policy of Nepal and its approach to big powers. The chapter argues that Nepal took advantage of the strategic competition and mistrust between the big powers during the Cold War. In the post-Cold War era it has taken advantage of the communication gap between China and India. Nepal has striven to maintain an equal distance with the two countries, but it has not antagonised India, in the light of the geographic reality. Nepal managed this due to the fact that before 1990 the monarchy was the only power centre. In the 1990s political parties emerged as major players. But political fragmentation and rivalry between them led to frequent change of government and the monarchy retained its dominant status. After the decline of the monarchy, although the Maoists declared that they would continue with the policy of 'equidistance', their tactics have not succeeded so far. In the changing geopolitical situation, Nepal will avoid pitting regional powers against each other, and be considerate of their sensitivities rather than supporting the interests of any power in the region to the disadvantage of the other.

Chapter 3 focuses on Nepal-India relations in the post-monarchy period. Despite a century-old relationship, there have been many ups and downs due to several factors. Since 1955, the ruling elites of Nepal have adopted an anti-India posture because of various reasons—psychological, geographical, political, economic and social—apart from some other external factors. This Chapter analyses construction of anti-Indianism and the actors engaged in perpetuating such perception. Since the demise of the monarchy in 2006 and emergence of the CPN (Maoist) as the largest party in the CA elections in 2008 there has been a spike in anti-Indianism. The political instability and growing influence of major powers in Nepal is of concern to India.

Chapter 4 seeks to highlight the increased Chinese presence in Nepal and the shift in China's foreign policy with regard to its southern border. This shift coincides with political changes in Nepal, and the chapter tries to objectively assess these developments and their implications for the region. There are two schools of thought on the increasing Chinese presence in Nepal. One school believes that China's presence in Nepal is driven by Tibet issue. It wants to take care of its security concerns by deepening its economic engagements with Nepal. However, this economic engagement is not just happening with Nepal; rather this is a global phenomenon. Another school believes that China's Nepal policy is not limited to Tibet policy. It wants to neutralise India's influence by taking advantage of equidistance policy of the Maoists. That is why China has diversified its engagements from state level to people-to-people level. The chapter also attempts to identify and analyse new trends in China's policy towards Nepal with the overall objective of providing a comprehensive understanding of China's policy towards Nepal from 2006 onwards.

Chapter 5 examines the US interests in the region. Since 1950, US policy towards Nepal has been influenced by three factors—Nepal's strategic location; containment of the domino effect of Communist permeation in South Asia and emergence of China and India as economic and military powers. Most importantly, from the US point of view, Nepal could also be an ideal place to extend support to the Tibetan refugees. Washington also considers Nepal as the gateway between India and China and understands their influence in South Asia. While the first two factors dominated US foreign policy towards South Asia till the early 1970s, the last factor has dominated its Nepal policy since the late 1990s. However, the US reframed its Nepal policy in 2001 when the Maoist movement acquired greater influence in Nepal. Despite some improvement in Sino-US relations, the US still have sympathy towards the Tibetan refugees and wants Nepal to allow them free passage between Dharamshala and Tibet. The US presence, with its inclination to facilitate (if not enable) the Tibetan resistance, may force both the countries into a turf war in Nepal.

Chapter 6 deals about role of the EU and the major European countries in Nepal. It looks at their engagements with Nepal both at bilateral level and at the EU level. Like the US and other big powers, some European countries strategic interests in the region are influenced by the US policy towards South Asia and other global issues. Although EU members are collectively engaged in community development, governance and peace building, some member-countries had supplied arms and ammunition to the monarchy to fight the Maoist insurgency. There has been a perception in Nepal that the demand of ethnicity-based federalism was promoted by some EU member countries.

Chapter 7 discusses Pakistan's relationship with Nepal. From Pakistan's point of view, Nepal is strategically an important country because of its location, widespread anti-India sentiment and the sense of insecurity prevalent within the country. Despite remaining economically fragile and politically unstable, Pakistan has been consistently providing development assistance to Nepal. An inventory of Pakistan's sector-wise annual aid assistance to Nepal indicates that it was more focused on the Nepalese districts that border India. Pakistan took advantage of an open border between Nepal and India and used Nepalese territory as a launching pad for ISI activities against India. A conflict-ridden and politically unstable Nepal suits Pakistan's interests in the region. In the absence of a democratically elected government and strong public order, the ISI would get a free hand to execute its anti-India propaganda.

Chapter 8 concludes that other major powers, including China, have taken advantage of the Nepalese elites' strained relationship with India. The elites seem to believe that the presence of extra-regional powers will help them to neutralise India's influence. In the post-monarchy period, some Maoist leaders tried to play the China card against India. They were unsuccessful in their efforts, perhaps because of improvement in bilateral relations between India and China. Despite that, Nepal has the potential to take advantage of the relations between the two neighbours given their security concerns in the region. On the other hand, it remains a challenge for Nepal to maintain a balance in its approach towards both the countries. Further, given the geopolitical reality and rapid changes in regional and global politics, Nepal's first option of playing the 'US card' against regional powers and its second option of using the China card against India and vice versa, may not have proven to be as effective as it was earlier. The growing Chinese influence in Nepal might gradually convert Nepal's China card into 'Nepal card' for China and the new political forces/actors in Nepal would try to rebalance India by taking China into cognizance south of the Himalayas. The study also finds that despite the growing influence of China and others in Nepal, geography might still determine the nature of external power presence and their role in that country.

There are few research studies done on the engagement of external powers with Nepal during major political transitions since 2006. The book focuses on this aspect and briefly deals with pre-2006 political developments and the role of external powers in Nepal. Therefore, primary and secondary data in this particular period is scarce. However, due care was taken to collect reliable data from official sources (statements, publications, reports etc.) as well as analyses and reports in the media.

*

NOTES

1. A country has the ability to influence world politics substantially because of its geography, population, strong economy and military capacity. Although many sovereign countries meet these criteria, this study discusses only the role of India, China, the US, major European countries and Pakistan because of their greater involvement in this part of the world.
2. Among the external powers, the US, China, India, the UK and Germany are considered

as 'major powers' present in Nepal. Given their influence in international politics, economy and strategic issues, the book has dealt extensively on the objectives and role in Nepal. Terms like 'external powers', 'major powers' and 'big powers' are used interchangeably. In this study, these major powers are treated as external forces for Nepal. Since Nepal is situated in South Asia, other than India, these powers are also referred to as 'extra-regional powers'. It may also be noted that geographically, China is a neighbour of Nepal; however, it is categorised as an 'extra-regional power', because it is not part of the South Asian region.

3. Yubaraj Ghimire, "Big Power Deal Gives Chinese a Foothold in Nepal", *Straits Times Indonesia*, 10 March 2012, at http://www.thejakartaglobe.com/economy/big-power-deal-gives-chinese-a-foothold-in-nepal/503811 (accessed on 2 July 2013).
4. The Communist Party of Nepal (Maoist), hereinafter referred to as 'CPN (Maoist)', merged with the Communist Party of Nepal (Unity Centre-Masal) on 12 January 2009, to form the Unified Communist Party of Nepal (Maoist), hereinafter referred to as 'UCPN (Maoist)'. The UCPN (Maoist) witnessed a vertical split on 18 June 2012 which led to the formation of the Communist Party of Nepal-Maoist (CPN-Maoist), hereinafter referred to as 'CPN-Maoist'. The CPN-Maoist is headed by Mohan Baidya 'Kiran' and functions strictly in adherence with Marxism-Leninism-Maoism (M-L-M) principles. Pushpa Kamal Dahal alias Prachanda, hereinafter referred to as 'Prachanda', is chairman of the UCPN (Maoist). The names of the Maoist Party (ies) are mentioned in the book according to their actual names during a particular period or year.
5. Some Chinese scholars suspect that the US presence in Nepal was for intelligence purposes. However, there is no credible evidence in this regard. Rather, Senator Jim Webb before the Senate Foreign Relations Committee in February 2010 viewed Nepal as something of an interesting gateway between India and China. Interestingly Jane's Intelligence review in 2001 analysed that future Nepal governments would try to become close to Beijing. That would give an opportunity to China to use Nepal as listening posts about foreign presence including India in the sub-Himalayan region. For details see Nishchal Nath Pandey, *Nepal's Maoist movement and implications for India and China*, Manohar Publications, Delhi, 2005, p. 126.
6. Kunda Dixit, "A New Himalayan Game", *The Fletcher Forum of World Affairs*, 34(1), Winter 2010. Also see Percy Fernandez, "Lost Horizon: China-Tibet Conflict Nowhere Near Resolution" *The Times of India*, 14 March 2005. C. Raja Mohan, "Tibet static in China," *The Hindu*, 22 June 2003. Srinath Raghavan, "The boundary dispute with China", *Seminar* (584), 2008, at http://www.india-seminar.com/2008/584/584_srinath_raghavan.htm (accessed on 2 July 2013).
7. Siddharth Varadarajan, "U.S. and India part company on Nepal", *The Hindu*, 22 February 2006. Also see "Region: Calling the shots," *Himal Southasian*, Kathmandu, April 2011, at http://www.himalmag.com/component/content/article/4365-region-calling-the-shots.html (accessed on 2 July 2013).
8. The White House, "U.S.-China Joint Statement", 17 November 2009, at http://www.whitehouse.gov/the-press-office/us-china-joint-statement (accessed on 26 July 2012).
9. "China too has a role to play in Nepal," *The Indian Express*, Delhi, 4 February 2010, at http://www.indianexpress.com/news/china-too-has-a-role-to-play-in-nepal-us/575463/0 (accessed on 2 July 2013).
10. Abanti Bhattacharya, "China and its Peripheries: Strategic Significance of Tibet," Issue

Brief, No. 220, May 2013, Institute of Peace and Conflict Studies (IPCS), New Delhi, p.01.

11. Kunda Dixit, "A New Himalayan Game", n. 6, pp. 125–34.
12. Prashant Jha, "A Nepali Perspective on International Involvement in Nepal", in Sebastian v. Einsiedel, *et al.* (eds), *Nepal in Transition: From People's War to Fragile Peace*, Cambridge University Press, Cambridge, 2012, pp.356-357.
13. AI Ping, Vice-Minister at the International Department of the Communist Party of China (CPC), during an unofficial visit to Kathmandu from 30 June - 2 July 2012, expressed Chinese concern over prolonged debate on ethnicity-based federalism in Nepal. For details see, "Focus on economy, not ethnicity", *The Himalayan Times*, Kathmandu, 30 June 2012. Also see, Prashant Jha, Editorial: "The message from the north", *The Hindu*, 5 October 2012.
14. "US national interest determines Nepal policy", *ekantipur*, Kathmandu, 12 December 2011, at http://www.ekantipur.com/the-kathmandu-post/2010/12/12/oped/monday-interview/215969/ (accessed on 2 July 2013).
15. Siddharth Varadarajan, "U.S. and India Part Company on Nepal", n.7.
16. Since all European countries are not members of the European Union (EU), the book discusses the EU's engagement with Nepal separately, alongside that of the major European countries.

CHAPTER 2

Foreign Policy Challenges of the Republic of Nepal

Nepal occupies a unique position in South Asia. It is a small and landlocked semi-buffer state[1] located between two Asian powers, who have fought a war with each other. It shares huge geographic, historical and cultural linkages with both the countries. There are many empirical studies on the foreign policy of small and buffer states, but there are very few studies on a country with the special characteristics of Nepal—landlocked, and located between two rival powers.

Nepal figured prominently in world politics during the Cold War. It lost its importance, to some extent, with the China-US rapprochement in 1972 and then again with the end of the cold war. But it has always figured prominently in the power politics of the Himalayan region. Since the mid-1990s, Nepal has gained some importance because of the strategic developments following the start of the Maoist movement (in 1996), the emergence of China and India as Asian economic powers, and the US's global campaign against terror launched in 2001. The presence of the US in the region has altered the geopolitical dynamics of the region. Traditionally, India, which considered South Asia as its natural sphere of influence, has not been quite comfortable with the idea of sharing its influence with extra-regional powers in this region. Given the changing relationship between the US and India, from 2000 onwards, the former has, to some extent, endorsed the latter's policy towards Nepal. However, the two countries differ significantly in their perspectives towards Nepal. For example, the US was opposed to India's move to engage the Maoists in 2005. On the other hand, China was suspicious of the US presence in Nepal, because of its apprehensions that the presence of external powers, especially the western countries, in Nepal might instigate anti-China movements spearheaded by Tibetan refugees in Nepal.

Theoretical Debate on the Foreign Policy (FP) of Small States[2]

There are many definitions of small states. While some have argued that geography, population, and level of international influence constitute the major objective criteria, others are of the view that many small countries do conform to that framework as they have played major role in international politics despite being small in size. Since the material aspects were not sufficient to define the small states, two scholars (Robert Rothstein and Robert Keohane) argued that the psychological dimension must form part of any objective criterion to define the small states; while some states believe they are unable to protect their territorial integrity in their own capacity.[3] This definition may not be sufficient to explain the behaviours of small states. In fact, there are many big countries which have joined military alliances to defend their territory. Therefore, a state's capacity to defend itself or secure itself should not be the only criteria for defining small states. For example, Nepal does not fall into small state category in terms of geography and size of population if one takes into consideration the definition given by the United Nations (UN). Although the UN does not differentiate between small and big states and treats them equally, there is a Forum of Small States (FOSS)—with population under 10 million—within the UN. The FOSS was formed at the initiative of Singapore in 1992 in New York as an informal grouping of small states. The Commonwealth and World Bank define a small state as sovereign state with a population size of 1.5 million or less.[4] Population wise, Nepal, does not qualify as a small state. However, if the criteria of economy and military power are taken into account, especially in the background two big neighbours—India and China—that it has, it may be considered as a small state. In fact, many scholars, including those from Nepal, consider Nepal as being a small state in the regional geopolitical context. Therefore, this study analyses the foreign policy behaviour of Nepal as a small state.

In the current century, as in the past, studies on International Relations (IR) have been driven by the politics of the big powers or mainly, the five permanent members of the UN Security Council, and reflect the hegemony of the P5. They have the power to veto any UN resolution that affects them or any of their allies. They often justify interventions in the name of preservation and protection of human rights, stability and world peace, without taking into account the interests or sentiments of other countries. No small state has the luxury of ever acting in this way, because for them "diplomacy [not demonstration of power] is the tool of statecraft".[5] Therefore, when (offensive) Realists argue that states are seeking to maximise their power, it is true only in a limited sense in case of small states. In the past, small states, like Cuba and Taiwan, have taken advantage of the competition between big powers, but very few of them have the ability to manoeuvre or influence world politics. In the post-Cold War period, small states have more international visibility and feel secure because of the UN and other multilateral organisations that are playing active international role to defuse crises. However, some small states, which had played key roles during Cold War period, have lost their influence in the post-Cold War period. Nepal could be one of them. Although it did not play any major role internationally, it certainly played a major role at the Himalayan sub-regional level. It managed to leverage its own interests by engaging both India and China—sometimes playing one against the other. It also invited super powers to neutralise their influence.[6]

There is a dominant view (Neo-Realism) in IR that the foreign policies of small states are affected more by international politics and less by domestic developments. M.L. Elman observes that: "The received wisdom in the field [International Relations theories] is that domestic determinants will be less salient when studying small state behaviour because external constraints are more severe and the international situation is more compelling."[7] This premise may not, however, apply to all small states. In the case of Nepal, its foreign policy is determined by its domestic requirements and regional political developments, especially those relating to China and India. Their strategic rivalry benefits Nepal much more than the other states of the same size and capability.[8]

A small state's ability to pursue an independent foreign policy further declines if it is landlocked and economically dependent exclusively on one country. Even a third power is less effective in terms of becoming a balancer or protector due to its physical remoteness.[9] Although Nepal tried to diversify its foreign policy during the 1960s by establishing relationships with other countries, it did not yield the desired results. Nepal established diplomatic relations with the US in 1947, before it did with any of its neighbours. Interestingly, on several occasions, both China and the US expressed their inability to offer any help to Nepal when its relations with India were strained. Informally, both recognised the southern Himalayas as India's sphere of influence.

S.D. Muni has observed that both internal and external variables have determined the foreign policy of Nepal. As far as external variables are concerned, it has been observed that the small countries in South Asia, including Nepal, took advantage of the big power politics in the region during the Cold War and enhanced their bargaining power vis-à-vis India. As far as internal variables are concerned, Nepal's internal politics has influenced the country's India policy more than India's policy towards Nepal. This is because of the frequent conflict between the forces who wanted to retain status quo and those have wanted change at the internal political level since the 1950s. The regimes in Nepal took advantage of international developments rather than influencing them in any manner.[10] At the same time, its dependence on India forced Nepal to take cognisance of India's sensitivities about its relationship with China. Thus, the foreign policy of Nepal has been operating at three levels: domestic/regime interests, sub-regional power politics, and global developments. The big powers have failed to bring peace and stability to Nepal and South Asia despite their presence in the region since the 1950s.

Figure 2.1: External Impact on Nepal's Foreign Policy

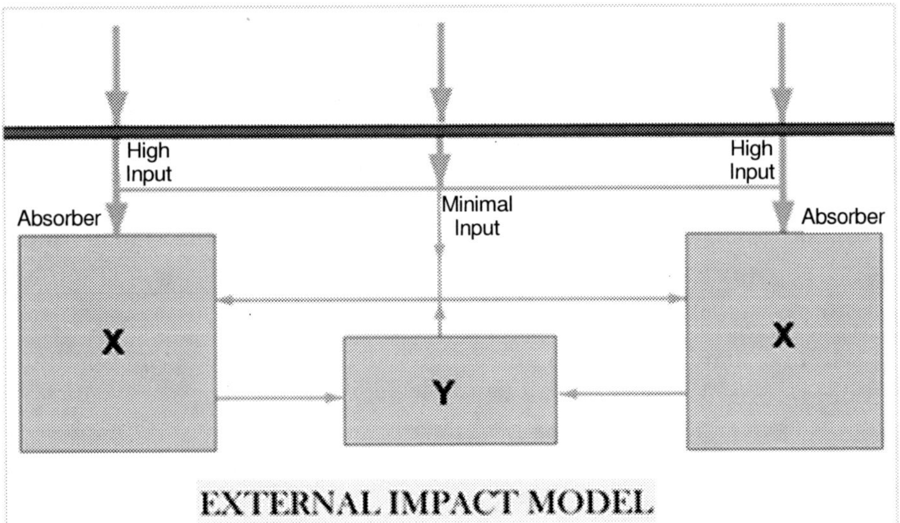

Source: Author.

The impact diagram (figure 2.1) explains that small and landlocked countries located between two big powers are less affected by international developments because the big powers surrounding it absorb the pressure. However, since small countries are part of the international system and regional sub-system, they are more influenced by their immediate neighbours rather than any extra-regional powers. In the case of Nepal (Y), this model explains the foreign policy behaviour of Nepal. Since Nepal is situated between India (X) and China (X), its foreign policy is mostly affected by its immediate neighbours and less by international developments. According to Barry Buzan and Ole Waever: "Smaller states will usually find themselves locked into an RSC [Regional Security Complex] with their neighbours, great powers will typically penetrate several adjacent regions, and superpowers will range over the whole planet."[11] There have been occasions, when small states have invited third parties to counter-balance their neighbours. But even if Nepal takes the help of a third power, it may not be effective vis-à-vis India, and at the same time its geostrategic location would demand that it maintains a non-antagonistic relationship with China. For example, Western countries have been trying to influence Nepal on the Tibet issue for the last 50 years. But Nepal has ignored them and adopted a policy that has largely suited the Chinese interests. Similarly, despite the pro-monarchy policy (especially against the Maoists) followed by the US since 2001 and its opposition to the 12-point agreement, the US felt necessary to support India's 2005 peace initiative in Nepal given its influence in this region. As one Nepalese analyst observed "On regional issues, with exception of those related to Pakistan, the US administration was content to give India the lead,"[12] for larger strategic gains. Moreover, given the complexity of the regional power-play and asymmetry of Nepal with its neighbours, Nepal is well-placed to take advantage of the economic development of both India and China without having to play them off against each other.

Evolution of Nepal's Foreign Policy

As a small and landlocked country, Nepal's foreign policy priorities were to preserve and protect its territorial integrity from its neighbours.[13] During the Panchayat regime any threat to the monarchy was considered as a threat to the sovereignty of the country and vice-versa. Thus the survival of the monarchy became synonymous with state security. As a result, Nepal's foreign policy was designed to protect its territorial integrity by maintaining a balance between India and China; adherence to the UN principles and being part of regional organizations. Its foreign policy was also specially formulated to mobilise international support and recognition with the purpose of fulfilling its political and economic requirements.[14] Articulating Nepal's foreign policy priorities, in view of its geographic reality, King Prithvi Narayan Shah said that Nepal was like a yam between two boulders, and should maintain an equal relationship with China (then Tibet) and India. S.D. Muni has observed that the foreign policy objectives of small states like Nepal are motivated by security (territorial integrity and military), stability (political and economic) and status, but these motivations may not be enough to decipher Nepal's foreign policy. Therefore, some structural factors that influence it need to be examined. The structural factors may be constant (e.g. geography, history, socio-cultural ties with its larger neighbour) or variable (e.g. nationalism and political system).[15] To fulfil its foreign policy objectives Nepal adopted the strategy of (i) taking advantage of differences and clash of interests between India and China (ii) reducing dependence on both neighbours by diversifying its foreign relations, (iii) and mobilisation of international contacts for building counter-pressures.[16]

The Rana rulers established a good relationship with British India by acknowledging the British Empire as the pre-eminent power in the region. This policy continued till the departure of the British from the subcontinent. While India was passing through its post-independence political transition, the Ranas established diplomatic relations with the US and other countries to counterbalance India, who wanted the Ranas to keep pace with political changes in the region (in other words, bring about political reforms) and seek international recognition. Meanwhile, the communist victory in China in October 1949 and its aggression on Tibet during 1950-51 altered the security situation in the Himalayas. China's view of Tibet as the palm of a hand and adjacent territories like Nepal, Bhutan and some parts of Indian territory like Sikkim, Ladakh and Arunachal Pradesh as the fingers increased the vulnerability of Nepal. Worried over these developments, India and Nepal signed two Treaties in July 1950: the Treaty of Peace and Friendship, and the Treaty of Trade and Commerce. Given the growing dissatisfaction against the Rana autocracy and demand for establishment of democracy, which was spearheaded by the Nepali Congress (NC), India helped to establish a constitutional monarchy and multiparty democracy. This was to ensure a progressive, stable and strong Nepal, which would be sensitive to India's security concerns. Some Nepalese believe that India exploited the anti-Rana feelings of the democratic forces to compel, the then rulers, to sign the 1950 Treaty. But the fact of the matter was that while both Nepal and India were negotiating a standstill agreement, the communist victory in China and its aggression on Tibet altered the geopolitical dynamics in the Himalayan region. An intelligence input over a possible Chinese military move into Tibet by the mid-1950s heightened security concerns for both India and Nepal. Nepal might have been interested in entering into a new agreement with India after British withdrawal from India and objections of the Soviet Union (now the Russian Federation) to Nepal's entry in the UN in May 1949 on sovereignty issue.[17] Since then, the Friendship Treaty has remained the guiding force in India-Nepal relations. Moreover, India and Nepal shared a special relationship given India's role in the restoration of monarchy. One of the main reasons for India's support for restoration of the monarchy was to do away with the unpopular 'Rana' regime and gradually facilitate the rise of democracy or some sort of representational elected government that embodies the will of the people. Till 1955, India largely influenced the foreign policy of Nepal.[18] However, after 1955 the monarchy became increasingly assertive and was reluctant to allow the democratic forces to function independently. The monarchy perceived India as being inimical to its interests as it feared that India's support to democratic forces would dilute its power.

Nepal's foreign policy took a new shape after King Mahendra assumed power in 1955. He deviated from his father's India-dependent foreign policy and formulated an independent foreign policy by diversifying Nepal's relationship with other countries. The major driver for this change was his desire to consolidate the monarchy, weaken the democratic movement and mobilise international support for the monarchy. Since India was proposing a mixed (constitutional monarchy) political system, he tried to neutralise India's influence by signing a parallel Treaty of Peace and Friendship with China in 1960. He also tried to reduce Nepal's dependence on India by seeking more development aid from Western countries. In all these efforts he took advantage of the differences between China and India and at the same time he was not hesitant to play a role in the 'containment policy' scripted by the Western powers. His policy was compatible with the interests of external forces in the Himalayas. China appreciated Nepal's efforts towards neutralising India's influence and offered "political support for the Nepal king's domestic policies together with generous economic assistance" (details of the Chinese engagement with Nepal are discussed in Chapter 4).[19] China in fact took advantage of the rift between King Mahendra and the then Indian establishment. China did not react immediately after King Mahendra's dissolution of the first democratically elected government and the royal coup. Its silence was a signal that the monarchy was a stable power centre. Its support to the authoritarian regime was reflected when the Chinese Vice-President Chen Yi praised King Mahendra's leadership while welcoming the Nepalese delegation to the Joint Committee on Nepal-India Boundary Commission to Beijing in February 1961. Subsequently, China also assured King Mahendra of all kinds of economic and military support.[20] Moreover, being a small country under constant threat to its survival, Nepal adopted the principle of non-interference in the internal affairs of others and articulated it at the UN and in other international fora.

King Mahendra's son Birendra, who assumed power in 1972, followed his father's domestic and international policies, but went one step ahead by declaring Nepal a Zone of Peace (ZoP) in 1975. Pakistan and China endorsed this seven-clause declaration which was immediately accepted by more than 70 other countries who endorsed it on the condition that it should be accepted by Nepal's neighbours. India, however, did not endorse it. A major objective of the ZoP proposal was to neutralise India's influence in Nepal by undermining the 1950 Friendship Treaty. Despite knowing that India would not endorse the proposal, the king went ahead with the plan to consolidate his regime by fomenting anti-India feelings. The ZoP remained a major objective of Nepalese foreign policy till the establishment of multi-party democracy in 1990, but did not figure prominently in Nepalese foreign policy articulation because India ignored it altogether. The proposal, it may be noted, was made soon after the formation of Bangladesh. The US was among the countries that were interested in pressurising India in the aftermath of the emergence of Bangladesh.[21] The king was also worried about India's support to the democratic forces in Sikkim. He might have been apprehensive that the Nepalese monarchy could face a similar future. Moreover, the proposal came while the monarchy was facing stiff resistance from the Nepali Congress, which was using Indian territory for its campaign for restoration of democracy. Under Clause 5 of the ZoP proposal, India would have been forced to take action against the NC and the monarchy would have maintained the status quo forever. The proposal was also similar to Pakistan's proposal for declaring South Asia as a nuclear weapon-free zone.

Foreign Policy During Multiparty Democracy

With the introduction of democracy and multiparty system the role of monarchy in politics diminished to some extent. The political parties were not interested in the ZoP proposal. Thus during the post-1990s the ZoP proposal fell into disuse. Nepalese foreign policy acquired a new shape with the promulgation of the 1990 Constitution. Its relations with India significantly improved. The democratically elected governments focused more on maintaining a balanced relation with both India and China.

Nepal attracted international attention once again with the onset of Maoist insurgency in 1996. The complex relationship that Nepal shared with India and the US underwent change with the onset of the Global War on Terrorism and a consensus emerged between the three countries. Nepal-US relations were strengthened with the exchange of high-level visits. During this period US aid to Nepal, which had been reduced between 1970 and 2001, was doubled. Review of existing Treaties between India and Nepal dominated discussions during bilateral visits. However, during the royal takeover in

February 2005, King Gyanendra tilted towards China and Pakistan to counterbalance the Indian and the Western opposition to his action.

Though at one time the Chinese authorities branded the Maoists as "anti-government forces" and suspected their intentions, the Maoists had retained King Mahendra's policy of maintaining equidistance from both India and China—which former Prime Minister Pushpa Kamal Dahal alias Prachanda (hereinafter referred to as 'Prachanda') had defined as 'non-alignment'—and remaining neutral. This policy has also been followed by the succeeding coalition government led by Communist Party of Nepal (Unified Marxist Leninist)—hereinafter referred to as 'CPN-UML'. The Maoists have even gone a step further and projected India as an enemy state. In their political resolutions, India has been projected as an interfering neighbour and China as a benign power.[22]

While China was looking for a reliable political power center, that could offer political stability in Nepal in the absence of the monarchy, the Maoists' policy helped it to push forward its strategic and economic policies. However, political parties in general and the Maoists in particular have contradicted their own declared equidistance policy. During their private and official visits, these leaders have reiterated the continuation of strong bilateral relations with India. During Prachanda's visit to Delhi in September 2008, both the countries in the joint statement had agreed to reactivate the existing bilateral mechanism in the evolving context and to review, adjust and update the 1950 Treaty while giving due regard to special features of bilateral relations. Interestingly, three years before the visit, Prachanda as head of the CPN (Maoist) outfit, had identified India as a hegemonic and interventionist neihgbour and had also vowed to bring changes in the Indian political system aided by the Indian Maoists. Baburam Bhattarai, vice-chairman of the Maoist party, in an interview to this author in June 2009 said: "(T)he equidistance policy is just a party decision to satisfy our neighbours. In reality, we are more dependent on India than China".[23]

Nepal and Multilateralism

India's neighbours, including Nepal, on many occasions have branded it as an interventionist power. This perception has emanated mostly due to historical issues, regime incompatibility and multiple asymmetries between India and its neighbours. These neighbours have been adopting certain policy measures to overcome what they see as their disadvantaged position. They resort to strategies like multilateral diplomacy, seeking the help of external forces and multilateral agencies, ganging up against India for reducing Indian influence in the region by forming regional organisations like SAARC and portraying India as a hegemonic power.[24]

Nepal has, on many occasions, successfully utilised multilateral forums and the UN to neutralise and minimise the influence of neighbouring countries in its internal matters. For example, Nepal was a founding member of both the Non Aligned Movement (NAM) and SAARC. In both these multilateral arrangements, Nepal has successfully raised the concerns of small states and has sought to establish that it is not influenced by any country; that being a sovereign country, it has created a space for itself at the international level. According to Muchkund Dubey, for example, Nepal and Bhutan, with the "support of other smaller member countries have used the SAARC forum to put pressure on India to provide transit through the Indian territory to trade with Bangladesh, and to the ports of Chittagong and Mongla for their trade with other countries."[25] Pakistan and other major powers have taken advantage of the prevailing India phobia in Nepal.

Nepal and NAM

As Nepal was asserting its sovereignty after the fall of British colonialism in the subcontinent, it sought a separate identity by becoming part of NAM. From Nepal's point of view, NAM was a message to the big powers that all states are equal and no state or group of states should dominate others. In the first NAM summit in Belgrade (1961), King Mahendra had emphasised on greater economic cooperation between countries and opposed the idea of military alliances and blocs. The message was indirectly to its neighbours to prevent them from pressurising Nepal to gang-up against other countries. Kirti Nidi Bista, a former prime minister of Nepal, said that by joining NAM Nepal wanted to send "a message to various countries that Nepal would never involve itself in bilateral conflicts or wars by pitting one against the other (India vs. China or India vs. Pakistan), which was honoured at the time."[26] In fact, as part of the NAM, Nepal demilitarised its territory by ousting Indian military missions and check-posts. Perhaps, Nepal took the decision to give an impression to international community that the Treaty of Peace and Friendship signed between India and Nepal in 1950 was not a military alliance.

While reiterating Nepal's view on world peace and development, King Mahendra, in the second NAM summit in Cairo, highlighted the relevance of NAM for small states given the intense competition for military blocs between the US and then Soviet Union. He appealed to the NAM member countries to bring out some special policies to contain the influence of big powers in the internal matters of small states. Moreover, the subsequent rulers of Nepal had almost followed the policy laid down by King Mahendra.[27]

In the era of globalisation, Nepal felt that the world was becoming interdependent. However, the NAM continued to provide a platform to Nepal to express its concerns, which it could not do at a bilateral level. The importance of NAM for Nepal was once again apparent when Prime Minister Baburam Bhattarai ignored the advice of some Western diplomats to not attend the 16th NAM summit in Tehran in August 2012. Addressing the Tehran summit, Bhattarai appealed to his audience to make "NAM a voice for the voiceless and power for the powerless and asking to make a pledge to work in a coherent, cooperative and concerted manner for justice and peace at home and more importantly for justice and peace in the world."[28] Given the changing geopolitical scenario and suspicion of interference by external powers in the internal politics of Nepal in the post-monarchy period, Deputy Prime Minister and Minister for Foreign Affairs Narayan Kaji Shrestha emphasised the need to strengthen the UN and NAM so that they could work to ensure "a country's [emphasis on small state] sanctity of sovereignty" and uphold its "political independence", and "unequivocally resist" any "interference in the internal affairs of other countries".[29]

Nepal and SAARC

Nepal has been firmly committed to making South Asian Association for Regional Cooperation (SAARC) a dynamic regional organisation. While the UN and NAM took care of Nepal's political and strategic needs, SAARC provided a platform for its economic interests.[30] There were occasions when Nepal along with other SAARC members tried to put pressure on India on sharing of river waters, dams and other economic issues and also tried to reduce India's influence by recommending the inclusion of extra-regional powers as observers.

Nepal and BIMSTEC

Nepal is also part of BIMSTEC and other regional initiatives like the Asian highway and Asian railway networks. Nepal was not a founding member of the BIMSTEC. It decided to join the new sub-regional mechanism in 1997 and obtained the observer status on 19 December 1998. Nepal thought to take advantage of the new sub-regional grouping for rapid economic growth. Although it wanted to become the permanent member of the BIMSTEC, the process was delayed due to a five-year moratorium set in 1997 on the consideration of applications for new membership. Nepal was granted full membership in 2003. Since then Nepal has been actively participating in various meetings of the BIMSTEC.[31] Nepal may have tried to take advantage of BIMSTEC due to slow progress shown by SAARC. It might as well have thought of improving its economic cooperation with BIMSTEC member countries and taking advantage of BIMSTEC's emphasis on connectivity and poverty alleviation. Interestingly, it was the first member of the BIMSTEC that depended on India and Bangladesh for access to the sea. Nepal has been demanding special facilities for landlocked countries in the BIMSTEC Free Trade Agreement (FTA). As a small country, Nepal believes that multilateralism would be the appropriate forum to raise the concerns of the Least Developed Countries (LDCs) on economic issues. In 2005, Bangladesh and Nepal disagreed on India's proposal over the Rules of Origin (RoO) issue and both demanded that the LDCs in the BIMSTEC should be allowed a "less stringent value addition norm".[32]

Nepal and the United Nations

Nepal joined the UN in December 1955. During this period the subcontinent witnessed some major geopolitical readjustments. There was a fear of Chinese aggression on the Himalayan kingdom. Mao Zedong had claimed Chinese dominance over Tibet and the Himalayas in 1950.[33] Moreover, the Nepalese ruling classes did not feel fully safe and secure from external intervention despite the 1950 Treaty with India. This was also the period when Nepal strove for an independent foreign policy. Its first effort to become a member of the UN in May 1949 was thwarted by the then Soviet Union's allegations that its independence and sovereignty was compromised by its 1923 Treaty with British India. For Nepal, joining the UN symbolised international recognition of its sovereignty.[34]

Nepalese leaders while addressing the world community in the UN General Assembly had expressed the view that joining the UN was a strategic move for Nepal to safeguard its independence and territorial integrity. In the UN, Nepal has been raising the plight of the small countries. In the post-monarchy period, in its Interim Constitution of 2007, Nepal has reiterated its commitment to support the UN at various levels. Deputy Prime Minister and Minister for Foreign Affairs Narayan Kaji Shrestha said at the 67th session of the UN General Assembly held on 28 September 2012:

> While every country has the legitimate right to pursue its enlightened national interests...the wider respect and observance of the principles of sovereignty, territorial integrity, political independence and non-interference are the bedrock principles of international relations. These

> principles cannot and should not be made subject to political test under any circumstances.

He also argued that given the global political scenario, "the UN must ensure that it works for the advancement of the world's poorest and most vulnerable countries".[35]

Nepal and LDCs

Nepal also assumed a distinctive identity in the UN by seeking more global attention for the LDCs. According to a publication from Nepal's Foreign Ministry, it obtained the position of Chair of the Global Coordinating Bureau of LDCs, in September 2009. Once it assumed the position, it:

> ...urged for the effective partnership between LDCs and their development partners in order to achieve the goals set by the Millennium Summit for development and poverty reduction. Nepal has also taken the position that the debt burden of the LDCs should be written off; the commitments of donors to allocate 0.15-0.20 per cent of GNP as ODA to LDCs should be fulfilled; and duty-free and quota-free access be given to the markets of the developed countries for the exports of LDCs.[36]

Nepal has been supporting the shared interests of LDCs in the UN and other important regional and multilateral forums since it took over the responsibility of chairmanship of LDCs Global Coordination Bureau in September 2009.[37]

It has also been Bureau Member of the Group of the Landlocked Developing Countries (LLDCs) (2010-12). In view of the increasing debt burden of the LDCs and LLDCs, Nepal has been demanding the easing—and where possible writing off—of such debts. It also supported the Highly Indebted Poor Countries (HIPC) initiative and expressed the belief that this initiative should be extended to LDCs as well.[38] Nepal has achieved its national objective more through multilateral forums than through bilateral relations. Therefore, it always emphasises the UN's role in ensuring collective security. Nepal as an LLDC articulated its view that grant of transit by any country is not a "favour" but is a right affirmed by the principles of international law and practice.[39]

Nepal utilised the UN platform to flag its constraints as an LLDC with the support of other landlocked countries. Apart from lobbying for more transit facilities through India at the UN and its special institutions like UNCTAD and ECAFE, Nepal also demanded a separation of the Treaty of Transit from Treaty of Trade after the UN passed a resolution on February 1957.[40] Along with Afghanistan, Austria, Bolivia and others it also demanded a special study for identifying the problems of accessing seaports at the Conference of Plenipotentiaries in the UN in 1957. On the basis of that demand, the UN organised a Conference on the Law of the Sea in Geneva in 1958. Nepal played a major role in preparing the 'seven principles', which were accepted in the conference as demands from landlocked countries. LLDCs also presented their demand for an international convention to be passed on transit issues after a detailed discussion.[41] Accordingly, the UN organised an international conference of landlocked countries in Geneva in July 1965 to discuss these issues. Nepal, with eight other landlocked countries, also lobbied for inclusion of the problems faced by landlocked countries in UNCTAD II in 1968 in Delhi. They demanded special facilities for landlocked countries as developing countries. In all these conventions, there were disagreements between Nepal and two of its closest neighbours – India and Pakistan.[42]

Demanding reduction of transactional cost for LLDCs, Nepal's Foreign Minister Narayan Kaji Shrestha pointed out at the 67th session of the UN General Assembly that, to make international trade more competitive, the cost of transit transport should be reduced. While delivering a statement on behalf of Nepal at the 11th annual ministerial meeting of the LLDCs in New York [on 26 September], Shrestha said that "the implementation of the Almaty Program of Action is a must to help LLDCs overcome their inherent geographical difficulties and provide them with support to eradicate poverty and hunger, achieve sustained economic growth and facilitate better integration into the world economy through increased flow of trade and investment."[43]

United Nations Mission in Nepal

Nepal is always perceived to be more comfortable with the presence of the UN than any other external force on its territory. Therefore, in the post-Maoist insurgency period, Nepalese leaders preferred the UN to any other agency for playing the role of a monitor in the peace process. Despite India's significant role in concluding the November 2005 12-point agreement and its support to the Jana Andolan-II, the Nepalese leaders did not consider India as a neutral observer of the peace process. They were apprehensive that this task of monitoring the peace process would increase India's intervention in Nepal. There was general perception in Nepal that India might fish in troubled waters and the Maoists were also suspicious about India. Interestingly it was reported that the NC and the CPN-UML leaders proposed the UN as a deal-maker, suspecting India to be sympathetic towards the Maoists.[44] They wanted India to use its good offices informally to support the successful completion of peace process and at the same time leaders of major political parties worked towards a consensus among themselves in favour of UN's role in monitoring the peace process. The government and the Maoists on 7 November 2006 reached an agreement to end the decade-old conflict and restored lasting peace through a six-point agreement. Subsequently, as agreed, the government and the Maoists signed the Comprehensive Peace Agreement (CPA) on 21 November 2006, promising to chart a new destiny for a "peaceful and democratic" new Nepal.

The UN established its Mission in Nepal under Resolution 1740(2007) on 23 January 2007. The Mission was entrusted with a four-point mandate, which included monitoring the management of arms and armed personnel of the Nepalese Army and the CPN (Maoist) as per the provisions of the CPA and providing technical support for holding the CA elections. The key objective of UNMIN was to support Nepal in creating the environment for a credible CA election that would further lead to establishing lasting peace in the country. In addition, the UN, through the Office of the High Commissioner for Human Rights (OHCHR) in Nepal has been monitoring the human rights situation in the country.

India might have agreed to a limited UN role in order to support its new-found benign image. In an interaction with this author, a senior official of India's Ministry for External Affairs in September 2012 said:

> India was not in favour of mediation because that would have given a chance to anti-India elements to project India as an interventionist neighbour. Anyway India had been projected as big brother in Nepal. It would have been a disaster for India had it accepted the mediation offer or tried to do that.[45]

India, initially, was also not very happy with the unilateral efforts made by some senior UN representatives to monitor the peace process. According to a retired senior diplomat "the UN record of peacekeeping in other conflict theatres has been patchy and its staff did not have sufficient knowledge about the conflicts in Nepal. Moreover, India [could not] trust anyone for protecting India's interests."[46] Despite that immediately after the formation of the Interim Government, the Special Adviser of the UN Department for Political Affairs, Tamarat Samuel, landed in Kathmandu on a ten-day visit on 6 May 2006. He wanted to resolve the trust deficit between the Maoists, India, the Nepali Congress (NC) and the CPN-UML over the involvement of external forces in the monitoring of the peace process. The UN officials also discussed its role with Indian officials. Therefore, while Nepalese leaders proposed UN mediation, India did not oppose it wholeheartedly but suggested UN presence with limited mandate.

India's suspicions in this regard turned out to be true. The UNMIN failed to distinguish between the original and duplicate cadres of the Maoists. While the UNMIN finally verified 19,602 armed cadres of the PLA, Prachanda disclosed to cadres at the Shaktikhor cantonment on 2 January 2008 that the party had only 7000-8000 armed cadres in July 2006.[47] This suggests that many of the cadres who surrendered to the UN were not members of the Maoist army. There was also a gap between the number of armed cadres and number of weapons deposited before the UNMIN by the CPN (Maoist). One researcher who is very close to top Maoists leaders disclosed to this author (in Delhi in October 2012) that a large chunk of sophisticated weapons seized during the armed struggle period by the Maoists are still with the Prachanda faction; he also claimed to know where the weapons were stashed. An inventory of the Maoists' attacks on the state armoury since 2001 indicates that the rebels had "seized more than 12 trucks of sophisticated arms and ammunition ... [which] included Israel-made Galil ARM 5.56 mm rifles, 81 mm mortars, shoulder-propelled grenade launchers, self-loading rifles, light machine guns, AK-47s, INSAS 5.56 rifles, wireless sets and tons of ammunition"[48] in a single attack on army barracks in Dang district on 23 November 2001. In an interview to *Naya Patrika*, Kathmandu, 13 January 2008, Prachanda said, "The day we captured the barracks in Dang, I was told that the weapons were sufficient to continue fighting for four years."[49] The Maoists launched eighteen major attacks on the security forces from February 1996 to March 2005 and seized an unspecified number of weapons.[50] Besides, their poor management of the former Maoists and their arsenal, the UN officials were also reportedly in touch with some Terai-based armed groups and crossed over to the Indian side to interact with them to find evidence about their linkages with India. They did this without taking formal permission from the Indian government. *The Times of India* reported that three officials from UN agencies visited the Muzaffarpur district of Bihar in September 2007 to hold secret talks with the Janatantrik Terai Mukti Morcha and the faction led by Jwala Singh. The Indian Embassy in Kathmandu objected to this visit.[51]

Foreign Policy Under the Interim Constitution

To adapt to the changing realities, Nepal's FP was spelt out afresh under the Interim Constitution (IC) in 2007. According to Article 26 (15, 16), of the IC, the foreign policy of Nepal was to be guided by the principles of the United Nations Charter, non-alignment, *Panchsheel,* international law, world peace along with continuous efforts to ensure peace for Nepal through international recognition, by promoting cooperation and good relations with other countries in economic, social and other spheres on the basis of equality. Nevertheless, the IC largely followed the foreign policy parameters of the 1990 Constitution.

The objective of its foreign policy as defined by the IC was to "enhance the dignity of Nepal in the international arena by maintaining the sovereignty, integrity and independence of the country."[52] Nepal agreed to follow the basic principles of international law such as:

1. Mutual respect for each other's territorial integrity and sovereignty;
2. Non-interference in each other's internal affairs;
3. Respect for mutual equality;
4. Non-aggression and peaceful settlement of disputes; and
5. Cooperation for mutual benefit.[53]

The Interim Constitution also provided for ratification and approval of previous Treaties and agreements in Parliament. According to Article 156(2),

> The laws to be made pursuant to clause (1) shall, inter alia, require that the ratification of, accession to, acceptance of or approval of treaty or agreements on the following subjects be done by a two-thirds majority of the total number of members of the Legislature-Parliament existing:

(a) peace and friendship;
(b) security and strategic alliance;
(c) the boundaries of Nepal; and
(d) natural resources and the distribution of their uses.

Article 156(4) says that "Notwithstanding anything contained in clauses (1) and (2), no treaty or agreement shall be concluded that may be detrimental to the territorial integrity of Nepal."

From August 2008 to March 2013,[54] Nepal has had four governments—the UCPN (Maoist) and CPN-UML both leading two of each. There has been a perception in Nepal that India was sympathetic to the governments of Madhav Kumar Nepal and Baburam Bhattarai. It may be noted that India's bids were ignored for most of the mega projects in Nepal during these two regimes. For example, the machine-readable passport project was given to France by Madhav Kumar Nepal's government. Three mega projects—Lumbini, Pokhara airport and West Seti—went to Chinese companies during Baburam's premiership. Also, while Indian companies[55] were facing difficulties in operating in the hydro, garment, hotel and infrastructure sectors in Nepal on account of the unfavourable business environment there, Chinese companies started investing in those sectors. All the four governments, instead of striving to enhance the dignity of Nepal in the international arena, adopted the policy of equidistance to neutralise perceived Indian influence, prompted by party ideology and individual agenda.

There have been major changes in Nepal's foreign policy outlook since the Maoists assumed power in August 2008. The Federal Democratic Republic of Nepal has emphasised independence in the conduct of its foreign policy. The Maoist government re-defined their policy of 'equidistance' as a policy of 'non-alignment' and neutrality. The practical application of this was that instead of feeding the people of Humla district with Indian rice transported by helicopter from Nepalganj, the government would get rice from the nearby markets in Tibet.[56] Prachanda, the then prime minister, visited Beijing in August 2008 to attend the concluding ceremony of the Olympic games. In April 2009 China proposed a revised Peace and Friendship Treaty with Nepal to improve its own standing in that country. The proposal, however, did not materialise in the event of cancellation of Prachanda's visit, which was scheduled in May 2009. Earlier, China was more focused on the Tibet issue, but it diversified its interests in Nepal after the Maoists adopted the policy of maintaining equidistance between India and China. One Nepalese scholar has observed:

> The new trend evident over the past three years [since 2008] now has China's interest in Nepal shifting from being almost exclusively focused on Tibet-related security issues (essentially preventing any 'Free Tibet' activity out of Nepal) to being part of Beijing's larger geostrategic plan for South Asia.[57]

On the other hand, the UCPN (Maoist), which had not abandoned its 'revolutionary political objective', was eager to seek China's support to counterbalance India. To oblige China, the Prachanda government took strong action against the Tibetan refugee movement in Nepal and increased border security to prevent transit of Tibetan refugees across the border with China.

Several high-level visits were exchanged between China and the Maoist government in Nepal. These included Prime Minister Prachanda's trip to Beijing in September 2008, followed by the visit of Defence Minister Ram Bahadur Thapa a few days later. China's Foreign Minister Yang Jiechi's visited Nepal in December 2008. During Thapa's visit in September 2008 China agreed to provide security assistance.[58] China also agreed to provide technical assistance for the merger of the Maoist armed cadres with the Nepalese Army. China also agreed to provide economic assistance worth NPR 1.2 billion to support Nepal's infrastructure and technical development.

Like the kings in the past, the democratic governments since 2008 too sought to reduce India's influence in Nepal, with the Maoists (before the split) even projecting India as an enemy state in their manifesto. The Maoist demands mentioned therein are: (i) regulated or closed border, (ii) more trade and transit facilities, (iii) formation of Greater Nepal, (iv) civilian nuclear units with help from China, (v) demarcation of borders, and (vi) diversification of trade and free arms import.

After becoming prime minister and breaking the tradition of visiting India first, Prachanda visited Beijing to underscore Nepal's sovereignty and independence. Although he undertook first official visit to India, his first foreign trip to Beijing had indicated that the Maoists would prefer China to India. During his visit to the Nordic countries in March 2009, Prachanda articulated the view that sustainable peace was not possible in Nepal without economic prosperity and support from the international community. He requested Norway to invest in hydropower development and other sectors of mutual interest.[59] Even after his resignation, the Maoists mobilised international support to come back to power and projected India as an interventionist power.

The Maoist policy of equidistance was also followed by the succeeding coalition government led by Madhav Kumar Nepal of the CPN-UML, but with some moderation in policies vis-à-vis India. The new prime minister visited India soon after assuming office. Interestingly, his visit to Beijing in December 2009 was a high-profile one and the two countries agreed to further strengthen their relationship. China took the visit very seriously since this was the first official visit of the Nepalese prime minister to China after it became a Republic. One of the longest and most detailed joint statements was issued at the end of that visit. The two countries agreed to "lift their bilateral relationship to a higher level by establishing a comprehensive partnership of cooperation",[60] which hinted at taking the relationship to a higher level from the previously stated "good-neighbourly partnership" to "closer ties between China and Nepal". China's top legislator Wu Bangguo,[61] during an interaction with Madhav Nepal clarified that the objective of the comprehensive partnership was "strategic". The joint statement further widened the window of opportunities for China in Nepal.

Madhav Kumar Nepal's successor Jhalanath Khanal further facilitated Chinese presence in Nepal. One scholar observed that: "Although both Madhav Nepal and Prime Minister Khanal belong to the same party [CPN-UML], the latter, who became prime minister through a secret deal with Maoist

Chairman [Prachanda], is perceived more positively by Beijing."[62] During this period, several Chinese political and business delegations visited Nepal. Surprisingly, in his six-month tenure, Khanal did not undertake any official visits to Nepal's two important neighbours.

The Maoists returned to power for the second time with Baburam Bhattarai as the prime minister in August 2011. He restored the tradition of making the first official visit to India at the invitation of India's Prime Minister. While articulating Nepal's foreign policy priorities in the changing global and regional order, he said that Nepal needs to reorient its foreign policy and become a 'vibrant bridge' between the two Asian economic giants. In this regard, road and rail connections between Tibet and India through Nepal needed to be augmented. He noted that the "country's focus on India, China and US will be instrumental in developing Nepal."[63] Despite the UCPN (Maoist)'s declared policy of equidistance, Bhattarai believed that Nepal is economically more dependent on India than China.

The growing presence of China in Nepal, could be a major challenge for it to maintain a balance between the two neighbours. While earlier India had a major share in the Nepalese economy and investments, the environment has recently become more competitive for India. Both countries exert pressure on Nepal if it enters into any agreement with the other. There is also domestic pressure to maintain a balance in the relationship. For example, after the conclusion of BIPPA agreement between Nepal and India, there was pressure both from China and some top leaders of the UCPN (Maoist) on Bhattarai's government to enter into a similar agreement with China. In an effort to maintain a balance in the hydro-power sector in Nepal, the Interim Constitution's directive on foreign policy was ignored—for the first time in the last four years—to allot the West Seti project to China. There has been a constant demand from the radical Maoist factions to allocate more hydro and infrastructure projects to China in order to neutralise India's influence.

However, given the controversies related to the West Seti project and the delay in the process, China sensed a conspiracy. These doubts emanated from Nepalese media stories that Baburam Bhattarai government was supported by India. This perception was strengthened further when Baburam Bhattarai told the media in advance about Chinese Prime Minister Wen Jiabao's visit to Nepal in December 2011. Perhaps the Chinese establishment was apprehensive about protests/demonstrations by Tibetan refugees in Nepal during the Premier's visit. As a result, the visit was postponed to January 2012. Moreover, China has never been comfortable with a pro-India regime in Nepal. It has the impression that such a regime might not take strong action against Tibetan refugees in Nepal. Since China had limited options of replacing the Baburam Bhattarai government, it expressed its displeasure by not responding positively to the Nepal Government's request to fix a meeting between Bhattarai and Wen Jiabao on the sidelines of the UN Conference on Sustainable Development at Rio in June 2012. The message was repeated thereafter when China reportedly facilitated Netra Bikram Chand's visits before the split in the UCPN (Maoist) in June 2012 and during an unofficial visit of Ai Ping.[64] During his visit, surprisingly, Ai Ping did not meet the prime minister. Although China claimed that it was against the split in the party, surprisingly, it did not put serious pressure on the Baidya faction to merge with the parent party during Baidya's China visit in July 2012. Rather, China acknowledged that the CPN-Maoist party was a "nationalist force".[65]

Since the Maoists' declared equidistance policy had been a non-starter because of both the domestic situation in Nepal and the regional power balance between India and China, the Maoists had moderated their policy by emphasising on economic and development programmes. They proposed a 'trilateral cooperation' between Nepal-India-China. The proposal came initially as a triangular strategic dialogue from the UCPN (Maoist) chairman, Prachanda, on 26 October, after his five-day visit for attending the Shanghai Expo 2010.[66] The proposal was reiterated by Prachanda after signing the MoU with the Asia Pacific Exchange and Cooperation Foundation (APECF) on 7 November 2012 for the Lumbini development project and again during his official visits to Beijing and New Delhi in April 2013. India was lukewarm about the proposal even before Prachanda could formally discuss with Indian decision makers. Sensing India's negative response, Prachanda modified his proposal during an interaction with Indian intellectuals at ICWA on 29 April and said, "trilateral cooperation in various mutual projects in Nepal is very much possible. It is our vision for the future. Let me also clarify that by no means do I wish to undermine or replace our centuries-old bilateral relations."[67] In the same meeting, he also emphasised that a prosperous and developed Nepal can address the security concerns of the region effectively. Although India did not respond to the proposal, it certainly cannot ignore it, given the changing geopolitical dynamics in the sub-Himalayan region. India will also benefit economically in case of joint investments in the hydro and agriculture sector. Most importantly, it could be a challenging task for Nepal to identify project areas given the strategic sensitivity of the region.

Proposed Nepalese Foreign Policy by Constitutional Committee

Since Nepal has become a federal, democratic republic, the committee on the International Relations and Human Rights in a 40 page report has recommended that Nepal's foreign policy should be updated in the changed context. The report says that Bhutanese, Tibetans and other refugees are a burden on Nepal, and Nepal should send them back with respect, through bilateral and multilateral diplomatic channels. Tibetan refugees should be allowed to stay on condition that they do not indulge in anti-China activities, which would affect Nepal's commitment to the one-China policy. Nepal should also formulate an appropriate policy to prevent the entry of refugees from Afghanistan, Sudan and Somalia. The report recommends that the scope of the Nepalese foreign policy should be diversified to support the economic and social development of the country. Nepal should also remain committed to international organisations like the UN, World Bank, IMF, ADB, WTO, etc.[68]

Conclusion

It has been observed that small countries have seldom challenged any big powers without the support of a powerful country. Rather they have utilised the presence of big powers to their advantage. "These states relied for security upon their strong neighbours or the balance of power among the mammoth states. The small states are consumers rather than producers of security."[69] In the case of Nepal, it has been seen that various regimes have linked their own insecurity with the country's sovereignty and territorial integrity to ensure their own survival. This has created anarchy in society and these leaders have resorted to blaming Nepal's neighbours to cover up for their own omissions and commissions.

A cursory analysis of Nepal's foreign policy behaviour indicates that Nepal's foreign policy has become more neighbourhood centric. Nepal has reiterated its intention to address security concerns of India and China. While earlier Nepal was looking West for development aids, it now looks for more investments from its immediate neighbours. Barring the early 1950s and 60s, the external power has been less effective in neutralising the influence of China and India in Nepal. Often it is seen that after national security and interests, Nepal has given priority to its neighbours security concerns.[70] Quoting Yadunath Khanal, a Nepalese diplomat, one Nepalese scholar has observed that: "[Nepal's] foreign policy will break down at the point where either India or China loses faith in us [Nepal] and concludes that her [Nepal's] vital national interests and sensitivities do not receive proper recognition in our conduct of relations."[71] Moreover, in the Twenty-First Century, the Himalayas no longer form a natural security barrier. In the event of the emergence of new Asian leaders in international politics, Nepal may seek better relationships with its neighbours instead of seeking help from other major powers to address its economic and security concerns. The following behaviour of Nepal can be discerned while analysing its foreign policy in the post-monarchy period. It has increased sensitivity to the security concerns of two immediate neighbours (India and China) which reflects a new thinking unlike that of the King Gyanendra regime. However, it continues to adhere to the old equidistance policy. Taking a view that both India and China are important for Nepal, it has now proposed a trilateral cooperation with them for regional peace, stability and development. Nepal also continues to prefer multilateral and regional arrangements to ensure effective bargaining power. To mark its presence internationally, it is committed to play a pro-active role in the UN, LLDC and other international fora. Most importantly, Nepal emphasises special relations with two neighbours within a diversified foreign policy for its rapid economic progress, to build modern infrastructure and also to attract development aid.

*

NOTES

1. Many scholars do not consider Nepal as a buffer state because they believe that Nepal is not a neutral country. John Chay and Thomas E. Ross (1986, pp. 25-30) observed that a "country with buffer state status is the result of two powerful states desiring a stable or neutral zone located between them. The buffer serves to keep the peace by functioning as physical barrier between the potential combatants." Since its formation Nepal has behaved as a neutral country. It did not take sides during 1962 Sino-India conflict. It has been adhering to *Panchsheel* as part of its foreign policy. It does not have any military alliance with its two neighbouring countries. Nepal was also one of the founder members of the non-alignment movement. However, geographically, it does not act as a major physical barrier between the two countries given the long borders between China and India towards the east and west of Nepal. Since Nepal's role as a buffer is limited to separating the two rival powers and it mainly acts as a political and cultural buffer between India and China in the sub-regional context, it could be regarded as a 'semi-buffer'.
2. Scholars have defined small states in terms of geography, economy, population and military capability. For example, Miriam Fendius Elman (1995) has projected the US as a small state prior to the mid-1800s. Elman uses the word small in the context of economy and power. Geographically, demographically and economically in comparison to India and China, Nepal is a small state but not in comparison with the Maldives and Bhutan. In terms of military capability and economics it is a small state. Therefore, Nepal is deemed

as a small state in terms of geography, military and economic size in this study.

3. Jeanne A.K. Hey, (ed.), *Small States in World Politics: Explaining Foreign Policy Behavior*, Lynne Rienner Publishers, London, 2003, pp.2-3.
4. Commonwealth Secretariat, The Commonwealth, London, at http://www.thecommonwealth.org/Internal/180407/ (accessed on 11 July 2013). Also see Baldur Thorhallsson "Small States in the UN Security Council: Means of Influence?", *The Hague Journal of Diplomacy*, 7 (2012) 135-160, at http://uni.hi.is/baldurt/files/2012/08/Small-States-UN-Security-Council-by-Thorhallsson.pdf (accessed on 11 July 2013). Also see "The Position of Small States in the 21st Century", 2 September 1983, Ministry for Foreign Affairs of Iceland, at http://www.mfa.is/news-and-publications/nr/1983 (accessed on 3 March 2014).
5. Annette Baker Fox, "The Power of Small States: Diplomacy in World War II,", in Christine Ingebritsen *et at.* (eds), *Small States in International Relations*, University of Washington Press, Seattle, 2006, p. 40.
6. Jeanne A. K. Hey, (ed.), *Small States in World Politics: Explaining Foreign Policy Behavior*, n.3, p. 1.
7. Miriam Fendius Elman, "The Foreign Policies of Small States: Challenging Neorealism in its Own Backyard", *British Journal of Political Science*, 25, 1995, p. 172.
8. M.G. Partem, "The Buffer System in International Relations", *Journal of Conflict Resolution*, 27 (1), March 1983, p. 5.
9. Ibid.
10. S.D. Muni, *India and Nepal: A Changing Relationship*, Konark Publishers Pvt Ltd, Delhi, 1992.
11. Barry Buzan and Ole Waever, *Regions and Powers: The Structure of International Security*, Cambridge University Press, Cambridge, 2003, p. 46.
12. Prashant Jha, "A Nepali Perspective on International Involvement in Nepal," in Sebastian v. Einsiedel, *et al.* (eds), *Nepal in Transition: From People's War to Fragile Peace*, Cambridge University Press, Cambridge, 2012, p.356.
13. S.D. Muni, *Foreign Policy of Nepal*, National Publishing House, Delhi, 1973.
14. Lok Raj Baral, "Nepal's Security Policy and South Asian Regionalism," *Asian Survey*, 26 (11), November 1986.
15. S.D. Muni, *Foreign Policy of Nepal*, n. 13. Also see Sangeeta Thapliyal, "Mutual Security: The Case of India-Nepal," Lancer Publishers, New Delhi, 1998, pp.6-8.
16. S.D. Muni, "The Dynamics of Foreign Policy," in S.D. Muni (ed.), *Nepal: Assertive Monarchy*, Chetana Publications, Delhi, 1977.
17. S.D. Muni, *India and Nepal: A Changing Relationship*, n.10, p.33. See A.S. Bhasin, *Documents on Nepal's Relations with India and China*, 1949-1966, Academic Books Ltd, Bombay, 1970, pp. 1-22. Also see "A Report on Emerging Challenges of Nepal's Foreign Policy", *National Level Seminars* (Report), Institute of Foreign Affairs, Kathmandu, June 2012, p.29.
18. S.D. Muni, *Foreign Policy of Nepal*, n. 13.
19. S.D. Muni, *India and Nepal: A Changing Relationship*, n.10, p. 24.
20. Lok Raj Baral, *Oppositional Politics in Nepal*, Himal Books, Kathmandu, 2006, p. 188. Also see Leo E. Rose, *Nepal: Strategy for Survival*, Mandala Book Point, Kathmandu, 1971 (reprint 2010), p. 235.
21. S.D. Muni, *India and Nepal: A Changing Relationship*, n. 10, p. 71.

22. The UCPN (Maoist) party until its split on 18 June 2012, identified India as its 'principal enemy'. While the new faction called the CPN-Maoist (Baidya) has identified India as its 'principal enemy', the UCPN (Maoist) changed its political line by not branding India as its enemy in the Hetauda Convention in February 2013. For details see "CPN-Maoist names new principal enemy" *Republica*, Kathmandu, 1 November 2012, at http://www.myrepublica.com/portal/index.php?action=news_details&news_ id=44215 (accessed on 13 July 2013). For details on political debate see Prashant Jha, Editorial: "Maoists in Nepal: the differences within," *The Hindu*, 6 December 2010. Also see Nihar Nayak, "Maoist's New Political Line and Challenges," IDSA Comment, 18 February 2013.
23. Author's interaction with Baburam Bhattarai in Kathmandu in June 2009.
24. Muchkund Dubey, *India's Foreign Policy: Coping with the Changing World*, Pearson, Delhi, 2013, pp. 58-59.
25. Ibid., p. 59.
26. Kirti Nidhi Bista, "Getting it right", *Republica*, Kathmandu, 17 September 2012, at http://www.myrepublica.com/portal/index.php?action=news_details&news_id=41841 (accessed on 13 July 2013).
27. See "Speeches of Heads of the Nepalese Delegation to the Non-Aligned Movement (1961-2009)", Institute of Foreign Affairs, Kathmandu, 2011, pp. 06-16.
28. "In Iran, PM reiterates Nepal's loyalty to NAM principles", *The Himalayan Times*, 31 August 2012.
29. "Nepal for stronger UN and NAM: DPM", *ekantipur*, 30 August 2012, at http://www.ekantipur.com/the-kathmandu-post/2012/08/29/nation/nepal-for-stronger-un-and-nam-dpm/238980.html (accessed on 13 July 2013).
30. Deputy Prime Minister and Foreign Minister Narayan Kaji Shrestha's keynote address at the conference on "Institutionalisation of the Foreign Policy of Nepal" on 17 August 2012 in Kathmandu. For details visit at http://ifa.org.np/seminar-on-institutionalization-of-nepals-foreign-policy/ (accessed on 12 February 2014).
31. "BIMSTEC," Ministry of Foreign Affairs, Government of Nepal, at http://www.mofa.gov.np/en/bimstec-170.html (accessed on 12 July 2013).
32. "Bimstec members partly solve ROO issue," *The Financial Express*, Delhi, 6 October 2005, at http://www.financialexpress.com/news/story/150379 (accessed on 12 July 2013).
33. S.D. Muni, *India and Nepal: A Changing Relationship*, n. 10, p. 33.
34. Ibid. Also see A.S. Bhasin, *Documents on Nepal's Relations with India and China, 1949-66*, Academic Books, Bombay,1970, pp.1-22.
35. Deputy Prime Minister and Foreign Minister Narayan Kaji Shrestha's keynote address at the conference on "Institutionalisation of the Foreign Policy of Nepal", no. 30.
36. "Nepal and the United Nations (1955-2012)," Ministry of Foreign Affairs, Government of Nepal.
37. "DPM Shrestha calls for international support for LDCs", *The Himalayan Times*, 28 September 2012.
38. *Nepal and the United Nations (1955-2012)*, n. 36.
39. Sita Shrestha, "Nepal in the United Nations," in S.D. Muni (ed.), *Nepal: Assertive Monarchy*, Chetana Publications, New Delhi, 1977, p. 174.
40. Recognising the need of landlocked countries for adequate transit facilities in promoting international trade, the General Assembly on 20 February 1957 invited the Governments

of Member states to give full recognition to the needs of landlocked Member states in the matter of transit trade. For details see "Land-locked countries and the expansion of international trade", The General Assembly, UN, 1028 (XI), 20 February 1957.

41. Sita Shrestha, "Nepal in the United Nations," n. 39, pp. 172-03.
42. Until 1971, Nepal tried to use East Pakistan as a transit route as an alternative to India.
43. "DPM addresses LLDCs meeting, holds talks with world leaders", *Republica*, 27 September 2012. Also see Deputy Prime Minister and Foreign Minister Narayan Kaji Shrestha's statement at the 10th Annual Ministerial meeting of the Landlocked Developing Countries in September 2011, at http://www.unohrlls.org/UserFiles/File/LLDC%20Documents/10th%20ministerial %20meeting%202011/nepal.pdf (accessed on 13 July 2013).
44. On 24 July 2006, Prachanda wrote to the UN Secretary-General that "the letter [of 2 July 2006] was written and sent unilaterally and secretively without any consultation with us [the Maoists] in utter violation of the spirit of ongoing negotiation between the Government of Nepal and the C.P.N. (Maoist)." For details see "CPN-Maoist Chairman Prachanda's Letter to the UN Secretary-General", South Asia Terrorism Portal, at http://www.satp.org/satporgtp/countries/nepal/document/papers/cpn_maoist.htm (accessed on 12 February 2014).
45. Author's interaction with a senior official of India's Ministry for External Affairs in Delhi in September 2012.
46. Ibid.
47. On 11 July 2006, the Maoists claimed that they had 36,000 "real" fighters. See Prachanda's Shaktikhor speech on http://www.youtube.com/watch?v=6EoQYZ2oa6M (source: Nepalnews.com, accessed on 28 February 2014).
48. Anirban Roy, *Prachanda: The Unknown Revolutionary*, Mandala Book Point, Kathmandu, 2008, p. 71.
49. Ibid., p. 72.
50. Details of the attacks are available in Nanda Kishor Pun alias Pasang, *Red Strides of the History*, Agnipariksha Janaprakashan Griha, Kathmandu, 2008. Pasang was chief of the People's Liberation Army (PLA), the military wing of the CPN (Maoist).
51. "India sees red over UN officials' meet with Nepal Maoists", *The Times of India*, 7 November 2007, at http://articles.timesofindia.indiatimes.com/2007-11-09/india/27989022_1_nepal-maoists-kathmandu-janatantrik-terai-mukti-morcha (accessed on 4 December 2012).
52. Ministry of Foreign Affairs, Government of Nepal, at http://www.mofa.gov.np/en/nepals-foreign-policy-102.html (accessed on 12 February 2014).
53. Ibid.
54. Baburam Bhattarai, elected in August 2011, was the fourth Prime Minister of Nepal after the Constituent Assembly elections.
55. The list of Indian joint ventures or companies, whose business was affected adversely in Nepal are: Surya Nepal (Garment), Nepal Lever, Manipal Medical, GMR (hydro), ITC Surya, Satluj Jal Vidyut Nigam (holding expansion plan) and Soaltee Hotels Limited.
56. C.P. Gajurel, "No Special relation between Nepal and India," *The Telegraph Weekly*, Kathmandu, 25 December 2008, at http://www.telegraphnepal.com/backup/telegraph/news_det.php?news_id=4576 (accessed on 16 July 2013). The paper was formally submitted at the Institute of Foreign Affairs-FES (Friedrich Ebert Stiftung, Germany)

Seminar in Kathmandu, 23 December 2008. C. P. Gajurel wrote this while he was a Politburo member of the Communist Party of Nepal (Maoist). He is presently vice-chairman of the Communist Party of Nepal-Maoist (Mohan Baidya faction). This faction in January 2013 identified India as its "Principal Enemy".

57. Purna Basnet, "China's Success," *Himal Southasian*, Kathmandu, April 2011, at http://himalmag.com/component/content/article/4350-chinas-success.html (accessed on 13 July 2013).
58. Peter Lee, "Sino-Indian rivalry fuels Nepal's turmoil," *Asia Times*, Hong Kong, 14 November 2009, at http://www.atimes.com/atimes/South_Asia/KK14Df01.html (accessed on 13 July 2013). For more information see Anand Gurung, "Reversal of Role: Is China playing 'Nepal Card' now?," *Canada Tibet Committee*, 6 March 2006, at http://www.tibet.ca/en/newsroom/wtn/5641 (accessed on 13 July 2013). Also see "China agrees to provide Rs 200 million worth security assistance," *Nepal News*, Kathmandu, 7 December 20008.
59. "PM in Norway, holds talks on energy deal," *The Rising Nepal*, Kathmandu, 29 March 2009. For details of Prachanda's interaction with journalists and Nepalese in Norway see "Prime Minister Prachanda in Norway," *Democracy and Class Struggle*, 30 March 2009, at http://democracyandclasstruggle.blogspot.in/2009/03/prime-minister-prachanda-in-norway.html (accessed on 13 July 2013).
60. "China, Nepal to advance bilateral ties," *Xinhua* (English), 30 December 2009, at http://news.xinhuanet.com/english/2009-12/30/content_12731012.htm (accessed on 13 July 2013). Also see Joint Statement declared during the visit on 30 December 2009, Beijing, at http://www.fmprc.gov.cn/eng/wjdt/2649/t649608.htm (accessed on 12 February 2014).
61. Chairman of the Standing Committee of China's National People's Congress (NPC).
62. Purna Basnet, "China's Success," n. 57.
63. "Govt to establish think tanks on foreign and strategic issues: PM," *The Kathmandu Post*, 15 January 2012, at http://www.ekantipur.com/the-kathmandu-post/2012/01/15/nation/govt-to-establish-think-tanks-on-foreign-and-strategic-issues-pm/230440.html (accessed on 13 July 2013).
64. Vice Minister of International Department for South Asian Affairs of the Communist Party of China (CPC).
65. "Chinese leaders caution Baidya against foreign interests in federalism", *Nepal News*, Kathmandu, 26 July 2012, at http://www.nepalnews.com/archive/2012/jul/jul26/news18.php (accessed on 31 July 2012).
66. "Dahal returns from China; prescribes trilateral talks for strategy on Nepal" *Nepal News*, 27 October 2010, at http://www.nepalnews.com/home/index.php/news/2/10090-dahal-returns-from-china-prescribes-trilateral-talks-for-strategy-on-nepal.html (accessed on 13 July 2013).
67. "Vision for tomorrow: India-Nepal Ties," edited excerpts from Dahal's speech at Indian Council of World Affairs (ICWA) in New Delhi on 29 April 2013, *Republica*, 1 May 2013, at http://www.myrepublica.com/portal/index.php?action=news_details&news_id=53965 (accessed on 12 July 2013).
68. English translation of the Report of the Legislative Parliament Committee for International Relations and Human Rights, Constituent Assembly 2008, Nepal.
69. Amry Vandenbosch, "The Small States in International Politics and Organization", *The Journal of Politics*, 26(2), May 1964, p. 301.

70. Yuba Nath Lamsal, Editorial: "Nepal's Foreign Policy In 21st Century," *The Rising Nepal*, Kathmandu, date of Publication is not available, see at http://www.gorkhapatra.org.np/rising.detail.php?article_id=57960&cat_id=7 (accessed on 13 July 2013). Also see Jay Raj Acharya, "Foreign policy Priorities of New Nepal", *The Telegraph Weekly*, Kathmandu, 7 January 2009, http://www.telegraphnepal.com/backup/telegraph/news_det.php?news_id=4645 (accessed on 28 February 2014).
71. Shambhu Ram Simkhada, "Nepal's National Interest and Foreign Policy," Major Policy Issues, Nepal Constitution Foundation, Kathmandu, see at http://www.ncf.org.np/upload/files/507_en_Nepals%20national%20interest%20&%20foreign%20policy.pdf (accessed on 13 July 2013). Nepal Constitution Foundation is an independent, non-governmental, not-for-profit civil society organisation based in Kathmandu.

CHAPTER 3

Protecting the Sphere of Influence: India's Relationship with Nepal

In the era of globalisation and a multi-polar world order, events in a particular region of the world can have trans-national ramifications. Therefore, no single country can deal with challenges without the support and cooperation of other countries. In this context, India believes that all its neighbours, big or small are crucial for its economic growth and stability. As in the case of any other country, India's foreign policy too is "dedicated to the furtherance of [its] national security and developmental priorities in a globalised and interdependent world."[1] At the same time, India's priority has been to "ensure a peaceful, secure and stable neighbourhood"[2] through cooperation and by making its neighbours stakeholders in India's growth by linking them to the larger Indian economy. But misunderstandings arise—in spite of best intentions—that are used by some analysts in different countries to malign India for its alleged 'hegemonic' intentions.

Strategic Relevance of Nepal for India

Nepal is an important neighbour of India and occupies special significance in its foreign policy because of the geographic, historical, cultural and economic linkages that span centuries. The Nepal-India relationship is determined more by geography and history than any other considerations. The two countries not only share an open border and unhindered movement of people, but they also have close bonds through marriages and familial ties, which is unique in Asia. The open border is a symbol of their deep trust and friendship.

Articulating India's strategic interests in Nepal, Jawaharlal Nehru in December 1950 said: "From time immemorial, the Himalayas have provided us with a magnificent frontier...We cannot allow that barrier to be penetrated because it is also the principal barrier to India."[3] India also shares an open border with Nepal. Therefore, "[t]he political instability and adverse security situation in Nepal [has been] a cause of deep concern to India."[4] There is evidence that anti-India elements have taken advantage of the chronic political instability and poor governance in Nepal.

The Himalayas as a natural frontier may have become less relevant in an era of nuclear weapons, globalisation, technology and the improvement in the Sino-Indian relationship in recent years. The Chinese have also shattered the myth of the Himalayas as a natural barrier by extending the Qinghai–Tibet railway line till Lhasa. Beijing plans to extend it to Nepal in the near future and later further into the South Asian hinterland.[5] Moreover, in the post-monarchy period, Nepal wants to become a transit country rather than a semi-buffer between China and India. It also wants to benefit from the economic growth taking place in its neighbourhood.

Despite this, Nepal will undoubtedly continue to be of strategic importance for India for various reasons. Nepal is the only country in South Asia whose citizens are given national treatment in India. It also has topographical similarities with the northern borders of India. Therefore, India's "heartland is vulnerable to Chinese attacks during a conflict situation. The Chinese Army can negotiate Himalayan barriers in Nepal without much resistance"[6] and it would have a clear advantage by occupying strategic heights in the mountainous terrain. The Rasuwagadhi-Syabrubesi-Kathmandu-Birgunj road could be the shortest route across Nepalese territory between India and China. According to Nepal government sources, technically, the Syabrubesi-Rasuwagadhi road is "more reliable than the Kodari Highway".[7] The Syabrubesi-Rasuwagadi highway runs at a height of around 6,000 ft across the Himalayan range and is almost unaffected by snow and landslides. This route could emerge as an alternative to the Arniko Highway, which is narrow, vulnerable to landsides and snows for ferrying large oil tankers and containers. Once this road is opened, Nepal will be able to transport gas and petroleum products from China through this route.[8]

India has built physical defences all along the India-China border but it remains vulnerable along Nepal's border with China. Moreover, given the Chinese security build-up in Tibet over the last 15 years, India's vulnerability has increased even further. China has vastly improved the roads and improved military infrastructure on its side of the border in Tibet. It has reportedly deployed nuclear-capable intermediate missiles in the area and around 300,000 troops across the Tibetan plateau.[9] Apart from the huge road connectivity to TAR, China reportedly set up 23 airfields in TAR exclusively for military purposes by 2001. Quoting a *People's Liberation Army (PLA) Daily*, a researcher has revealed that at least 50 airports have been constructed by a single PLA Air Force (AF) Engineering Division under China's Western Development Programme of which TAR is an integral part. China has also constructed more than 10,000 km of roads specifically for the defence of TAR's borders.[10] This has become a major concern for India. Although India has upgraded its physical and air defence by adding to its existing strength, it is still unable to match the Chinese preparations. Therefore, Nepal's valleys are more important than its mountains for defending Indian territory in case of any hostilities.[11] In this context, the military modernisation in the two countries will have an impact on Nepal. Since the future conflict might not be the same as in 1962, both the countries will try to make further investments in strategic locations in Nepal.

For India, a sovereign Nepal constitutes a political bulwark against China. India believes that Nepal will always abide by the UN principles and will not allow any third country to attack India through its territory. Similarly, Nepal, as a small neighbour of China and a part of the so called Chinese aggressive five-fingers concept, would prefer to maintain its close relationship with India as a deterrent for any potential Chinese aggression.

Conflicts Over the Peace Treaty

The India-Nepal relationship has been further strengthened by numerous Treaties and agreements signed by the two sovereign nations. The Treaty of Peace and Friendship, concluded on 31 July 1950, is one of them. The Treaty acknowledges each other's sovereignty and territorial integrity without seeking to alter their natural relationship. It has to some extent institutionalised the open border and has facilitated socio-cultural and economic linkages.

The Treaty, however, has for various reasons become an emotional issue in Nepal and the demand for its abrogation has regularly featured in election manifestos of different political parties. The Rana regime fell within six months of signing it. Subsequent regimes in Nepal have been expressing their reservations over the Treaty. However, the people of Terai who have strong links with people across the border in India want the continuation of this Treaty. One of the significant parts of this Treaty has been the granting of resident status to each other's citizens. Although Nepal does not reciprocate on this clause, it has enabled many Nepalese citizens to take up government jobs in India. Over time Nepal has enacted much legislation to dilute the original spirit of this Treaty. The monarchy too believed this Treaty as an instrument of Indian influence. The Treaty has been politicised over time to serve the political interest of the particular constituency that draws it support from the anti-India sentiments in Nepal.

With the introduction of multi-party democracy in Nepal in 1990, other issues such as border encroachment and hydro projects, etc, were taken up by some political parties. In 1994, for example, the CPN-UML campaigned vigorously on these issues. The 40 demands of the CPN (Maoist) in 1995 also focused on the 1950 Treaty and aroused intense anti-India feelings during the People's War. However, except for King Mahendra, no other monarch, raised this issue with India. During the constitutional monarchy period, the Nepalese Foreign Minister Kamal Thapa of the royalist Rashtriya Prajatantra Party (RPP)—a coalition partner of the Nepali Congress which led the government—visited India in August 1998 with a 'non-paper', which for the first time, made some suggestions for its revision. The CPN (Maoist), in its manifesto for the 2008 Constituent Assembly (CA) elections, promised to abrogate the Treaty and maintain equal distance between India and China. The CPN-UML also promised to review 'all unequal Treaties', while the NC manifesto remained silent on the matter.[12] Yet, even after India expressed its willingness to revise the Treaty, there has been a lack of political consensus in Nepal over the issue and no alternative or specific proposal has been given by Nepal regarding the provisions they want to revise. The politicisation of this Treaty is also evident from the fact that no political party wants to abrogate it.[13]

In September 2008 India and Nepal agreed to form a high-level committee headed by foreign secretaries to examine the Treaty and suggest possible revisions. There is a view in India, however, that this issue is being needlessly hyped. For instance, former Indian ambassador to Nepal Deb Mukherjee in an interview to *The Telegraph* in May 2008 said:

> This demand has been raised several times in the past and we [India] have said, fair enough, renegotiate or restructure. In fact, Clause 10 of the treaty clearly says it can be abrogated by either side on a year's notice. And I remember that during the Foreign Secretary-level talks in 2001, we had reminded the Nepali delegation of the clause and said, why don't you do it? We should be prepared to discuss all options.[14]

India's former Foreign Secretary Shyam Saran also dismissed the contention of Prachanda that the Treaty was an 'unequal pact', and pointed out that under the pact "Nepali citizens enjoy special privileges in India".[15] The issue figured prominently in the joint statement during the visit of Prachanda to New Delhi as prime minister in September 2008. The two countries agreed to "review, adjust and update" the Treaty and other agreements, while duly considering the special features of the bilateral relationship.

From an Indian perspective, the Treaty seems to have limited relevance in the changed global security environment. Former Indian Ambassador to Nepal, K.V. Rajan, has observed that:

> Its relevance for India's security in today's context is limited and questionable. China is no longer the only security concern in the sub-region. Pakistani activities in and through Nepal...environment and climate change, also have serious long-term implications for the security of both countries.[16]

Apart from addressing mutual security concerns, the Treaty also covers other social-economic issues. It has been observed that people have criticised more the 'letter of exchange' that followed the Treaty than the Treaty itself. Nevertheless, both countries have periodically acknowledged each other's value and importance and have also described the relationship as 'special' on various occasions. For example, Maoist leader and former Prime Minister Baburam Bhattarai noted: "Practically, we are more closely integrated with India, with an open border and closer economic ties. So we have more interaction with India and more problems also, which sometimes creates misunderstanding."[17] Therefore, in view of the changed geopolitical dynamics, the Treaty should be updated in accordance with contemporary reality.

India and Nepalese Nationalism

India has always supported popular governments in Nepal. It played a major role in bringing the monarchy, the democrats and the Ranas together in the 1950s; and supported the movement for multiparty democracy in 1990. India played an important role in bringing the Maoists and the seven political parties together to sign a 12-point agreement in November 2005. This agreement significantly led to the mainstreaming of the Maoists as stakeholders in Nepal's multiparty democracy and brought an end to a decade-long insurgency. Since then it has been constantly supporting the peace process in Nepal.

Despite that, there have been ups and down in the century-old India-Nepal relationship due to several factors[18]—psychological, geographic, political, economic and social, apart from some external factors. The perception of the Nepalese elites about India being an interventionist or hegemonic power has percolated down to the common people. The ruling elites, including the political parties, exploited this sentiment to either protect their regime or for acquiring power. Lok Raj Baral has observed that these 'strained relations' highlighted in the name of 'nationalism' have been useful for regime continuity. Even so, Nepal's rulers have never lost sight of the geopolitical reality.[19]

Nepal feels vulnerable and insecure because it is landlocked, and its sense of insecurity is, ironically, fuelled by the very cultural affinities that are also touted as the greatest asset of the bilateral relationship. Trailokya Raj Aryal argues that: "With so many similarities between Nepal and India, naturally, Nepal had no other options but to contrast itself with India."[20] There is a tendency to define Nepalese identity as distinctly different from that of India. In Nepal, it is fashionable to be anti-India, especially in Kathmandu, as a mark of nationalism and patriotism. In fact, some political parties in Nepal turn anti-India when they are in the opposition, and accuse the government of being guided by 'foreign elements'. In Nepal, foreign elements indirectly implies India. But once in power, they change their position.[21] Many of the political parties whether in power or in opposition seek India's indulgence to retain or gain power.

The monarchy used anti-Indianism as a rallying point, both to create a popular support base for itself and to generate a sense of national unity amongst the people. The monarchy viewed India's latent support for democracy with suspicion, even though it benefited immensely from India's support to the democratic movements in early 1950s, as it led to the removal of the Ranas. Unfortunately, later, King Mahendra and his successors thought that India was playing the 'democracy card' in Nepal to protect its security interests. On several occasions, both the right and left-wing political forces in Nepal (the royalists, communists and the Maoists) have promoted anti-Indianism for their own political benefit. Since the mid-1950s, they have been frequently using the 1950 Treaty, the Koshi and Gandaki Treaties, and since 1990s the Mahakali Treaty—to foment anti-India sentiments. Similarly, the alleged border encroachments by India, poor treatment of Nepalese workers in India and unresolved trade and transit issues have also been used for the purpose of fomenting anti-Indianism. Some Kathmandu-based intellectuals and journalists too indulge in anti-India rhetoric to take benefits from other countries known for their adversarial stance towards India.[22]

Nepal-India Relations in Post-2006

Interestingly, this trend has reached new heights since the abolition of the monarchy and with the emergence of the CPN (Maoist) as the largest party in the CA elections of 2008. While earlier this phenomenon was confined to the elites in Kathmandu, it has since become more visible in rural areas due to the constant anti-India propaganda by the Maoists and especially after the resignation of Prachanda as prime minister in May 2009. Some Nepalese Army officers and royalists even believe that India is responsible for the abolition of the monarchy and the rise of the Maoists. Senior army officers argue that India's refusal to supply arms in 2005 after the royal coup indirectly strengthened the Maoists. The Maoists on their part accused India of not trusting them and also hold it responsible for the ongoing political instability in Nepal and the delay in the drafting of the Constitution under the first CA. They believe that the bureaucrats in South Block lack a clear understanding of Nepalese politics. Interestingly, although some leaders in the NC and the CPN-UML share similar feelings, they do not want to antagonise India by going public on the issue.

There has been a general perception that India could not accept the emergence of the CPN (Maoist) as the largest party. Some other sections argue that India tried to cultivate the Maoists just after the CA elections but was betrayed by them.[23] After Prachanda's resignation the pro-Maoist political pundits were of the view that India was not comfortable with Maoists as the largest political party given the ideological differences between them. The Maoists accuse India of interfering in the internal affairs of Nepal and encouraging encroachments into Nepalese territory along the borders. They have also tried to convince the people that India does not want political stability in Nepal.[24] They say that India played a role in the pulling down of the Maoists government headed by Prachanda. It is often said that the Madhesi parties reportedly supported the Madhav Kumar Nepal government (that succeeded Prachanda's in May 2009) at India's behest. It was also alleged during this period that India was against the integration process of the Maoist combatants into the security forces. Such arguments completely disregard the fact that major political parties like the NC, the CPN-UML, and the Nepalese Army were also opposed to integration despite inter-party agreements. It would be worth mentioning that India was blamed for the May 2009 developments which led to various anti-India demonstrations by the Maoists. This damaged India's reputation at the international level. Interestingly, Prachanda confessed later on 7 August 2013 that the "[Former Nepalese Army Chief General] Katawal saga was the result of his immature working style after taking [over] the reins of government. Obviously, it was our [the Maoists] mistake to take action against the Army Chief who was due to retire in three months."[25]

The Maoists' resolutions against India and their ploy to take advantage of PLA cadres' integration into the Nepalese Army for capturing state power in

Kharipati conclave in November 2008 further added to the confusion in India's Nepal policy and affected India-Nepal relations. The Maoists' ambiguous political line and subterfuge kept Nepal in a constant state of political instability since May 2009, which became a matter of concern for India and the international community. India continues to fear that anti-India elements will take advantage of lingering political instability and has been expressing its concerns in this regard during bilateral visits. India's economic and political engagement with Nepal had been affected due to the Maoist campaign against India, which had included targeting Indian business houses and joint ventures by organising labour strikes, political protests as well as extortions by Maoist-affiliated front organisations.

Many in Nepal think that 'India's over-reaction to Nepal's assertions of sovereignty' (even when they do not affect legitimate Indian interests) has fuelled anti-Indianism over the years. Other aspects of India's 'misconceived' Nepal policy, as pointed out by the Nepalese, are: India's inconsistency in supporting various political players and thereby giving one or the other a sense of political insecurity; the recurring effort to micro-manage Nepal's internal politics (an effort which can be said to date back to the 1950s); its intrusive profile in Nepal's internal politics (a historical pattern rather than occasional aberration); a hegemonic attitude, which is all too apparent to most Nepalese, despite New Delhi's professions of respect for Nepal's sovereignty. Other irritants include: the allegation that Indian embassy lobbied for an Indian company to get the machine-readable passport (MRP) printing contract without following due process; holding up of the Kantipur printing consignment at the Kolkata seaport; the unseemly manner in which Nepalese leaders are treated by Indian diplomats and leaders (the alleged threatening of a Constituent Assembly member of the Maoist party in 2011),[26] and making unsubstantiated statements regarding linkages between Nepalese Maoists and Indian Maoists.

In the post-May 2009 period, there is a feeling in Nepal that India does not have a consistent Nepal policy. Over the last few years, both at the diplomatic and political levels, India has been playing a passive role in the peace process and in Constitution drafting. Given the multi-layered stakeholders' linkages that define India's relations with Nepal, people in Kathmandu often debate as to who formulates India's Nepal policy. Previously, the Nepal policy used to be handled by the political leaders, and the relations between the political leaders of both country made things easier. But this is no longer the case, with few Indian political leaders being active in Nepal-India affairs. The absence of any high-level political engagement from the

Indian side has added to misunderstandings and misperceptions. For example, seven Nepalese prime ministers[27] have visited India over the past 12 years but these have not been reciprocated by India. In exchange, only three high level visits were made by the Indian side, including two by S. M. Krishna, the former Minister for External Affairs. In fact, there was a huge difference in the Nepal policy between United Progressive Alliance (UPA)-I and the UPA-II.[28] Prashant Jha, a journalist and security analyst, has observed:

> India's influence has reduced due to some reshuffle in the Nepal desk of MEA[Ministry of External Affairs] and absence of left parties in the UPA government. All those persons involved in the 12-point agreements are either sidelined or no more associated with that. India's involvement in the internal matters of Nepal is now more open than earlier.[29]

However, this discourse changed after Baburam Bhattarai became the prime minister. Surprisingly, the anti-India cacophony in the media declined to some extent after the Maoists assumed power in August 2011, for the second time in four years. This was mainly because Baburam Bhattarai is supposed to have a strong support base amongst intellectuals and media houses in Nepal and there was a perception in Kathmandu that India was supportive of his government. Subsequently, almost all the bilateral mechanisms between the two countries were revived and several meetings were held to discuss issues relating to energy and water, trade and commerce, security and border management.

India's relations and engagement with Nepal in general and Maoists in particular gained some momentum after Jayant Prasad took charge as India's ambassador to Nepal on 25 August 2011. He assumed office while Nepal's peace process was passing through uncertainties and the term of the CA was extended for the third time. Political parties were entangled in debates over contentious issues and were looking for India's support. India was concerned about protracted political stalemate in Nepal after the resignation of Jhalanath Khanal of the CPN-UML. Since then, India reportedly used its good offices to further improve bilateral relations. The bilateral meetings that could not take place in the last two years were reactivated. Some of the important bilateral meetings[30] held between India and Nepal are as follows:

- 17 January 2012: Joint Home Secretary-level mechanism meeting held in New Delhi.
- 24 January 2012: Nepal and India Joint Commission on Water Resources (JCWR) meeting held in Kathmandu.

- 5 September 2012: The Nepal-India Border Management Coordination Meeting held between border district administration and security officials in Siliguri.
- 4 December 2012: Meeting of the border guarding forces Sashastra Seema Bal (India) and Armed Police Force (Nepal).
- 2 January 2013: The Nepal-India Transit Treaty renewed without any changes to the existing Treaty.
- 12 April 2013: The Nepal-India Consultative Group on expanding military cooperation.
- 1 June 2013: Annual joint Home Secretary level meeting held in Kathmandu. Both the countries agreed to exchange information to combat terrorism and criminal activities across their open border.

With slow progress in the peace process (PP) despite a Maoist-led government, the people gradually realised that it was intra-party factionalism within the main political parties that was responsible for the political stalemate, rather than India. After repeated failure to get Chinese support for government formation in Kathmandu since 2008, the Maoists had realised that antagonising India would cost them dearly. Their tactic was not to oppose India but to engage it in a constructive manner, despite their suspicion that India would not welcome Maoist ascendance in Nepalese politics. At the same time, the anti-Indianism of the break-away Mohan Baidya faction had become very strident and was trying to build its political base on this posture.

The spate of anti-Indianism that was reflected through various statements, and writings in the media picked up again after appointment of Chief Justice (CJ)-led election government in March 2013. Some groups—those not part of decision-making process—accused foreign powers of interfering in the domestic politics of Nepal and suggested that India had played major role in the appointment of the CJ-led government. These groups include the ultra-rightist, the leftists and some civil society leaders, who have their own vested interests. These groups thought that India had been facilitating an alliance between the Madhesis and the Maoists. The anti-government forces, especially the CPN-Maoist (Baidya faction) and fringe ultra nationalist parties had come out with statements that establishment of a CJ-led interim government was an 'Indian design'. Speculations about India's role circulated in Nepal after Indian envoy to Kathmandu, Jayant Prasad, reportedly met President Ram Baran Yadav followed by his meeting with the CJ, who was introspecting on the proposal and agreed to it after this visit.[31]

Surprisingly, the Prachanda and Baburam Bhattarai factions in the UCPN (Maoist) were of the view that India was not in favour of strengthening the

Maoists in Nepalese politics, and preferred to restrict to participating in the Constitution-drafting process. Especially, after Baburam Bhattarai's resignation as the Prime Minister in March 2013, his sympathisers had spread the word in Nepal and also to the international community that India did not want the second CA elections to be held under the Maoists. The Maoists, who began to be favoured by New Delhi after the Hetauda general convention[32] of March 2013, were surprised by New Delhi's invitation to Sher Bahadur Deuba and Sushil Koirala of the Nepali Congress and Madhav Kumar Nepal of the CPN-UML to visit India and hold meetings with Sonia Gandhi following Prachanda's Delhi visit. After these visits, the misunderstanding within the UCPN (Maoist), especially between Baburam Bhattarai and Prachanda, aggravated further. The Prachanda faction, which was under the impression that Baburam Bhattarai has been India's favourite, accused him of not lobbying strongly for arranging a meeting between Prachanda and Sonia Gandhi. India's policy of re-balancing democratic forces and encouraging home-grown ideas to resolve political disputes in Nepal thus was again misread by many political analysts in the county.

The CPN-UML joined the ultra-nationalist groups' chorus against the appointment of Lokman Singh Karki as the chief of the Commission for Investigation of Abuse of Authority (CIAA) in May 2013. It had decided to make 'nationalism' its campaign agenda during the proposed November 2013 CA elections. As reported in the media, the party felt that: "foreign factors are at play in Nepalese politics after the dissolution [of] the CA in May [2012] and the appointment of controversial Chief Secretary Lokman Singh Karki as [chief of] CIAA is the continuation of such interference."[33] The party also claimed that the CPN-Maoist was more nationalist compared to other parties.

The observations of the CPN-UML and the CPN-Maoist on foreign interference led to further polarisation in Nepal polity and while the country was preparing for the proposed November elections. The election preparation was delayed due to the non-cooperation of 33 political parties and strong resistance at local level from the CPN-Maoist in the process of voter registration and issue of citizenship cards. There was also lack of consensus amongst the top four political parties over contentious issues like fixing the percentage of the threshold level for proportional representation, number of seats in the CA, delineation of constituencies, declaration of properties by aspiring candidates, and preventing participation of candidates with criminal charges. In all these issues, the High Level Political Committee (HLPC) had failed to garner any consensus despite several rounds of discussions. The HLPC had also failed to convince the CNP-Maoist and other political parties for discussing their opposition to the elections under the CJ-led government.

At the same time, certain sections in Nepal believe that India should play a constructive role in the peace and Constitution-drafting process rather than being involved in petty politics. The political forces in Nepal also do not rule out the importance and necessity of India for Nepal's political stability and economic prosperity—in fact, every political party wants India's support for its own benefit.[34] Ramesh Nath Pandey, former foreign minister of Nepal, observed: "India has very good relationship with many leaders of Nepal cutting across the party line. But it is yet to introduce a comprehensive policy towards Nepal focusing on economic engagements."[35] Therefore, there is a strong view in Nepal that India needs to take advantage of its leverage in the country and help to forge consensus on government formation and critical constitutional matters.

The Nepalese want India to accept the changes in the demographic and economic profile of Nepal over the last decade. With remittances from foreign countries including the Gulf, Nepal now has an expanding middle class and is less dependent on India for employment. The Nepalese middle class has undergone sea change over the years because of exposure to the outside world, access to knowledge, and information technology. They have few personal or familial relationships across the border, unlike the past when only the feudal elites and the poorer Madhesis in the southern plains used to have such relations.

Madhesi Movement and India

There is a perception in Nepal that India has been backing the demand for federalism. The *Pahadis* (hill people) believe that India has been encouraging the demand for 'One Madhesh One Pradesh'. Many in Nepal see this as an attempt on the part of India to balkanise the country, while others think that India wanted a single province as a buffer zone on the southern flank of Nepal. The perception gained currency in the early 2000s as India was attempting to carry out special development programmes in the underdeveloped and neglected Terai region to prevent Nepalese Maoists from gaining influence there, given their strategic linkages with Indian Maoists. Historically, Nepalese nationalism, as promoted by King Mahendra, is dominated by the ethos of the hill people and the people from Terai were regarded as being close to India and were discriminated against. Therefore, the demand for special autonomy in Terai was raised as early as the late 1950s. The Maoists expanded their base to the region cashing in on anti-monarchy sentiment. Moreover, India was unhappy with monarchy for not protecting its security interests.

From that time onwards, a number of India-funded development projects were diverted to the Terai region. After the CA elections, India reportedly used this constituency to promote its interests in Nepal. On one occasion India attempted to use Madhesi parliamentarians to keep the Maoists out of power.[36] The Maoists and some Nepalese analysts argue that Shyam Saran's visit to Kathmandu in 2010 as special envoy of the Indian prime minister was for the purpose of preventing the Madhesis from supporting any Maoist-led coalition government.[37]

Former Prime Minister G.P. Koirala, hinting at India's hand in the Terai crisis, had also said, "The ongoing Madhesh crisis [2007] can be solved within a minute if Nepal and India jointly work together for it."[38] This indicates that senior political leaders were under the impression that India had links with those agitating in the Madhesi movement and sought India's help for resolving outstanding issues in Terai. A similar observation was made by Prachanda during the 2007 Madhesi protests against the Interim Constitution. If this perception gains further ground, it can lead to greater anti-Indianism in Nepal, and allow more space for China and Pakistan to make Nepal a hotbed of anti-India activities.

Madhesis' sympathy towards India is more a cultural than political issue, given their centuries old relationship with the people of India and their desire to maintain it. The Nepalese political parties have not been sympathetic to their plight and the discrimination against them, even after the formation of the Democratic Secular Republic of Nepal. The *Pahadis* continue to look at Madhesis with suspicion and this may further complicate the situation. As noted by a former Deputy External Affairs Minister of India, Surendra Pal Singh: "As long as they [Madhesis] keep their cultural links or other types of links with another country, naturally they will be looked at with suspicion."[39] However, the fact of the matter is that both the hill people and those of Terai origin have a strong cultural affinity with India, apart from property and business interests.

The Madhesis on their part believe that India's Nepal policy is more Kathmandu-centric. They accuse India of neglecting the Madhesi movement. Upendra Yadav, the then president of the Madhesi Janadhikar Forum, said in an interview:

> India, especially South Block and the Indian Embassy, have been against the Madhes and Madhesi Janadhikar Forum (MJF). They created the Terai

> Madhes Loktantrik Party (TMLP) to weaken us. In fact, one of the reasons the pre-election alliance did not happen was because India was trying to boost up TMLP.[40]

One senior leader of the Sadbhavana Party told this author that: "Eighty per cent of India's aid is being utilised in the hilly region." The Madhesis have also accused India of engineering divisions in the MJF in June 2009. Keshav Mainali, president of the Chure Bhawar Ekta Samaj, observed that: "It is only...when India wants controversial issues to erupt [it uses]...Madhesh [to its advantage]....India's stand on the Nepalese Madhesi issue is self-contradict[ory]."[41] There is already a debate in the Terai region that the Madhesi groups have failed to take any concrete decision about their future because of India's support to the liberal democratic parties, who have been opposing ethnicity-based federalism.[42] One scholar observed that:

> Even the Madhesi political and rebel leaders are not happy with Indian intervention because such intervention can hurt their own political future in their constituencies. Some consider Madhes issue as a solely internal issue/conflict of Nepal because there is nothing to do with a bilateral matter.[43]

Given the rigid positions taken by the major political parties in Nepal over the demands raised by the Madhesi groups, the region may witness some serious ethnic unrest—the pointers are already there. According to Keshav Mainali:

> Some scholars identify pre-symptoms of civil ethnic war in a case like this. Already, there is serious aggression in Madhesh against any people of hill origin. Pahadi officials are not able to work in Madhesh. Most of them are being transferred from the region. Some of them have already been killed, tortured, displaced, their houses burnt. They are no longer safe there and are treated as enemies of Madhesh and Madheshi.[44]

It is estimated that around "300 people have lost their lives in the (Madhesi-Pahadi) conflict"[45] since 2006. Given the cultural and familial linkages between the Madhesis and the Indians in the region, the absence of a clear Indian response to the suffering of Madhesis could destabilise governments in New Delhi and at provincial levels, especially in Uttar Pradesh (UP) and Bihar. Upendra Yadav has said on record:

> We are people of Indian origin, but remember we are Madhesis and Nepalis. This is our struggle. India can give us moral support, which is not forthcoming at the moment. The people of Bihar and UP are with us, but the Government of India is not taking any notice. If the situation

in Madhesh worsens, India will be badly affected. The implications could be terrible.[46]

Instability in Nepal is likely to have an adverse impact on India's political, economic and security interests. Any upheaval in the Terai bodes more ill for India. The anti-Indianism flowing especially from the Madhes movement will again have adverse impact on India's economic and security interests in the border region. Since the Terai is closely linked with India, a troubled Terai may affect every major highway, custom point and industrial zone, as well as Nepal's trade with India and other countries.[47]

India, however, is faced with a dilemma—any constructive attempt by India to salvage the Terai situation is likely to be interpreted as unnecessary intervention in the internal affairs of Nepal and upset its *Pahadi* constituency, whereas, passive indifference to developments in Terai will be construed as shirking of Indian responsibility by the Madhesis. India cannot afford to ignore developments in Nepal, and especially the discrimination against the people of Terai region.

Therefore, it is in the interests of both the countries and for the internal cohesion in Nepal that the people of Nepal, including the Madhesis, to settle the issue through dialogue and consensus within the framework of the new Constitution. Similarly, the Madhesis need to conform to the constitutional norms of Nepal. Both the *Pahadis* and Madhesis should overcome their mutual mistrust and devote themselves to the nation-building process.

Trade and Economic Assistance

India is the largest investor and trade partner of Nepal. India accounts for 44 per cent of Nepal's Foreign Direct Investment (FDI) and 60 per cent of Nepal's external trade. For uninterrupted economic growth and trade with other countries, India has opened 22 transit routes with Nepal, far more than stipulated by the international convention. In addition, India has agreed to open two land routes in Brahmadandi and Tanakpur in western Nepal. These two routes would facilitate in-land trade between the northern far-west and southern far-west of Nepal via India. It will reduce the distance and cut transportation costs for Nepalese traders. The open border has made a huge contribution to the development of both the countries.

India has been consistently providing economic assistance for Nepal's national development since 1951. Up to August 2011, India had provided economic assistance for 411 development projects in Nepal, including NPR 6,300 crore in 2010-11 alone.[48] India has also been a major job market for both the skilled and unskilled labourers of Nepal and is ranked second in the remittance contributor countries/destinations for Nepal. There are around 40,000 Gorkhas serving in the Indian Army and another 5000 in the paramilitary forces of India. There are also 150,000 pensioners, including their dependents. Their pay and pensions make a significant contribution to the Nepalese economy. A GEFONT-Note prepared by Umesh Upadhyaya, entitled "Issue of Protection of Migrant Workers and their Families", states that there are around seven million Nepalese workers in India. The All India Migrant Nepali Association estimates that most of them have merged into the population of India while about 50 per cent of them retain their official Nepalese citizenship.[49]

India is the biggest and most easily accessible market for Nepalese finished industrial goods and is the cheapest source of raw material for Nepalese industries. Table 3.1 shows that India still remains the largest trade partner of Nepal with around US$2 billion worth of business. At the same time, it cannot be denied that India is gradually being overtaken by China in the Nepalese economy. The prolonged political instability and growing anti-India sentiment in Nepal has affected the bilateral economic cooperation and has shrunk the inflow of FDI from India (see Table 3.2). In fact, in the last one decade, India has been struggling to uphold its old position in the major sectors.

Table 3.1: Nepal's Trade with India, China and US

Export						*(Value NPR '000)*
Country	*2005/6*	*2006/7*	*2007/8*	*2008/9*	*2009/10*	*% Change*
India	40,714,700	41,728,800	38,555,700	43,574,482	39,902,811	-8.4
China	892,583	377,991	736,405	1,847,934	1,008,696	-45.4
US	6,993,442	5,571,274	4,598,900	4,878,573	3,867,223	-20.7
Import						*(Value NPR '000)*
Country	*2005/06*	*2006/07*	*2007/08*	*2008/09*	*2009/10*	*% Change*
India	107,143,100	115,872,300	142,376,500	165,119,002	214,261,109	29.8
China	12,083,497	16,678,616	22,255,845	32,852,910	39,218,203	19.4
US	1,677,499	4,259,983	3,718,141	3,808,616	5,384,826	41.4

Source: Federation of Nepalese Chambers of Commerce and Industry.

Apart from growing anti-India sentiment, Indian business houses find unfavourable business atmosphere to invest in Nepal. A survey by Federation of Indian Chambers of Commerce and Industry (FICCI) showed that industries in Nepal are "badly hit by acute shortages of power and raw materials. Petrol and diesel supply have run out and the labour unrest has struck at the very heart of businesses."[50] There are also concerns relating to delays in the completion of hydroelectric projects like the proposed 6000 MW Pancheshwar dam. An Indian official has been quoted as saying, "We view the developments in Nepal as very disturbing as far as the Pancheshwar dam is concerned."[51]

Table 3.2: FDI by India, China and US in Nepal, 2006/07-2012/13

Fiscal year (July 16 to July 15)	*India*		*China*		*US*	
	No. of Industries	*Foreign Investment (NPR in mln)*	*No. of Industries*	*Foreign Investment (NPR in mln)*	*No. of Industries*	*Foreign Investment (NPR in mln)*
2005/2006*	331	11547.00	121	3005.82	98	4509.45
2006/2007	22	1719.54	25	263.13	12	60.10
2007/2008	29	3645.40	15	231.30	9	81.98
2008/2009	28	2341.31	51	875.24	8	44.00
2009/2010	27	3993.54	58	715.75	10	51.30
2010/2011	38	7007.26	69	1187.40	8	81.4
2011/2012	24	2298.00	77	986.03	24	182.16
2012/2013	41	2809.07	97	2771.8	24	380.50

Note *: The figures for 2005/06 are cumulative total up to that year.
Source: Table complied by author based on data obtained from Department of Industries, Ministry of Industry, Government of Nepal, Industrial Statistics (relevant years).

Despite the Bilateral Investment Promotion and Protection Agreement (BIPPA), between the two countries, Indian companies still do not want to take risks for investment in Nepal because of the Maoists' opposition. Also a new controversy appears to have arisen in Nepal with regard to BIPPA. Not only the hardliners, led by Mohan Baidya, but also a section of the UCPN (Maoist) standing committee members on 25 October 2011 argued that as BIPPA was finalised 'without sufficient discussions' within the party and it should be scrapped.

As regards economic assistance for development projects, India has consistently been increasing the volume of assistance since 2006. Given the diversified engagements between the two countries, economic assistance from other countries has also gone up especially in the sectors where Indian assistance is felt insufficient.

Infrastructure

During 2004-2013, India provided assistance worth NPR 118 crore to Nepal for laying the 904 km optical fiber cable along the East-West Highway. It has built 807 kms out of the 1024 km of the East–West Highway. Twenty-two bridges were constructed by India on the Kohalpur-Mahakali section of

Table 3.3: Number of Development Projects in Nepal Supported by India's Economic Assistance

Year (number of projects as on 31 March)	*Small**	*Large and Medium*	*Total*
2004	16	10	26
2005	56	22	78
2006	100	24	124
2007	174	26	200
2008	247	28	275
2009	294	30	324
2010	340	30	370
2011	366	35	401
2012#	390	35	425

*The Small Development Projects are implemented on the basis of a MoU signed between India and Nepal. Projects costing less than NPR 5 crore.
31 January.
Source: Embassy of India, Kathmandu.

the East–West Highway. India supported construction of eight roads and one bridge at a cost of NPR 32.83 crore. It also funded the upgrading of the road from Dakshanikali (Kathmandu) to Kulekhani (Makwanpur) and Gaur Municipality to Sukhdeo Chowk in Rautahat district at a cost of approximately NPR 25 crore. In the Terai region, India proposed to construct 19 link/postal roads. It had also been providing assistance for electrification, provision of drinking water, strengthening of cross-border linkages, cross-border railway links, flood control and preservation of the unique cultural heritage of Nepal.[52]

Education and Health

A major part of India's economic assistance to Nepal is being spent on education—approximately NPR 490 crore—across almost all districts in Nepal. Quoting official sources, one media report said India offered more than 1900 scholarships annually to Nepalese students at various levels. More than 15,500 students have received training provided through the Embassy of India since 2005-06. Other than that over 800 Nepalese students have benefited from financial and technical crash-courses in India under Indian Technical and Economic Cooperation (ITEC) scholarship programme launched in 2000 and India spends more than INR 500 million annually on ITEC activities. It also spends around NPR 462.57 crore for multiple health programmes operating both in rural and urban areas.[53]

Training of Nepalese Officials in India

The government of India has sponsored study-cum-training programmes for more than 500 officials of the government of Nepal since 2007. The total expenditure on these study visits/training programmes has been about NPR 8 crore. These programmes targeted at capacity-building and skill enhancement of senior officials have been instituted at the specific requests of the Government of Nepal.[54]

Common Challenges and India's Concerns

Misuse of the Open Border

The presence of armed groups and organised crime syndicates in the border region constitutes a major security challenge for both the countries. The unregulated border enables these groups to cross over and move around with impunity. Suraj Vaidya, vice-president of the FNCCI, told this author in Kathmandu in August 2010:

> Due to political instability and poor law and order situation in Nepal, revenue collection is affected. In the border districts more consumer goods from India are being smuggled into Nepal than from Nepal into India. Security in the border area is a big problem. Life is miserable in Birgunj. People fear to send their children to school.

According to the Nepal Ministry of Home Affairs, around 109 armed groups were active in Nepal, the majority of who were based in the Terai region. Thirty-eight of these groups have a Terai-based nomenclature, 15 have a Madhesi-based nomenclature and another three have Terai-Madhesi nomenclature. Terai-based armed groups opposed the November 19 CA elections. Around 13 Terai based armed outfits had merged together and formed a new front called Janatantrik Terai Mukti Morcha (JTMM) against the State on 3 July 2013. Apart from that the international community was worried over lingering political instability and possibilities of some international terrorist outfits taking sanctuary in Nepal. In an effort to curb terrorist activities on Nepalese soil, under the Security Council's resolutions, it had seized assets of around 224 individuals and 64 groups, including Al Qaeda, in September 2013.[55] Although Nepalese officials have denied any information about Dawood Ibrahim's presence there, media reports have indicated that he visited Kathmandu several times and leveraged his connections with the ISI, Nepalese politicians, business houses, and the criminal underworld for large-scale *hawala* transactions.[56]

Infiltration of Terrorists and Insurgents

In recent years, Nepal has become a haven for terrorists, smugglers and anti-India elements sponsored by Pakistan's ISI. ISI agents have also been using the Kathmandu–Delhi bus service to enter Indian territory. The rise in the number of Muslim seminaries in the border region is a major concern for India. According to Tilak Kak the Director General of the Sashastra Seema Bal (SSB) around 1900 madarsas have come up in the border region and security agencies are monitoring the activities of 50 or 60 'sensitive' ones.[57] While reviewing the security situation on the Nepal-India border in 2013, the SSB found that over the past 20 years most of the materials used in major terror attacks in the Indian cities were brought into India through Nepal or Bangladesh.[58] Arguing for an Extradition Treaty with Nepal, then India's Minister of State for Home, Sriprakash Jaiswal, informed Parliament on 4 November 2006, that Pakistani militants had been using Nepalese territory as a hideout and as a base for infiltration into India. Maloy Krishna Dhar, a former joint director of the Intelligence Bureau, has also supported this view and held that two subsidiaries of the ISI—the Joint Intelligence Miscellaneous and Joint Intelligence X—have been systematically exploiting the sentiments of the Muslim population of Nepal in general and Muslim population in the Terai area in particular to foster anti-India sentiments. They have also been aiding some Islamist groups such as the Nepal Islamic Yuva Sangh, Jamaat-e-Islami Nepal, Nepal Muslim Seva Samiti and Nepal Muslim Ittehad Association.[59]

Media reports reveal that radical Islamist groups operating within India, such as the Indian Mujahideen (IM), use Nepalese territory as a safe haven, especially after Bangladeshi security forces raided their bases in Bangladesh.[60] According to the *Country Reports on Terrorism 2009* of the US State Department: "There is a possibility that members of extremist groups could transit Nepal, especially into India. The large ungoverned space along the Nepal/India border exacerbates this vulnerability, as do security shortfalls at Tribhuvan International Airport." In June 2009, Mohammad Omar Madani, the alleged Lashkar-e-Taiba (LeT) head in Nepal, was arrested in Delhi. According to media reports, Madani had set up a madarsa in the jungles along the border from where newly trained militants could be sent to India. The LeT presence in Nepal was confirmed in 1999 with the hijacking of Indian Airlines flight IC 814 from Kathmandu to Kandahar, Afghanistan.

The LeT also benefits from the illegal trading along the border.[61] The Pakistan-based terrorists, arrested for their role in the November 2008

Mumbai attack, disclosed during interrogation that funds for the attack were supplied by Nepal-based traders. Based on that information, the police arrested Aslam Ansari (Pakistani) and Nasim Ansari (Nepali) in the border town of Birgunj in December 2008.[62] The LeT generates half of its annual budget of about $10 million[63] from the illegal trade across the India-Nepal border.[64]

Other separatist movements in India such as secessionist outfits from Punjab during the 1980s also used Nepalese territory as shelter zone and for training camps. In the late 1980s, these outfits also used this soft border to infiltrate into India as the border between Pakistan and India is now fenced. Since 2003 many Northeast-based insurgent outfits like the ULFA and the NDFB too have been crossing over to Nepal. According to an Indian intelligence report, the ULFA, the Kamtapur Liberation Organisation (KLO) and NDFB had linked up with the CPN (Maoist) to work out a joint strategy for operations in the region.[65]

The Nepalese Maoists' links with Indian Maoists were a major concern for India until the former joined the peace process in 2006. The same concerns have re-emerged after the split of the UCPN (Maoist) in June 2012 and Mohan Baidya faction openly declared its ideological linkage with the Indian Maoists. They are members of Coordination Committee of Maoist Parties and Organisations of South Asia (CCOMPOSA) and have vowed to fight jointly against "Indian expansionism" in the region.

The links between these outfits go back to 1995, when some senior leaders of the CPN (Maoist) visited Maoist-affected areas of India. Prachanda acknowledged in 2000 that since Indian Maoist groups such as the PW, the MCC and others had experience of an armed struggle, "we made some investigation of [areas] in Bihar in India. We went to Andhra Pradesh to look at the struggle there and we tried to understand the practical situation and practical problems of armed struggle."[66] As the relationship deepened, the Nepalese Maoists and the PW formed the "India-Nepal Border Regional Committee to coordinate their activities in areas along the India-Nepal border in Bihar".[67] They were also reportedly acquiring arms through the rebel groups active in Northeast India. The links between Indian and Nepalese Maoists were reduced from strategic level to ideological level after the Nepalese Maoists joined mainstream politics. Despite that Mohan Baidya faction of the UCPN (Maoist) had been in touch with Indian Maoists.[68]

Trafficking

The border has become a major hub for trafficking in fake currency, small arms, narcotics and humans. The Indian Intelligence Bureau (IB) has estimated that around INR 1690 billion worth of fake currency is in circulation all over India.[69] A large part of the money used to fund the terror operation in Mumbai in November 2008 was obtained through the fake currency and hawala channels. Sabahuddin, an accused in the Mumbai attack, who was also the chief of operations for the LeT in Nepal, confirmed that it takes just INR 5000 to cross over from Nepal into India.[70] Although the border is open and does not require any documents for common people to cross over, sometimes suspicious and anti-national elements have to find backdoor channels for safer entry. Some instances of pumping of fake Indian currency are given below.

- 7 May 2013: Police arrested Shaikh Muhammad Fukran, a Pakistani national, with fake Indian currency notes from Tribhuvan International Airport. He had arrived from Qatar on a Qatar Airlines flight.
- 15 April 2013: Police arrested Julekha Bano, a Pakistani woman and her son Denish Essa, with fake Indian currency notes worth 4.7 million at Tribhuvan International Airport.
- 10 August 2010: Nepal Police arrested a Pakistani national, Muhammad Farooq, with fake Indian currency notes worth of 2.5 million.
- 9 July 2010: Nepal Police arrested three men, including an Indian and a Bangladeshi with counterfeit currency.
- 26 May 2010: Pakistani national Mohammed Jamil from Rawalpindi arrested from Tribhuvan International Airport with INR 1.55 million worth of counterfeit Indian currency notes. He had arrived in Kathmandu from Bangladesh.
- 15 March 2010: A 55-year-old Pakistani woman was arrested at the Tribhuvan International Airport with fake Indian currency worth INR 3 million.
- 1 September 2009: The Madhya Pradesh police arrested two Nepalese—Rajesh Gupta and Ateeq Ahmad—with fake Indian currency notes. They disclosed that the kingpin of the racket was Nepal's former crown prince, Paras, and the son of a former Nepalese minister, Salim Mian Ansari.
- 14 April 2008: A Pakistani diplomat, Naushad Alam Khan, was caught with fake Indian currency notes.[71]

The ISI uses Pakistan International Airlines (PIA) to transport counterfeit currency to its agents in Nepal and Bangladesh. After the flights from Pakistan were put under the scanner in Nepal, fake money began entering through Bangladesh, the Middle East, Tibet and even Sri Lanka into that country.[72] The ISI has been using women couriers, particularly those with young children and physically disabled persons, to minimise suspicion.

Illegal Trade

Both India and Nepal lose huge amounts of revenue due to illegal trade through the open border. The leakage of transit goods imported by Nepalese traders from third country through Indian territory is another concern for India. The trading items depend on demand and supply, subsidies, high transaction costs of official trade and tariff differentials. Gold, sugar, rice, motor vehicle parts and fertiliser are among the main items being smuggled to Nepal from India. According to an Indian Council for Research on International Economic Relations (ICRIER) document, "In 1990, informal exports from Nepal to India were US$626 million. In 2000-01, the estimates of informal trade show[ed] a two-way informal trade flow of $408 million."[73] A study conducted by the Nepal Council for Development Research (NCDR) suggests that Nepal's informal trade of agricultural commodities with India stands at around NPR 65 billion—more than 21 per cent of the total formal trade. The study estimated that informal imports of agro products from India are worth over NPR 54.75 billion a year.[74]

Border Encroachment and Migration

There are allegations and counter-allegations regarding encroachments by people residing in the border region. The issue has assumed a nationalistic dimension in Nepal. Some civil society groups in Nepal have alleged that there are as many as 54 disputed areas and approximately 60,000 hectares have been encroached by India.[75] Given the geographical dynamics of the border region, 'encroachment' is more a natural phenomenon than a man-made one. Rivers flowing from Nepal to India frequently change course during the monsoon, thus transferring some chunks of territory to either Nepal or India. Farmers from both countries encroach on this fertile land for cultivation. Former Nepalese Prime Minister Prachanda during a visit to India acknowledged the problem of inundation in the border areas and agreed to take effective steps to prevent it through bilateral consultation. The two countries have unofficially agreed that 98 per cent of the border is demarcated except for two disputed areas in Kalapani and Susta. This was confirmed by

India's then External Affairs Minister Pranab Mukherjee during his visit to Kathmandu in November 2008. Interestingly, the Maoist-led government in Kathmandu did not contradict this. The issue regained prominence only after Prachanda's resignation. The Maoists have also accused Indian security forces of encroaching on Nepalese territory in Dang district. However, such allegations are more political in nature and are raised by some political parties only to score points. It can be noted here that no concrete measures were taken by the Maoists when in power.

There are similar concerns on the Indian side also. Some groups in West Bengal have begun to demand the abrogation of the 1950 Treaty with Nepal in order to restrict movement of people from Nepal into Darjeeling and Siliguri. They want a passport-visa system and that citizenship rights should be granted only to those Nepalese who had entered India before the Treaty was signed. It is their belief that if the border is not regulated, new Nepalese migrants might outnumber the original inhabitants, and lead to a serious law-and-order problem in the hills and plains of Darjeeling district. Some sections of the Indian establishment have expressed concerns regarding the 'Greater Nepal' demand[76] in the Indian states bordering Nepal. Although these demands are not likely to escalate into a full-fledged separatist movement, anti-India agencies may use these groups for creating trouble in the border region.

The Nepalese, on the other hand, apprehend that India may capture Nepalese territory. Their insecurities arise from vast differences in territory size, population, military and economic strength of the two countries. The *Pahadis* of Nepal believe that the demand for Madhesh Pradesh is supported by India, and Nepal in the future may have to deal with a situation that Sikkim faced in 1974. Some, therefore, believe that any such Indian designs can be prevented only by closing the border, and by making changes in the 1950 Treaty.

According to the Treaty, neither country can unilaterally impose restrictions on the free movement of peoples across the border. However, Nepalese analysts allege that India has unilaterally imposed restrictions on Nepal in the past and that India has deliberately kept Nepal dependent and created insurmountable difficulties in the way of implementing a market-based development policy because it was not ideologically palatable to India between 1950–1990. Objectively, however, India has not violated the Treaty at any time. India did impose trade restrictions in 1989 when Nepal bought arms and ammunition from China in 1988 and restricted Nepalese trade to two points on the border as per international law and closed 20 other trading points. But, India never restricted civilian movement in the border areas.[77]

India's Perception of External Involvements in Nepal

India has apprehensions regarding the involvement of other major powers in Nepal due to its overwhelming geographic, cultural linkages and people-to-people contacts with Nepal. Security analysts in India believe that India understands the security dynamics in its neighbourhood better than others. India also believes that a democratic, stable and peaceful Nepal will be in India's interest. Therefore, since 1 February 2005, India has been playing a major role in political transition in Nepal.[78]

There are reports that Pakistan has been fomenting anti-India sentiments in Nepal. Since the 1960s Pakistan has made its presence felt in Nepal and its intelligence agencies have used Nepalese territory to export terror to India by taking advantage of the open border. Some Madhesi leaders indicated to this author that in view of the growing anti-India feelings in the Madhesi region, China, the US and other countries have been trying to build their constituencies in the region. For example, China has increased its presence through its Confucius Institutes and Pakistan through some madarsas.

The CPN-Maoist (Baidya faction) is known to have a strong anti-India bias. Other anti-India forces could gain influence over them, to take advantage of their easy access to separatist and Maoist outfits operating within Indian territory to foment anti-India activities. For example, the CPN-Maoist on 27 September 2012 prohibited Indian-registered vehicles entering into Nepal and all cinema halls from screening Hindi movies to develop a self-reliant national economy.[79] The party in its 7th National Congress in January 2013 adopted a new political line.[80] At the opening ceremony of the Convention, the Party Chairman, Mohan Baidya, identified India as the 'principal enemy' and warned Indian rulers against casting 'covetous eyes' on Nepal's national sovereignty.[81]

The growing influence of China and western players and their competition for political and strategic space in Nepal would keep India, and especially the northern provinces of India, vulnerable due to an open border.[82] There is a view in India that it will become increasingly vulnerable if the Chinese become more sensitive to an ever-increasing presence of Western forces in Nepal.

Conclusion

The growing anti-India sentiments in Nepal indicate that India has to some extent failed to manage the public perception in Nepal. There is also a decline in India's economic engagement with Nepal vis-à-vis China. Existing controversial Treaties, border disputes, political resistance to Indian hydro projects, attack on India's business houses, trade and transit issues, perceived Indian interference in internal affairs of Nepal, etc., are major irritants in India-Nepal relations. India believes that the contentious issues can be better resolved by a popular and strong government in Kathmandu. Therefore, there is a need for sustained multi-dimensional engagement with Nepal by taking into account the political transition there and adapt its Nepal policy to the new realities in the sub-Himalayan region. At the same time, India also needs to enhance its assistance to Nepal with greater focus on socio-economic and development programmes, and promote unhindered trade and investment.

*

NOTES

1. Introduction and Synopsis section of *Annual Report 2010-2011,* Ministry of External Affairs, Government of India, p.i, at http://www.mea.gov.in/Uploads/PublicationDocs/45_Annual-Report-2010-2011.pdf (accessed on 8 August 2013).
2. Ibid.
3. "6 December 1950, speech in Parliament", *Jawaharlal Nehru, India's Foreign Policy: Selected Speeches, September 1946–April 1961*, Publication Division, Ministry of Information and Broadcasting, Government of India, August 1961, p. 436.
4. *Annual Report 2005-06,* Ministry of External Affairs, Government of India, p.13.
5. Zhang Li, "To manage conflict in South Asia: China's stakes, perceptions and inputs", Asia Paper, October 2009, Institute for Security and Development Policy, Stockholm, p.81.
6. Author's interaction with a senior Indian Army officer in Delhi on 24 July 2012.
7. Tulsi Sitaula, Joint-Secretary and Chief of Construction Department, Ministry of Physical Planning and Works, Government of Nepal, interview to *Republica* on 30 December 2009, Kathmandu, at http://www.myrepublica.com/portal/index.php?action=news_details& news_id=13437 (accessed on 13 July 2013).
8. Nishchal Nath Pandey, *New Nepal: The Fault Lines*, Sage Publications, London, 2010, p. 130.
9. Frank Jack Daniel, "In Himalayan arms race, China one-ups India", *Reuters*, 30 July 2012, at http://in.reuters.com/article/2012/07/30/india-china-arms-race-special-report-idINDEE86T01720120730 (accessed on 31 July 2012).
10. For more details about China's military infrastructure developments in TAR, see Bijoy Das, "China's planning on border infrastructure: Post 1996 CBM period", IDSA Fellow Paper. The paper was presented in IDSA on 18 November 2011. Also see at http://www.gs.chinanews.com/news/2010/01-11/50611.shtml (accessed on 8 August 2013).
11. Eugene B. Mihaly, *Foreign Aid and Politics in Nepal: A Case Study*, Himal Books, Kathmandu, 2009, p. 172.
12. "Overwhelming support for Maoist proposal", *The Red Star*, a CPN (Maoist) publication, Kathmandu, I (6), 15-31 March 2008. The manifesto also promised to bring necessary changes in managing and controlling of Nepal-India border, initiation to conclude encroachment of Nepalese land at India border, end of Gorkha recruitment centre, etc.
13. Article 10 of the Treaty of Peace and Friendship between the Government of India and

the Government of Nepal was signed on 31 July 1950, says "This Treaty shall remain in force until it is terminated by either party by giving one year's notice."

14. "Nepal to Delhi: Junk sentiment and special ties," *The Telegraph*, Kolkata, 3 May 2008.
15. "India ready to renegotiate 1950 treaty with Nepal", *Oneindia News*, 6 May 2008, at http://news.oneindia.in/2008/05/06/india-ready-to-renegotiate-1950-treaty-with-nepal-1210072316.html (accessed on 8 August 2013).
16. K.V. Rajan, "Should the 1950 treaty be scrapped?", *The Hindu*, 3 May 2008, at http://www.thehindu.com/2008/05/03/stories/2008050352481000.htm (accessed on 8 August 2013).
17. "Nepal won't jeopardise any genuine Indian interest", former Nepal Prime Minister Baburam Bhattarai's interview to Prashant Jha, *The Hindu*, 3 September 2011, at http://www.thehindu.com/opinion/interview/article2419048.ece (accessed on 8 August 2013).
18. K. Majumdar, "Indo-Nepal Relations: The Past, The Present and The Future", in Lok Raj Baral (ed.), *Looking to the Future: Indo-Nepal Relations in Perspective*, Anmol, New Delhi, 1996, p. 31.
19. Lok Raj Baral (ed.), *Looking to the Future: Indo-Nepal Relations in Perspective*, Anmol, New Delhi, 1996, p. 7.
20. Trailokya Raj Aryal writes that Nepalese politicians do fuel "anti-Indianism to safeguard our [Nepal's] own interests". For details see "Rethinking anti-Indianism in Nepal", *Republica,* Kathmandu, 25 April 2010, at http://www.myrepublica.com/portal/index.php?action=news_details&news_id=17877 (accessed on 8 August 2013).
21. Dipendra Jha, "Uprising ahead", *Republica*, 13 May 2013.
22. This view was expressed during the author's interview with some Nepalese scholars in Kathmandu in June 2011 and November 2013.
23. Author's interaction with Pradeep Giri, central committee member of the Nepali Congress in Kathmandu in June 2011. Also see Prashant Jha, "A Nepali Perspective on International Involvement in Nepal," in Sebastian v. Einsiedel, *et al.* (eds), *Nepal in Transition: From People's War to Fragile Peace*, Cambridge University Press, Cambridge, 2012, pp.337-339.
24. The UCPN (Maoist) had sent its senior leaders in January 2010 to the border points allegedly encroached upon by India to foment anti-India sentiments. Before that the party on 22 December 2009, had declared months-long protests against India's interference in Nepal and encroachment of Nepal's territory. For details see "UCPN-Maoist announces fourth phase of protests", *The Rising Nepal* (The *Gorkha Patra* in Nepali), Kathmandu, 22 December 2009, at http://www.gorkhapatra.org.np/detail.php?article_id=28513&cat_id=4 (accessed on 1 August 2013). Also see "India expresses displeasure over Maoists' anti-India campaign", *Asian Tribune*, 19 January 2010, at http://www.asiantribune.com/news/2010/01/19/india-expresses-displeasure-over-maoists%E2%80%99-anti-india-campaign (accessed on 1 August 2013).
25. For details see "Dahal concedes his three mistakes," *ekantipur*, 7 August 2013, at http://www.ekantipur.com/2013/08/07/top-story/dahal-concedes-his-three-mistakes/376050.html (accessed on 7 August 2013). UCPN (Maoist) Chairman, Prachanda said this at a programme organised in Pokhara, Nepal.
26. "Nepal parliament to look into Indian Embassy 'threat'", *The Times of India*, 9 August 2010. Also see Siddharth Varadarajan, "The danger in India's Nepal policy", *The Hindu*, 16 August 2010.

27. List of high level visits between Nepal and India during 2006-2012:

    Nepal

    - Prime Minister G.P. Koirala visited India in 2006. A comprehensive economic package of INR 1000 crore was announced during this visit.
    - Prime Minister Pushpa Kamal Dahal visited India from 14-17 September 2008. India agreed to implement the Naumure hydroelectric project on Rapti river, besides providing INR 20 crore assistance for Koshi breach relief.
    - Prime Minister Madhav Kumar Nepal visited India from 18–22 August 2009. India allowed the Visakhapatnam port to be used for movement of transit traffic to and from Nepal. He assured India that it would not allow Nepalese territory to be used for any activity against India, which was reciprocated by India.
    - President Ram Baran Yadav visited India between 15-18 February 2010 during which four MoUs/agreements were signed.
    - Prime Minister Baburam Bhattarai visited India from 20-23 October 2011. A number of agreements, including BIPPA were signed.
    - President Ram Baran Yadav visited India between 24-28 December 2012.

    India

    - India's Minister of External Affairs, S.M. Krishna, visited Nepal from 15–17 January 2010.
    - S.M. Krishna visited Kathmandu in April 2011 and raised concerns over the deteriorating law-and-order situation and its possible repercussions in Indian investments in Nepal.
    - Finance Minister Pranab Mukherjee visited Kathmandu on 27 November 2011 and signed the Double Taxation Avoidance Agreement (DTAA).
28. In the UPA-I, the Communists were part of the coalition, while the UPA-II was formed without them.
29. Author's interaction with Prashant Jha in Kathmandu on 29 June 2009.
30. Other bilateral developments in 2012:
    - 6 January 2012: India decided not to pursue the demand for placing sky marshals on flights originating in India and signing of a revised Extradition Treaty and the Mutual Legal Assistance.
    - 18 January 2012: India agreed to allow Nepal to make direct transshipment of goods from its custom stations and dry ports.
    - 16 February 2012: Nepal and India concluded first-ever Nepal-India energy minister-level talks.
    - March 2012: India declared to give INR 2.7 billion in grants to Nepal in 2012-13.
    - 3 March 2012: India consented to open all forms of railway cargo to facilitate Nepal's trade with its southern neighbour and third countries.
    - May 2012: Nepal and India signed a Letter of Exchange for the final implementation of the Railway Service Agreement.
31. "Indian envoy secretly calls on prez", *ekanipur*, 17 February 2013, at http://www.ekantipur.com/2013/02/17/top-story/indian-envoy-secretly-calls-on-prez/367230.html (accessed on 8 August 2013).
32. In March 2013, the 7th General Convention (GC) of the UCPN (Maoist) party (Prachanda faction) at Hetauda adopted that the party will adhere to competitive politics

(democracy) and work towards consolidation of peace and the drafting of the Constitution. It also pledged its commitment to republicanism and 'economic revolution' (development oriented pro-people policy in line with party ideology). For the fist time since the unset of Maoist armed struggle in 1996 in Nepal, one Maoist faction, the UCPN (Maoist), did not include name of any 'principal enemy' (earlier India, the US and some political parties were termed as enemies that the party had to constantly work against).

33. "CPN-UML picks nationalism as party's election agenda", *ekantipur*, 12 May 2013, at http://www.ekantipur.com/2013/05/12/editors-pick/cpn-uml-picks-nationalism-as-partys-election-agenda/371498.html (accessed on 8 August 2013).
34. Author's interaction with Uddhab Pyakurel in Kathmandu on 21 June 2009. Pyakurel is a Kathmandu-based political analyst and faculty of Kathmandu University, Nepal.
35. Author's interview with Ramesh Nath Pandey, former Minister for Foreign Affairs, Nepal, in Kathmandu on 24 June 2009.
36. Siddharth Varadarajan, "The danger in India's Nepal policy," *The Hindu*, 16 August 2010, at http://www.thehindu.com/opinion/columns/siddharth-varadarajan/the-danger-in-indias-nepal-policy/article572789.ece (accessed on 2 August 2013).
37. Gopal Khanal, "The Saran doctrine", *ekanipur*, 19 August 2010, at http://www.ekantipur.com/the-kathmandu-post/2010/08/18/oped/the-saran-doctrine/211736/ (accessed on 2 August 2013).
38. Krishna Hari Pushkar, "Seeds of ethno-civil war in Terai", *Nepal Monitor*, 20 December 2007, at http://www.nepalmonitor.com/2007/12/seeds_of_ethno-civil_war_in_nepal_terai. html (accessed on 8 August 2013).
39. Lok Sabha calling attention notice on "Anti-Indian riots in South Nepal", 29 June 1971.
40. Prashant Jha's interview with Upendra Yadav, "Koirala must resign", *Nepali Times*, Issue 401, 23–30 May 2008.
41. Keshav Prasad Mainali, "India's stand on Madhesh issue is self-contradicting," *The Telegraph Weekly*, Kathmandu, 1 July 2008, at http://www.telegraphnepal.com/news_det.php?news_id=3654 (accessed on 8 August 2013). Manali is President Chure Bhawar Ekta Samaj.
42. Author's interaction with a senior leader of the NSP (Nepal Sadbhavana Party) in Patna on 29 February 2009.
43. Krishna Hari Pushkar, "India's Neighbourhood Intervention in Madhesh", *Nepal Monitor*, 14 February 2008, at http://www.nepalmonitor.com/2008/02/inviting_indias_neighbourhood_intervention_in_madhesh.html (accessed on 20 January 2014).
44. Keshav Prasad Mainali, "India's Stand on Madhesh issue is self-contradicting," n. 41.
45. Ibid.
46. "I will talk, but not to compromise", Upendra Yadav's interview to *Tehelka*, Delhi, 14 July 2007.
47. Keshav Prasad Mainali, "India's Stand on Madhesh issue is self-contradicting," n. 41.
48. *Maitree*, August 2011 (a monthly journal published by Indian Embassy in Kathmandu).
49. Umesh Upadhyaya, "Issue of Protection of Migrant Workers and their Families," General Federation of Nepalese Trade Unions (GEFONT), Kathmandu, pp.269-276.
50. "Nepal events hitting India Inc: FICCI", *Hindustan Times*, 6 May 2009, at http://www.hindustantimes.com/StoryPage/StoryPage.aspx?sectionName=HomePage&id=f72535b7-ed67-45c6-bf91-cd8493bba7a3&ParentID=c9fcc197-033e-4766-8a19-

9b9128b5bdfe&Headline=Nepal+events+hitting+India+Inc%3a+Ficci (accessed on 8 August 2013).

51. "Nepal crisis may hit Pancheshwar dam", *Business Standard*, Delhi, 07 May 2009, at http://www.business-standard.com/india/news/nepal-crisis-may-hit-pancheshwar-dam/357257/ (accessed on 8 August 2013).
52. For more information see "Economic Cooperation", Embassy of India, Kathmandu, Nepal, at http://www.indianembassy.org.np/ (accessed 2 May 2014).
53. Ibid. Also see "Over 800 Nepalese students benefit from Indian scholarships", *NDTV*, 26 December 2013, at http://www.ndtv.com/article/india/over-800-nepalese-students-benefit-from-indian-scholarships-463525 (accessed on 11 January 2014).
54. See n. 52.
55. For information about the presence of armed groups in Nepal, see Narayan Manandhar, "Nepal's armed groups", *Republica,* 29 August 2009, at http://www.myrepublica.com/portal/index.php?action=news_details&news_id=9156 (accessed on 8 August 2013).
56. Pushpita Das, "Towards a Regulated India-Nepal border", *Strategic Analysis*, 32 (05), September 2008, p. 884.
57. For details see "1900 madrassas mushrooming along Indo-Nepal border," *rediff*, 24 March 2006, at http://www.rediff.com/news/2006/mar/24border.htm (accessed on 25 October 2013).
58. SSB chief Arun Chaudhary disclosed this during an interaction with journalists before the 50th Raising Day celebrations of the force on 18 December 2013. For details see "Numbers in Pak's Nepal mission increasing: SSB chief," *Deccan Herald*, 18 December 2013, at http://www.deccanherald.com/content/375461/numbers-paks-nepal-mission-increasing.html (accessed on 11 January 2014).
59. Maloy Krishna Dhar, *Fulcrum of Evil: ISI-CIA-Al Qaeda Nexus*, Manas Publications, New Delhi, 2006, p. 207.
60. "IM has shifted to Nepal after Bangladesh crackdown", *The Times of India*, 10 March 2010.
61. Jason Miklian, "Illicit Trading in Nepal: Fueling South Asian Terrorism", PRIO South Asia Briefing Paper #3, 2009, International Peace Research Institute, Oslo (PRIO).
62. "Terror-Funding Pak Kingpin in Nepal Police Net," *The Times of India*, 21 December 2008. Also see "Nepal Nabs Fake Money Kingpin," *The Telegraph*, Kolkata, 21 December 2008.
63. "Lashkar-e-Toiba," Terrorist outfit profile, South Asian Terrorism Portal, at http://www.satp.org/satporgtp/countries/india/states/jandk/terrorist_outfits/lashkar_e_toiba.htm (accessed on 8 August 2013).
64. Jason Miklian, "Illicit Trading in Nepal: Fuelling South Asian Terrorism," n. 61.
65. "Militant Groups", *Frontline*, Delhi, 21 (01), 03-16 January 2004.
66. "Red Flag Flying on the Roof of the World", Li Onesto interview with Prachanda, General Secretary of the Communist Party of Nepal (Maoist), *Revolutionary Worker,* No.1043, 20 February 2000, at http://www.revcom.us/a/v21/1040-049/1043/interv.htm (accessed on 8 August 2013). Also see at http://www.rwor.org
67. P.V. Ramana, "South Asia's Maoist Web", *rediff*, 14 October 2004, at http://www.rediff.com/news/2004/oct/14spec2.htm (accessed on 8 August 2013).
68. "Split in Nepal Maoists spells trouble for India", *The Times of India*, 2 July 2012, at http://articles.timesofindia.indiatimes.com/2012-07-02/india/32507561_1_nepal-maoists-maoist-army-indian-maoists (accessed on 3 August 2012).

69. "Secret template leak responsible for fake notes", *Zee News,* 12 August 2009, http://zeenews.india.com/news/business/secret-template-leak-responsible-for-fake-notes_554751.html (accessed on 8 July 2011).
70. "How terror travels to India in a bus", *rediff,* 02 April 2009, at http://www.rediff.com/news/2009/apr/02how-terror-travels-to-india-in-a-bus.htm (accessed on 8 July 2011).
71. List of Pakistan activities in Nepal are collected from English language newspapers published both in Nepal and India.
72. Joginder Singh, "Fake currency and its linkage with crime Origin of fake currency and its use", *Organiser,* India, 6 September 2009. Singh is former Director, Central Bureau of Investigation (CBI).
73. Nisha Taneja, *et al., India-Nepal Economic Cooperation,* Indian Council for Research on International Economic Relations, November 2009, p. 36.
74. "Informal trade of farm products with India estimated at Rs 65b," *Republica,* 20 February 2012, at http://www.myrepublica.com/portal/index.php?action=news_details&news_id=32020 (accessed on 8 August 2013).
75. Pushpita Das, "Towards a Regulated India-Nepal border", n. 56, p. 883.
76. The Maoists had raised the issue of Greater Nepal until 2005. They had even floated a map of Greater Nepal which included the Indian towns of Varanasi, Ballia, Bahraich, Pilibhit and Jaunpur, mostly in the Indian state of Uttar Pradesh. They had brought out a book, *Nepal: Teesta Dekhi Satlej Samma* (Nepal: From Teesta to the Sutlej) and published calendars featuring a map of Greater Nepal (in 2005). However, Maoist leader Prachanda had called it a "media stunt".
77. Smruti S. Pattanaik, "Indo-Nepal Open Border: Implications for bilateral Relations and Security", *Strategic Analysis,* 22 (3), June 1998, p. 475.
78. Former India's Ambassador to Nepal and Foreign Secretary, Shyam Saran's interview on Dishanirdesh, Nepal Television, 12 July 2004, www.south-asia.com (accessed on 26 October 2007).
79. "CPN-Maoist bans Hindi movies, Indian plate vehicles", *Republica,* 27 September 2012.
80. Highlights of political document:

    International situation

    1. Indian expansionism is main exploiter of Nepal while American imperialism is increasing in South Asia;
    2. Main obstruction and threat to revolution is American imperialism;
    3. Rightist revisionism is main threat to world revolution;
    4. Imperialist countries including USA are weak, dependent on financial capital;
    5. To form front against imperialist and expansionist forces;
    6. To develop brotherhood among parties that follow Marxism, Leninism and Maoism.

    National Situation

    1. Nepal is neo-colonial and national sovereignty is in great danger;
    2. Principle enemy are stooges, bureaucrats and feudal class directed and mobilised by Indian expansionism;
    3. To form people's constitution through struggle;
    4. To form a front and working alliance among leftist, nationalist, federalist and democratic forces;
    5. Objective reality for revolution is forming in Nepal but subjective reality is weak;
    6. The nature of Nepal's revolution is long-run;

7. To reorganise people's communes;
8. To establish new democratic republican Nepal through [a] new democratic revolution;
9. Size of semi-proletariat in Nepal increasing hugely due to employees. Source: "People's constitution through struggle: CPN-Maoist", *Republica*, Kathmandu, 11 January 2013.

81. "CPN-M general convention kicks off", *Republica*, 10 January 2013.
82. David G. Wiencek, "China's geopolitical manoeuvring in the Himalayas," China Brief, 7 May 2005, Jamestown Foundation, at www.asianresearch.org (accessed on 26 October 2007).

CHAPTER 4

China in Nepal: From Political to Strategic Engagement

It has been noted with some anxiety in India, especially by the wider strategic community, that China has taken deliberate steps to improve its relations with almost all of India's neighbours—after the improvement in Indo-US relations since 2000 in general—especially with Nepal after the fall of the monarchy.[1] China's growing interest in Nepal is being viewed with particular concern by India. The increase in the number of visits by Chinese officials and leaders to Nepal, since the end of the monarchy and reinstatement of democratic government in that country in 2006-07, indicates that China is trying to scale up its engagement with Nepal. The concern in India arises from the hypothesis that the growing Chinese presence in Nepal could undermine both India's influence and its strategic equations with the Himalayan country.

China's Broad Foreign Policy Objectives

As a rising power, China has raised its stakes in global politics by maintaining its presence all over the world. Realising that "the world is undergoing unprecedented changes, and China is developing rapidly", China has formulated a new foreign policy to "go global and seize opportunities".[2] China has also managed to balance "firmness" with "flexibility" to deal with the global situation.[3] The perceived external threats to China's core interests—the maintenance of its territorial integrity, preservation of its system of government and continued economic and social stability—could be the main driving force behind its external behaviour.[4] China's *National Defense* document, which in 2010[5] reiterated the threats identified in 2008, reflected China's fears regarding its security situation. Some of the important external and internal challenges mentioned in the document are:

> Asia-Pacific security is becoming more intricate and volatile...The United States is reinforcing its regional military alliances, and increasing its involvement in regional security affairs...Separatist forces working for "East Turkistan independence" and "Tibet independence" have inflicted serious damage on national security and social stability. Pressure builds up in preserving China's territorial integrity and maritime rights and interests.[6]

The US has emerged as the country of greatest significance and concern for China in recent years. It is also worried about the future of Tibet, Xinjiang and Taiwan. China also aspires for a global economy that provides "strategic opportunities" for China and is dominated by it. It must be noted that there is no clear articulation of 'South Asia' as a region in the Chinese foreign policy pronouncements of 2011 and the countries in the region are clubbed as "Asian neighbours".[7]

Going back into history, Chinese interest in the region underwent a qualitative shift in the late 1970s, following changes in overall Chinese foreign policy to cope with the changing domestic and international environment. China implemented some economic and political reforms after the death of Mao Zedong and the elevation of Deng Xiaoping as president. At the international level, the end of the Cold War and the thaw in the Sino-US relationship brought about major changes in China's foreign policy. During this period China sought to resolve its border disputes with its neighbours, and became more outward looking apart from readjusting its foreign policy to suit its new economic agenda. As a Chinese observer has noted:

> China's foreign policy thus became more pragmatic and less ideological...Beijing embraced multilateralism and sought friends by strengthening bilateral ties with nations around the world regardless of differences in political system, ideology and culture.[8]

Until China joined the WTO in 2001, its foreign policy decisions were guided by Deng Xiaoping's idea of "keeping a low profile, and getting something accomplished."[9] Without losing sight of that principal objective, subsequent leaders made some minor adjustments in accordance with domestic and international requirements. For example, Hu Jintao made a shift from his predecessor's uni-directional foreign policy of "major power diplomacy" to multi-directional diplomacy and focused on strengthening relations with neighbouring countries, especially within Asia.[10] The new leader of the Communist Party of China (CPC), Xi Jinping, who assumed presidency in March 2013, is expected to stick to the foreign policy laid out by his predecessors and it is unlikely that he will make any major departure from it.

China's Approach to South Asia

While the Chinese approach to South Asia has been largely centered around India and Pakistan, of late, Nepal has begun to figure prominently in its foreign policy outlook. This region gets special attention in Chinese policy because of its 'all weather' friend and trusted ally, Pakistan, as well as its global economic competitor, India, both are located in South Asia. Ever since the economic reforms in 1991, India has emerged as a global competitor for China. A series of successful tests on Inter-Continental Ballistic Missiles (ICBMs) by India had raised eyebrows in China among scholars and top leaders about Indian technological prowess and China recognised India as an important actor in Asian politics. Further, the 2005 India-US civil nuclear deal, its pro-active foreign policy in international forums and military modernisation have placed India at the centre-stage of global affairs.[11] In view of the competition for influence between the two at the regional and global levels, it is logical that China would want to keep India tied up in internal and regional matters in order to hamper its global ambitions. Ideologically, too, the world's largest democracy, i.e., India is located in this region and China perceives that democratic forces (the US, India and Japan) led by the US, are ganging up against it. As a result, China has made major shifts in its foreign policy towards South Asia since 2000. This was visible after 2005, as China became increasingly concerned about India's expanding strategic ties with the US. The presence of Tibetan refugees in India added to the concerns. In fact, Chinese President Hu Jintao, during his visit to Delhi in March 2012, had discussed the possibilities of India participating in any Western 'containment strategy' with regard to China with Prime Minister Manmohan Singh. Since the Fall of 2011, when the Obama administration articulated its 'Asian pivot' policy as part of its strategic shift of focus from Europe to Asia and a 'rebalancing' role in the Asia Pacific region, the Chinese leadership too has refocused its attention on increasing its influence in the South Asian neighbourhood vis-à-vis with a view to balance perceived American strategy to contain China by strengthening its partnership with India.

China is thus continuing its policy of endearing itself to the South Asian countries. It has regularly sent political, economic, military and academic delegations to India's neighbouring nations. In the words of B. Raman:

> China has been seeking to build up for itself a strong South Asian presence which could cater to its strategic needs in the long term. It has made inroads in the South Asian countries in the recent years by taking advantage of their hunger for the development of their infrastructure and

their requirement of financial assistance for major infrastructure projects and for the exploration of their natural resources.[12]

The undercurrents of suspicion between India and its smaller neighbours have to some extent facilitated the Chinese policy of expanding its footprint in South Asia. Various countries in the region have often used the so-called China card to neutralise India's dominance and perceived hegemony in the region. Although China acknowledges that South Asia is India's rightful sphere of influence, it does not desist from seeking long-term relationships in the region. Unlike in Africa where China's presence has been growing, mainly for harnessing African resources, the South Asian region does not have an abundance of mineral deposits—except in India, and of course Nepal, which has huge hydro-potential. It is therefore pertinent to question China's growing interest in the region. Is it primarily economic or does it have a strategic dimension? One explanation is that during the Cold War, a large part of South Asia did not figure in the global strategic discourse because there was a quiet recognition of India's predominant influence in the prevailing regional security complex,[13] and therefore apart from India and Pakistan other countries of South Asia did not evoke much interest outside the region. However, in the post-Cold War era, the region assumed importance mainly due to the growth of the Indian economy, its successful democracy, existence of two nuclear-powered nations and emergence of the region as the hub of global terrorism.[14] According to B. Raman:

> The Chinese policy in the South Asian region has a mix of strategic and opportunistic dimensions—that is, working for carefully calculated long-term strategic objectives while not missing short-and medium-term opportunities that come its way. China has no contentious issues affecting its bilateral relations with these countries—as against many contentious issues in the relations of India with its neighbours—has also worked to its advantage.[15]

India's conditional investments—both political and economic—in its neighbourhood may have also helped China to strengthen its presence. There is a predominant view in the neighbourhood that despite India's claim of providing non-reciprocal aid and assistance to its neighbours, its policies are largely driven by narrow national security interests. While China could also be expanding its engagement for strategic reasons and put conditions on the smaller South Asian countries to protect its core interest, they seems to have a more benign view of China compared to their views on India.

It is true that China has also been imposing conditions on Nepal because it is concerned about the more than 20,000 Tibetan refugees living in Nepal who often cross over to Tibet to protest against China. It is also worried about a large number of Western funded NGOs and INGOs operating in Nepal. These funds are reportedly being used to convert the hill *Janajatis* to Christianity and create awareness about ethnicity-based federalism.[16] In Chinese perception, this is part of the long term strategy of Western forces to destabilise its southern territory.

The other factors that influence Chinese foreign policy in South Asia are: (i) the strategic location of South Asia in terms of a market for acquiring raw materials and selling finished goods, (ii) the region's proximity to international sea routes in the Indian Ocean and also to the two disturbed provinces of China, i.e., to Xinjiang and Tibet, (iii) its strategic ally—Pakistan—can be used to counter-balance India in case of a conflict situation, and (iv) supplying of military hardware to India's neighbours, which both fuels and sustains regional antipathy vis-à-vis India.[17] Therefore, over the period of time, China has improved its bilateral relations with Sri Lanka and Maldives to secure its supply lines in the Indian Ocean.

The Sri Lankan government, under Mahinda Rajapaksa, has almost endorsed China's concept of establishing a 21st Century 'Maritime Silk Route Economic Belt' in the Indian Ocean. It feels that the concept would reinforce the 'Strategic Co-operative Partnership', with China which was singed between the two countries in May 2013. The new Maldivian government led by President Yameen Abdul Gayoom has also hinted that many development projects of the country would get Chinese assistance. Further, China has used its passive presence in the strategically located Bay of Bengal region to monitor Indian Navy and ICBM programmes at Wheeler Islands and Chandipur by supplying two Ming-class submarines to Bangladesh. The nature of Chinese engagements in the region indicates that it wants to reduce India's influence in the region and secure its core interests. In this context, Nepal occupies a special place in China's South Asia policy. Chinese scholars specialising in South Asia and Nepal affairs are optimistic that the new leadership in China will continue to strengthen its relationship with South Asia, especially Nepal, because of Tibet and the presence of external forces in that country. Therefore, the new leadership will "definitely want to build [a] strong relationships with Nepal which shares border with Tibet."[18]

Where does Nepal Figure in China's Foreign Policy?

Nepal has a special place in Chinese foreign policy, though it is described as a country of 'peripheral' concern by many scholars in China. China has been following a modest policy towards Nepal ever since the two countries established diplomatic relations in 1955. However, even if Nepal may not have figured prominently in China's broad foreign policy, it has certainly assumed importance in China's neighbourhood policy over the past few years. There are several concerns that underpin the Chinese policy towards Nepal. Because Nepal shares the longest border with China—after India—and a large part of this border remains unguarded due to mountainous terrain. In their many joint statements the two countries have stressed on strengthening 'border area management'.

Geographically, Nepal has remained the southern gateway to Tibet and has had closer economic and cultural linkages with Tibet than China since times immemorial. For China, Nepal is a geographic and cultural buffer between Tibet and Tibetan refugees living in India. Beijing fears that Nepal could be used by other powers as a frontline state to challenge China's security interests. It suspects that the CIA and Indian intelligence agencies support Tibetan refugees who are trying to cross into China—the Himalayan mountain range does not always provide a natural defence against infiltration. Some Chinese analysts are in agreement with Maoist leaders that the US agenda in Nepal is basically designed to encircle China.[19] Wang Hongwei, a Chinese expert on Nepal, believes that India and the US are using Nepalese territory to act against China.[20] Expressing China's security concerns, in May 2001, the Chinese ambassador to Kathmandu confirmed that China had a vital interest in securing its strategic southern border by nurturing a credible relationship with Nepal.[21] Again in March 2006, Tang Jiaxuan, former Chinese Foreign Minister, while commenting on the deepening political crisis and the role of external forces in Nepal, said: "Beijing has always stuck to the approach of non-intervention towards Nepal's inside affairs, fully respecting any model of national development that the Nepalese people chose."[22] Some analysts also suggest that even if China does not expressly mention the role of external forces in Nepal, it is insecure about India's leverage in Nepal as well as the influence of the United States, the United Kingdom, and the European Union in that country. Therefore, China would always look for a credible nationalist force in Nepal, amenable to its influence, for political stability.[23] It also consistently emphasises that the government of Nepal must stick to the one-China policy and should not allow Tibetans to indulge in any kind of anti-China activities.

From the economic point of view, overall, China is the second largest trading partner of Nepal after India. Despite the economic boom in China, the Tibet Autonomous Region (TAR) continues to be the major exporter to Nepal. By 2011, the bilateral trade between Nepal and Tibet had touched US$945 million, up by 86.2 per cent year-on-year. In 1997, the volume of trade between Nepal and Tibet was just $60 million which crossed $200 million in 2000.[24] Nepal could be a major market and transit route to South Asia for industrial products in TAR.

More importantly, India has had strong historical, geographic, cultural and economic links with Nepal and the two countries share an open and peaceful border. There is a chronic suspicion in China that the Nepal-Tibet and Nepal-India border is being misused by the Tibetan refugees. Therefore, Nepal comes second in importance for China, after Pakistan, in South Asia. As a noted Indian analyst has pointed out, "[t]he importance of Nepal to China's strategic thinkers and planners arises not only because of its potential for being used against India in times of peace as well as war, but also because of its potential to India for being used to create instability in Tibet."[25] Although India has been reiterating since 2003 that "the Tibet Autonomous Region is an integral part of the People's Republic of China"[26] and despite repeated assurances that the Indian government would not allow anti-China activity by Tibetan refugees living in India, "Chinese leadership remain[s] wary of India's stance on the Tibet issue."[27] Therefore, ensuring Nepal's neutrality on the Tibet issue and precluding any possibility of India-Nepal collusion over the issue becomes important from the Chinese point of view. Its concern regarding India's stance on Tibet doubled when it appeared that India was about to change its position on Tibet after the Chinese denial of a visa in August 2010 to then general officer commanding-in-chief of northern area command Lieutenant General B.S. Jaswal on the grounds that he was responsible for Jammu and Kashmir.[28] Earlier, in 2008, India was unhappy with China for treating Jammu and Kashmir as a disputed area and issuing stapled visas to Indian citizens living there.

Therefore, China's policy towards Nepal has been different from its policies towards the other South Asian countries. China also has three major strategic interests in Nepal: (i) containing Tibetan refugees in the south of the Himalayas and controlling their anti-China activities; (ii) neutralising India's influence in Nepal and setting up a pro-China regime in Kathmandu, for which China has scaled up its engagement in recent years and has also taken soft diplomatic measures, i.e. people-to-people contacts, cultural relations, scholarships for students, economic aid and spread of Chinese Confucianism by setting up Confucius Institutes in Nepal; and (iii) investing in strategically important infrastructure projects like airports and important highways. The investments in Lumbini and Pokhara airports—for which the government of Nepal has finally decided to accept Chinese investment during Premier Wen Jiabao's visit—indicate that China is going all out to increase its leverage with the Nepalese people and government.

The frequency of high level visits since 2006 from China to Nepal reflects elevation of Nepal's position in China's external periphery policy. The short visit of China's premier in January 2012, after ten years, was undertaken at a time when China was concerned about the ongoing political instability in Nepal and was looking for new political partners in that country after the fall of the monarchy. The last Chinese premier to visit Nepal was Zhu Rongji in May 2001, when the Maoists were waging an armed struggle and the king was still in power. China has apprehensions that the Tibetan refugees may take advantage of Nepal's instability and strengthen their position. Moreover, the Chinese are not comfortable with the multi-party system of Nepal. It is easier for China to work with a single party in Nepal to further its interest. However, given Nepal's multi-party system and the dynamics of coalition politics; China finds it difficult to have an enduring partnership with any particular party. India's successful engagement with the Maoists in the recent past after Baburam Bhattarai-led Maoist government came to power added to Chinese concerns and, perhaps, prompted them to proactively cultivate—especially the CPN-Maoist (Baidya faction)—which is against the Prachanda faction and India.

This has also led China to reshape its foreign policy towards Nepal. Apart from sending many political, economic, military and academic delegations to Nepal, since 2008, it has posted one of its better diplomats as ambassador to Kathmandu. It has encouraged people-to-people contacts, opened more customs posts on the borders, increased the annual assistance to Nepal and, most importantly, strengthened its engagement at the institutional level, leading to greater interaction with the Nepalese Army, bureaucracy, police and armed police (mostly deployed along the borders). During Wen Jiabao's visit, the Chinese side pledged US$ 02 million for strengthening the Nepal Police by setting up an Armed Police Force College.

China's Continental Policy and Nepal

Chinese 'continental policy' at a broader level includes soft borders, easier immigration and co-option.[29] In the case of Nepal, China has been systematically trying to gain influence in the border regions by offering incentives to businessmen, local traders, villagers and government officials posted in the border districts, etc. It has started a special development programme in the 15-border districts of Nepal in 2008. The TAR government provided Yuan 3 million annually to these districts to execute various infrastructure-related projects, along with food assistance. Although the programme was initially for five years, it was extended perhaps under its newly declared policy in November 2013 for strengthening relations with South Asian countries.

In fact, the November 2013 policy was a reiteration of the 'extended peripheral policy' attempted by the previous Chinese leadership with added emphasis on developing strategic and economic cooperation with Pakistan and Nepal. In an interview to *The Kathmandu Post* in September 2011, Ai Ping, the former vice minister at the International Department of the Central Committee of the Communist Party of China (CPC) had stated that China had been working to develop good relations with its neighbours, including Nepal. He had said:

> China's developing of good relations with the South Asian countries is part of its general policy towards the surrounding countries of building friendship and partnership with its neighbours...Nepal is rich in natural resources such as hydropower, and China has the technology and capital. Therefore, there will be great cooperation opportunities in this field between us. The Chinese government supports its able enterprises to invest and participate in the hydropower and other infrastructure development in Nepal.[30]

During every bilateral visit China reiterates the three policy determinants of its relations with Nepal: (i) the relationship is based on the five principles of *Panchsheel*; (ii) China will not intervene in Nepal's domestic politics; and (iii) China would expect Nepal's support on issues that concern China's sovereignty and national interests, including Tibet and Taiwan. Tibet is the core issue in this policy framework. In fact, Nepal has reciprocated well on all the three fronts. Quoting an official source a Chinese scholar says that China's policy towards Nepal is based on an:

> ...emphasis on equality and trust on mutual basis, sovereignty and territorial integrity, non-intervention from outside powers, general reconciliation leading to peace and order as well as respect for any models for national building and development based on Nepalese own choices and interests.[31]

China's Nepal policy was reiterated after the anti-China protests of 2008 and the Maoist's ascendance. It emphasised the accommodation of each other's concerns. According to the former Chinese Ambassador to Kathmandu, Qiu

Guihong, China has adopted a fourfold policy to strengthen its relations with Nepal: "First, accommodate each other's political concerns. Second, enhance the economic cooperation on the basis of mutual benefit. Third, boost people-to-people and cultural exchanges. Fourth, strengthen coordination and cooperation in international and regional affairs."[32] China has sought to engage Nepalese political actors at all levels, primarily to secure its strategic interest and increase coordination in managing Nepal-Tibet Border.

When the Maoists emerged victorious in the April 2008 elections, China was uncertain about its approach towards them. There was a perception that the Maoists were backed by India and were catapulted on to the political center stage only after a comprehensive peace agreement in which India played a substantial role. However, media reports revealed that after several interactions with Maoist leaders, China began to feel quite comfortable with the Maoist-led government. In fact, in order to cope with the changing political landscape in Nepal and build contacts with the Maoists, in December 2007, Beijing had sent an unofficial delegation headed by Wang Jiarui, director of CPC Central Committee's International Department, to interact with Maoist leaders. The Maoists' ideological linkages with China and their keenness to neutralise India's influence in the region perhaps facilitated the process of engagement between the two.[33]

It has been reported that in their discussions with the Chinese, the Maoist leaders had given the impression that the future of democracy in Nepal could be guided by democratic centralism model of the CPC. Indeed, many in Nepal argue that the very fact that they have retained their Maoist tag despite joining competitive politics indicates that the party may be working towards a single-party system in the future, given that dictatorship of the proletariat has pride of place in the Maoist lexicon. Even after the Maoists joined the political mainstream, some hardline leaders of the Maoist party in Nepal had on a number of occasions suggested a people's republic similar to that of China. These ideas might have encouraged Chinese attempts to consolidate its position in Nepal continuously engaging the Maoists at various levels, to secure its strategic interests in the region.

Chinese Concern over External Powers in Nepal

During the Cold War, the United States had identified Nepal as being strategically important for preventing the spread of communism to South Asia. As part of its containment policy, the US had armed Tibetan rebels called the 'Khampas' in the late 1950s and encouraged them to launch an anti-China insurgency from Mustang district of Nepal to liberate Tibet from the Chinese occupation. The incident had made China realise its vulnerabilities because of the presence of the US and Western countries in Nepal. And, Nepal continues to be an ideal location for extending support to Tibetan refugees. Washington also considers Nepal as being strategically important for monitoring India and China and their relations and influence in South Asia.

When the Maoist movement entered into the 'strategic offensive' phase by middle of the 2004, followed by King Gyanendra's assumption of power in February 2005, the US administration felt political polarisation would further erode Nepal Government's ability to resist the Maoists. The Maoists should be prevented from capturing power by bringing the king and political parties together. Anticipating serious humanitarian ramifications and spread of Maoism to neighbouring countries, the US decided to augment its diplomatic leverage and resource support for development programmes.[34] For example, a US official observed in 2006 that, the king's take-over of power deteriorated the security situation in Nepal, and China might take advantage of the situation, which could "destabilize the region, spur new tensions between India and China, and potentially create a new terrorist haven in South Asia".[35]

China, on the other hand, became very suspicious about the undue US concerns regarding Maoist insurgency and the presence of US special troops in that country. Although China did not react openly, it reportedly monitored US activities in Nepal and diplomatically obtained assurances from the monarchy that it was committed to the one-China policy. In the post-conflict period, China also became suspicious of the presence of Western-funded I/NGOs, especially from Europe, which were said to be supporting the agenda of ethnicity-based federalism, and grew wary of the proactive role played by India in the peace and Constitution-drafting process in Nepal.

Ever since the political transition in Nepal in 2006, China has been perceiving developments in its periphery as constituting a national threat. Its 2008 Defense White Paper identified Tibet as a national security threat for the first time—the earlier versions had only mentioned Taiwan. The White Paper observed: "China is encountering many new circumstances and new issues in maintaining social stability...'East Turkistan independence' and 'Tibet independence' pose threats to China's unity and security."[36] A series of anti-China protests by Tibetan refugees in Kathmandu in March 2008 gave credence to this threat perception. The abolition of the monarchy—regarded by Beijing as a trusted ally—has also complicated matters for China.[37] Traditionally, China has been sensitive about separatist movements in its territory and about losing sphere of influence to external powers in its immediate neighbourhood. In response to that China has so far made more than 20 military interventions in its external periphery till the early 1990s because of the threat perception from neighbouring countries, its weakening control over its traditional sphere of influence and encirclement by strong powers.[38]

Against this backdrop, the protests by Tibetans in Kathmandu in 2008 alarmed the Chinese and, according to Kunda Dixit:

> ...convinced Beijing that any understanding with India about minimising American interference in Nepal had broken down. New Delhi, having just signed a nuclear cooperation deal with Washington and hence being openly in the 'US camp,' was either unable or unwilling to stop pro-Tibet activities in Nepal.[39]

Jessica Mathews, president of the Carnegie Endowment for International Peace, observed that: "The United States has already started partnering with an emerging power that shares a long border with China as it moves to open a special relationship with India."[40] However, the real or perceived fear of being encircled by the Western powers has compelled China to work relentlessly to bring the Himalayan countries into its sphere of influence, while the US is using the influence of its regional allies to advance its policy in the region. Therefore, a kind of Cold War-like situation is in the making in the sub-Himalayan region.

China is also concerned about its asymmetric presence in Nepal vis-à-vis India and the dominant role of liberal democratic parties in Nepalese polity. It was earlier worried about the external support to pro-democracy movements in the 1990s and again in 2006. It feared all along that democracy in Nepal would open the doors for India and Western governments, especially the United States, to launch a campaign of intervention and coercion against China.[41]

The unregulated open border between India and Nepal is another area of concern for China. Beijing considers this region to be extremely significant for its security, particularly because of its undemarcated border with India.[42] It believes that Nepal is being used as a transit route between Tibet and Dharamshala by illegal migrants. It is warily watching out for any new ethnic problems and infrastructure investments by other countries in the Nepalese districts that abut Tibet. Therefore, India's influence in Nepal has remained a major policy determinant for China in this region.

In this scenario, Beijing is interested in protecting Nepalese 'sovereignty' (a euphemism for reducing Indian influence) to maintain its buffer status. Liu Hong Chai, the international bureau chief of the CPC, in November

2008, assured the Nepalese people that: "any foreign conspiracy to disintegrate Nepal will be appropriately dealt with by China".[43]

Chinese Engagement in the Post-Monarchy Period

Exchange of High-Level Visits

Interestingly, the number of visits from the Chinese side has increased since the abolition of the monarchy (see Table 4.1). While only two high-level visits took place in 2006 end, the number increased as the political instability and internal disturbances in Nepal continued. Media reports in Nepal indicate that China had sent around 26 delegations to that country between 2006 and 2008.[44] While earlier visits were confined mostly to the top level and were at the invitation of the respective governments, delegations from the CPC, military teams and business delegations have dominated the visits in recent years. The year 2011 witnessed the highest number of Chinese high level official visits to Nepal.[45] The number of high level visits came down in 2012 in comparison to previous years perhaps because China had established some contacts with major political parties and it was pretty convinced that the one-China policy would remain core of Nepal's foreign policy towards China. This policy was in fact reiterated during the bilateral visits by almost all the parties that had been in power since 2008. Although the high-level visits came down in 2012, interestingly, some Nepalese scholars and journalists shared with this author in November 2013 in Kathmandu that the number of unofficial visits (members of the CPC) has gone up and most of the visits

Table 4.1: High-Level Visits from China and India to Nepal during 2006-2012

Year	*Official*		*Unofficial^*		*Total*	
	*China**	*India***	*China*	*India*	*China*	*India*
2006	2	3	–	—	2	03
2007	3	2	3	—	6	02
2008	6	1	1	1	7	02
2009	2	4	4	—	6	04
2010	3	2	2	—	5	02
2011	11	—	4	—	15	—
2012#	4	—	2	—	6	—

* Including military delegations.
** Including foreign secretary and special envoys.
#Till December 2012.
^ Party members and business delegations.
Source: Table complied by author. For China–data obtained from media sources. For India–Annual Reports 2006-2010, Ministry of External Affairs, Government of India.

are not reported in media. This phenomenon might have begun before 2012. Quoting Chinese official sources, *Xinhua* said in 2010 the number of bilateral personnel exchanges with Nepal touched 74,000.[46]

These visits served to broaden cooperation by identifying various areas of mutual interest in the fields of security, trade, infrastructure development, tourism, etc. China repeatedly promised economic, technological and military aid to Nepal. The Nepalese Government(s) was reportedly asked to follow the one-China policy, not to allow Nepalese soil to be used for anti-China activities, take strong action against Tibetan refugees and grant special facilities for Chinese investments in strategic sectors. A Chinese scholar has observed that "through these high-profile engagements, Beijing urged the Nepalese government to follow China's Tibet policy and at the same time, assured Kathmandu of a non-intervention approach toward the Himalayan neighbour regardless of the prevailing volatile political climate."[47] Beijing has also increased Track-II diplomacy with Nepal and invited Nepalese scholars to visit and undertake research work at Chinese think-tanks since 2008.

Some of the important visitors from China to Nepal were:

- 25 June 2013: Chinese State Councilor Yang Jiechi led a 19-member delegation for a two-day official visit to Kathmandu.
- 30 June 2012: Vice Minister of the International Department of the CPC, Ai Ping, led a delegation to Kathmandu.
- 2 April 2012: A 16-memeber Chinese delegation led by Vice Chairman of Standing Committee of the 11th National People's Committee Chen Zhili visited Nepal.
- 22 February 2012: Chinese Minister of State Forestry Administration Jia Zhibang undertook a four day official visit to Nepal.
- 14 January 2012: Prime Minister, Wen Jiabao, paid an official visit to Nepal.
- 23 March 2011: A 15-member military delegation headed by People's Liberation Army (PLA) chief, Chen Bingde.
- 6 December 2010: A cultural delegation led by Culture Minister Cai Wu.
- 17 September 2010: A high-level 40-member business team led by All-China Federation of Industry and Commerce (ACFIC) first Vice-Chairman Quan Zhezhu.
- 11 September 2010: He Yong, Vice-Premier and Secretary at the Secretariat of the 17th Central Committee of the CPC, led a 21-member delegation.

- 28 July 2010: A high-level team of security officials headed by Vice Minister for Public Security Chen Zhimin.
- 25 February 2009: Assistant Foreign Minister Hu Zhengyue led a 14-member delegation.
- 19 February 2009: Liu Hongcai, Vice Minister of the International Department of the Central Committee of the CPC led a delegation to take part in the inaugural ceremony of the Eighth Convention of the CPN-UML in Butwal.
- 10 February 2009: A high-level PLA delegation, one of the largest delegations in two months, visited Kathmandu.
- 6 December 2008: Lieutenant General Ma Xiaotian, Deputy Chief of General Staff of the PLA, headed a ten-member delegation.
- 1 December 2008: Foreign Minister Yang Jiechi visited Nepal.
- 24 July 2008: Vice-Minister for Foreign Affairs, Wu Dawei, visited Kathmandu.
- 4 March 2008: Assistant Minister for Foreign Affairs, He Yafei, was on a three-day visit to Kathmandu.

Compared to China, high-level political engagement from the Indian side is dominated by foreign secretaries and special envoys, with occasional visits by the external affairs minister. Since 1997, seven prime ministers of Nepal have visited India. The last Indian Prime Minister to visit Nepal was I.K. Gujral in June 1997. Table 4.1 indicates no major qualitative or quantitative improvement in bilateral relations with Nepal. The political imbalance in the relationship has been gradually eroding India's traditional leverages in Nepal. If the trend continues, other countries including China may consolidate their hold on Nepal in the near future at the expense of India.

Nepal's engagement with China has also increased manifold with the visit of delegations, both at the state[48] and non-state levels. Private visits by political leaders, journalists and academics are also sponsored by China as part of its public diplomacy exercise. During state visits Chinese authorities reportedly assured Nepal leaders of full support for laying the foundation for a 'New Nepal'. For the Nepalese Maoists, the growing Chinese engagement is a win-win situation in line with their policy of equidistance, which has been deliberately adopted to counterbalance India's influence in Nepal.

Political Engagements

In addition to engaging the Maoists, China wants to maintain good relations with other political parties as well. It is open to working with any political dispensation in Kathmandu as long as it is prepared to take strong action against political activities of the Tibetan refugees. It has penetrated and gained the confidence of hardline communist leaders of the CPN-UML and the UCPN (Maoist). Prior to Jhalanath Khanal, who is perceived to be close to China, became CPN-UML chief, a four-member Chinese delegation had reportedly visited Kathmandu on 10 May 2008 and met him and other Maoist leaders. A senior CPC delegation, led by Vice-Minister Liu Hongcai, was in Kathmandu in February 2009 to attend the inaugural ceremony of the 8th National Convention of the CPN-UML. It should be noted here that, Khanal's victory as chairman of the CPN-UML was crucial for the survival of the Maoist-led coalition government in 2008-2009. Khanal was also considered close to Prachanda. The opposition parties in Nepal suspected that China had played a role in facilitating the alliance between the two parties in February 2011 after which Jhalanath Khanal became prime minister. After the November 2013 CA elections, a Chinese delegation led by Qiu Guoheng visited Kathmandu and met political leaders of Nepal including CPN-UML leader Jhalanath Khanal.

Significantly, China has also begun taking an active interest in Terai politics. A high-level Chinese delegation had reportedly attended the general convention of the Madhesi People's Rights Forum in early 2009. Moreover, media reports indicated that CPN (Maoist) leader Matrika Prasad Yadav visited China in 2011. Apart from that, China wants to strengthen people-to-people contacts through the Chinese Study Centers in Terai. According to Bhim Prasad Bhurtel, executive director of the Nepal South Asia Centre, Kathmandu, "More recently 33 China Study Centers have been established in southern Nepal adjoining the Indian border."[49]

After the split in the UCPN (Maoist) party on 18 June 2012, there are perceptions in Nepal that the newly formed CPN-Maoist (Baidya faction) has been seeking political support from China. Although the exact nature of their relationship with China is yet to be established, some politburo members of the outfit are in touch with CPC officials and have undertaken several visits to Beijing on the invitation of the CPC. During their visits, the CPN-Maoist leaders have reportedly discussed the future political line of the CPN-Maoist and especially on funding issues. The CPC and the CPN-Maoist relationship became clear when both Chairman Mohan Baidya and Vice-Chairman C.P. Gajurel undertook an unscheduled[50] visit to Beijing to meet CPC officials. Interestingly, the visit was undertaken while the party was opposing the 2013-November elections and had decided not to participate in the electoral process until its demands were accepted by the High Level Political

Committee. Although the leaders had denied any kind of pressure from China about their participation in the elections and for re-unifying with the UCPN (Maoist), the party, interestingly, softened its conditions for dialogue with the HLPC after the visit. Further, on 5 January 2014, *Republica* reported that Chinese Vice-Minister Ai Ping during his visit to Kathmandu in December 2013 had discussed with the top leaders of both the Maoist factions about their merger and suggested to the Baidya faction to cooperate in the Constitution-drafting process. There was a perception in Nepal that Chinese mediation over merger of both the factions might actually succeed in future.

Strategic Partner

The Chinese engagement in Nepal goes beyond the political domain. At a meeting between the then Defence Minister Ram Bahadur Thapa and the Deputy Commander of the PLA, Lieutenant General Ma Xiaotian, held in Kathmandu in December 2008 and signed an agreement on military assistance worth US$ 2.6 million, which was discussed in September 2008, for the modernisation of the NA. That was the first such military assistance to the Maoist government. Beijing had keenly supported the Maoist government's proposal to integrate some 19,000 Maoist guerrillas into the Nepalese Army. During Prime Minister Wen Jiabao's visit to Nepal in January 2012, China announced a one-time grant of $20 million, for the rehabilitation of former Maoist combatants. During Madhav Nepal's regime Defence Minister Bidya Devi Bhandari visited China in March 2010 and the Chinese reiterated their keenness to provide military modernisation assistance to Nepal. During the then Chinese Army Chief General Chen Bingde's visit to Nepal in 2011, China signed an agreement for providing military aid to the tune of US$7.7 million to the Nepalese Army in an effort towards deepening the military relations. China's engagement with the Nepalese Army, which has been traditionally close to the Indian and the US Armies, "underlines that China has no 'favourites' on the Nepalese political landscape and has only 'interests' and Beijing will advance its interests no matter who it has to deal with or what it takes."[51]

China's wooing of Nepal as a new strategic partner has been confirmed by various Chinese officials. For example, on 16 February 2009 Foreign Minister Yang Jiechi said that China would prefer to work with Nepal on the basis of 'strategic partnership'. During former Prime Minister Madhav Kumar Nepal's visit in December 2009 President Hu Jintao vowed to enhance the bilateral relations to a 'comprehensive partnership of cooperation' and the two countries agreed to further strengthen political and economic ties. They agreed to promote exchange of high-level visits and contacts at all levels and make full use of the existing mechanisms.[52] China also proposed to strengthen the relationship through cooperation in five different areas for mutual benefit and peace and stability in South Asia during Zhou Yongkang's[53] visit to Nepal in August 2011. The areas identified were:

(1) exchange of high level visits;
(2) cooperation in trade and investment, agriculture, transportation, information technology, infrastructure development, hydropower construction and poverty alleviation;
(3) cooperation in areas of security, education, human resource development, tourism and cultural exchanges;
(4) cooperation between the CPC and various political parties of Nepal; and
(5) close coordination and cooperation on major global issues like global financial crisis, climate change, energy, food security, security and SAARC.[54]

China, in fact, immediately after the second CA election results, reconfirmed continuation of its strategic partnership relations with Nepal. Speaking at a programme organised by Nepal World Relations Council Chinese Ambassador Wu Chuntai stated "China has accepted Nepal as a strategic partner," and wanted to expand its relationships with Nepal in diverse fields.[55] As part of the comprehensive partnership of cooperation programme, China had been trying to compete with India in Nepal by offering scholarships to Nepal Police and Armed Police Force (APF) officers for the National Defence Course (NDC) at the National Defence University of the People's Liberation Army. This is besides the regular quota of a few Nepalese Army officers. For the first time, China granted a scholarship to a civilian officer of the then Kathmandu Chief District Officer (CDO), Jaya Mukunda Khanal. In April 2009, Chinese authorities took a ten-member team of Nepal Police, APF and National Investigation Department to China on a 15-day tour. A 20-member Nepalese team comprising bureaucrats and security officials went on a China-sponsored visit to Lhasa on 7 August 2009.[56] The main objective of this initiative could have been to win over the officials of the security agencies who could help in quelling anti-China activities in Nepal and to influence the deployment of security forces in the northern districts to curb the Tibetan movement in that region.

In view of the protracted political deadlock in Nepal over the formation of a new government and the adoption of a new constitution, China expressed its concerns that anti-China elements might exploit the prevailing political uncertainty. In the absence of a trusted regime, instead of following a regime-based policy, China has decided to engage with the key security organisations to suppress anti-Chinese activities both in Kathmandu and the border areas and maintain equidistance from all political parties in its future engagements. In keeping with this policy two important security delegations visited Kathmandu in 2010. Nepalese sources said the Chinese delegations announced an annual aid of US$1.47 million (10 million Yuan), excluding grant-in-aid assistance, to the ministry of home affairs to improve the efficiency of the security agencies for curbing anti-China activities by Tibetan refugees.[57] As part of the comprehensive partnership of cooperation, during Chinese State Councilor Yang Jiechi's visit to Kathmandu in June 2013, China pledged to provide NPR 3.6 billion in assistance for the construction of an APF training academy at Matatirtha, Kathmandu. The fact of the matter is that since 2010 Nepal has deployed the APF for border security, especially along the northern border to curb anti-Tibet activities.

Economic Engagements

Aid and Assistance

China[58] has expanded its financial assistance to Nepal to cover several sectors in the country. There has also been a significant increase in grant-in-aid since 2006/07 when Nepal underwent political transition.[59] Table 4.2 shows how China has increased its annual aid assistance to Nepal from US$0.14 million in 2005/06 to $35.48 million in 2010/11, while Indian aid went up from $4.75 million in 2005/06 to $92 million in the same period. After regime change Chinese aid assistance to the country has increased more than 200 times and India's more than 19 times. The figure shows the China's growing interests in Nepal. Interestingly, when former Chinese Premier Wen Jaibao visited Nepal in January 2012, he committed $1.18 billion in aid to be spent over three years. As already discussed China has been providing annual food assistance especially in the northern districts that borders Tibet. This programme was started in 2008, following the Tibetan uprising.

Table 4.2: China and India Development Assistance to Nepal

(*US$ million*)

Fiscal year	*2004/05*	*2005/06*	*2006/07*	*2007/08*	*2008/09*	*2009/10*	*2010/11*
China	0.14	0.14	12.07	1.39	36.60	29.41	35.48
India	8.65	4.75	61.91	38.61	95.45	100.70	92.55

Source: Chandra Ghimire, "New Age of South-South Development Cooperation: A Case Study of Nepal", (unpublished paper).

A sector-wise inventory of India-China development assistance to Nepal again reflects that both countries have focused more on infrastructure sector than social sectors. The foreign aid to Nepal from the two countries is mostly for strategic investments.

Table 4.3: Sector-wise Development Assistance to Nepal from India and China (FY 2006/07 to 2010/11)

(US$ million)

Year	*Country*	*Agriculture*	*Infrastructure*	*Public Service/ Security*	*Social Sector*	*Trade Industry/ Finance*	*Total*
2010/11	India	14.16	59.34	...	...	19.06	92.55
	China	0	35.04	0.44			35.48
2009/10	India	7.55	75.10			18.06	100.70
	China	...	29.41				29.41
2008/09	India		95.03			0.42	95.45
	China		36.60				36.60
2007/08	India		32.36	0.97	4.86	0.42	38.61
	China		1.39				1.39
2006/07	India		50.16		11.39	0.36	61.91
	China	1.88	10.20				12.07

Source: Chandra Ghimire, "New Age of South-South Development Cooperation: A Case Study of Nepal" (unpublished paper).

Table 4.3 reflects that China has also increased its development assistance for the public security sector. Earlier, it was only India that had provided aid for this sector. The second highest development assistance from these two countries went to the trade, industry and finance sectors. Interestingly, during this period, China provided limited aid for social development projects like schools and hospitals in Nepal, while India contributed US$ 4.86 million in 2007/08.

Major Loan Assistance

In 2008 the Chinese Assistant Minister for Foreign Affairs, He Yafei, pledged a loan of US$125 million for Upper Trishuli 3A and $62 million for the Upper Trishuli 3B projects to generate hydro power in Nepal. These projects were expected to be operational by 2012, however their current status is not known.[60] Chinese Vice-Minister of Commerce Fu Ziyiing and Nepal's Finance Secretary Rameshwor Khanal signed on 28 February 2011 an agreement for a loan of approximately NPR 7 billion for Upper Trishuli 3A. During Fu

Ziyiing's visit, China also agreed to provide NPR 547 million to Nepal as part of bilateral economic and technical cooperation and as assistance for the upgrading of the 27.4 km-long Kathmandu city ring road.[61] Six months after the Upper Trishuli 3A project deal, the two countries again signed a $50 million economic and technical cooperation agreement—which provided for a $24 million soft loan for a hydropower transmission line project and $2.5 million security project for enhancing the capabilities of the Nepal Police, besides an understanding to provide other concessional loans.[62]

Trade

The China-Nepal bilateral trade as of 2012 stands at NPR billion 72418.82 with China selling goods worth about NPR 69910.83 billion and Nepal exporting goods worth a mere NPR 2507.99 billion. Table 4.4 indicates that there is trade deficit of NPR –67402.84 billion. To bridge the trade deficit, China had agreed in April 2009 to provide zero tariff facility to 497 Nepalese goods to the Chinese market and it further increased to 7,787 products in November 2012. Despite the zero tariff facilities, Nepal is yet to utilise that in its favour. As a result, the trade gap has increased consistently since 2010. The traders in Nepal believe that poor implementation of zero-tariff barriers, lack of facilities for export of Nepalese goods, and poor trade related infrastructure have been major hurdles in reducing trade deficit.[63]

Table 4.4: Nepal's Trade with China from 2010 to 2012

(*All figures in NPR Billion*)

Year	*Export*	*Import*	*Trade balance*
2012	2507.99	69910.83	-67402.84
2011	761.98	51466.42	-50704.44
2010	996.99	41057.90	-40060.91

Source: Ministry of Foreign Affairs, Government of Nepal.

While there is a huge gap in Nepal-China trade, as mentioned earlier, Nepal has remained Tibet's top trading partner since 2000. Nepal-Tibet trade has grown roughly in an average US$ 70 million per year since 2000. While the bilateral trade between Tibet and Nepal in 2000 was around $200 million, it jumped to $542 million in 2010, up by 65 per cent from the previous year. The same touched $945 million by end of 2011.[64]

Investments

It is interesting to note that the number of joint ventures (JVs) with China have increased since 2008 after the political change took place in Nepal and the emergence of Maoists as largest party in the CA elections that very year. As Table 4.5 indicates, China was the third top investor by July 2008. The number of Chinese JVs in Nepal surpassed those with the US by July 2010. A further year-wise comparison shows that number of Chinese JVs surpassed Indians JVs in Nepal by July 2009-10. In terms of volume of investments, there were more investments from India than China in Nepal during the same period, but the number of projects from India shrunk. Between July 2008-09 and 2009-10, while India had added only 27 JVs, China had added 59 JVs in Nepal. Similarly, while only 39 Indian JVs were added by July 2011, around 69 JVs were added to the existing Chinese JVs during the same period. The same trend continued in the following fiscal year (July 2011-12). However, the only solace for India was that even though Nepal had fewer joint ventures with India, the investments were much higher than those with China till 2012.[65] Interestingly, for the year 2012-13, China had committed NPR 5.99 billion FDI, around 30.89 per cent of the total amount committed by foreign investors to Nepal. According to the Department of Industry (DoI), Government of Nepal, China surpassed the investments commitment from India, which dominated the FDI sector in Nepal, until the year 2011-12[66]. Apart from the political, strategic and the Chinese 'go global' policy factors, bilateral institutional arrangements like the Nepal-China Non-governmental Cooperation Forum, established in 1996, have also been playing a major role in promoting Chinese investments in Nepal.

Table 4.5: Joint Ventures in Nepal with India, US and China

Nepal's financial year is from July 16 to July 15

	2007/08		*2008/09*		*2009/10*		*2010/11*		*2011/2012*	
Total Projects	1,570		1,726		1,898		2,108		2,335	
	JVs	%	*JVs*	%	*JVs*	%	*JVs*	%	*JVs*	%
India	414	45	435	44	462	44	501	47.6	525	46.32
US	142	10.4	156	9.87	166	8.40	174	7.28	198	6.84
China	#	-	273	10.48	332	10.08	401	10.34	478	10.46

%—of total investments.

China might have secured third position.[67]

Source: Bureau of Economic, Energy and Business Affairs, US Department of State. The Bureau collected data from *Foreign Investment Division, Department of Industry, Nepal.*

It is believed that Chinese trade and investments in Nepal can grow with better connectivity between the two countries in the future. In this regard, Nepal government has requested Chinese government to extend its railways and improve the roads in the border areas. The objective of this is mostly to reduce dependence on India and take advantage of the economic growth in the neighbourhood. Not surprisingly, the concept of Nepal being a 'vibrant bridge', as reiterated by former Prime Minister Baburam Bhattarai, has become dominant in Nepal's foreign policy discourse. Therefore, a friendly Nepal provides China with an open overland gateway into South Asia, which is exclusively under New Delhi's sphere of influence. To consolidate this connection, Beijing has tried to make headway by increasing its economic engagement with this area.[68]

Interestingly, historic evidence suggests that China has had limited trade activities with Nepal. The China-Nepal trade is dominated by the trade between TAR and Nepal because of inhospitable trade route and the distance from the mainland. Nepalese traders find it too expensive to import goods overland from mainland China. Durga Lal Shrestha, president of the Nepal Trans-Himalayan Traders Association, says: "Importing through ship via Kolkata is some 40 per cent cheaper than importing via Khasa."[69] However, given the Chinese determination to cross the Himalayas by building railway lines (Lhasa-Shigatse) to the border with Nepal and opening two more new transit routes—the Syafrubesi-Rasuwagadhi and the Baglung Beni highway to Jamsom (Mustang)—Nepal could well become an important gateway for China to establish links with other countries in the subcontinent. China in fact has proposed to offer financial support to Nepal to connect the same railway line with Kathmandu.

Infrastructure Development

Development of infrastructure is an integral part of China's economic diplomacy. In the case of Nepal, China can also use it for strategic purposes. As noted earlier, China agreed to upgrade Kathmandu city ring road. China also agreed in 2011 to construct a dry port at Larcha in Sindhupalchowk, followed by a similar port in Rasuwagadhi. The Larcha dry port is being "constructed on turn-key basis with grant assistance worth Rs [NPR] 270 million from China."[70] Media reports said China had proposed to develop dry ports and cargo terminals on both sides of Yari-Pulam, Rasuwa-Jilong, Kodari (Tatopani)-Zangmu (Khasa) and Olangchung Gola-Riwu customs. The first three are proposed as international ports and Olangchung Gola-Riwu as a bilateral port. The two sides have already opened six customs points—Olangchung, Kimathanka, Tatopani, Rasuwagadhi, Mustang and Yari—for bilateral trade and movement of people (See Map-Appendix-I).[71]

Investment in strategic airports is also part of Chinese infrastructure development programme in Nepal. It has already signed agreements with Nepal to develop Lumbini and Pokhara airports. Chinese investment in the Pokhara airport was confirmed during Wen Jiabao's visit. The project was delayed due to project cost negotiations between both the countries. While the Nepalese side decided that the estimated project cost would be around US$167 million, the Chinese company, CAMC, had initially quoted $305.13 million. China in fact, assured Nepal of a concessional loan of $145 million for the project from the Export-Import (EXIM) Bank of China.[72]

Apart from Tibet and economic issues, China has been focusing more on hydro sector in Nepal since 2010. This message has been conveyed by Chinese political and business leaders during their visits to Nepal. A high-level 40-member business delegation in September 2010 told their Nepalese counterparts that they wanted to invest in hydro projects ranging from 10 MW to 500 MW or even more.[73] According to Nepal's Ministry of Energy, the Sunkoshi (10 MW) hydro project has already been completed with Chinese assistance. China has offered soft loans for Trishuli-3A (61 MW) and Nalsyaugad (400 MW). Two Chinese companies, Sinohydro and Hydrochina, are developing Upper Marshyangdi (50 MW) and Trishuli 2 (102 MW) respectively. Chinese contractors are also involved in the Upper Tamakoshi (456 MW), Chamelia (30 MW), Kulekhani III (14 MW), Lower Indrawati (4.5 MW) and Madi (20 MW) projects (see Appendix-II). Earlier, China was aiding the construction of small projects to generate goodwill amongst the local people, without having any major economic stakes.

Since geography no longer constitutes a constraint for China due to its current economic and technological expertise and improved relations with India as a potential market and trade partner, its investment strategy has shifted to hydro and infrastructure sector. The signing of an Memorandum of Understanding (MoU) between the China Three Gorges Corporation (CTGC) and government of Nepal on the 750-megawatt West Seti hydropower project in February 2012 indicates that China has been taking a greater interest in mega projects both for business and strategic purposes.

People-to-People Contact

China has started encouraging, and in many instances funding, the establishment of front organisations[74] in Nepal to spread Chinese language and culture. The latest in the series is the establishment of Nepal China Himalayan Friendship Society (NCHFS) and the Nepal-China Media Forum.

The objective of NCHFS is to expand its network in the 15 mountainous districts abutting China in the first phase.[75] China has also been funding several social development projects, including construction of schools, hospitals and other basic necessities to create a favourable constituency in Nepal. China has agreed to develop infrastructure in Lumbini at a cost of $3 billion in 2011. As discussed earlier, China has also come up with special packages for the economic development of northern Nepal.

Apart from mutual cultural visits, the number of Chinese tourists to Nepal has doubled in recent years and the number of direct flights between the two countries has increased. Over the years the number of Confucius Institutes has also gone up. According to official sources, as of 2012, China was offering 100 scholarships to Nepalese students for higher studies in China.[76] However, other sources indicated that China will double the number of scholarships to attract Nepalese students.[77]

Elements of China's Nepal Policy

China's Nepal policy has five elements. The first relates to China's periphery. The second could be in response to India's role in Nepal. A third may be prompted by the activities of Western countries in Nepal in general and the US policy towards Nepal in particular. The fourth is its increasing interest to invest in joint ventures and finally, to explore cultural linkages so as to bind the two countries through Buddhism. Underlying these factors are Chinese concerns relating to Tibetan separatism and the evolving Indo-US relationship. Nepal's small size and dependence on China for neutralising India's influence in domestic matters helps to promote Chinese objectives. Earlier, the king and pro-palace leaders preferred to have a close relationship with China to counter Indian influence, as India was perceived to be a supporter of democratic forces. King Mahendra effectively played the China card during the 1950s and 1960s. His son Gyanendra continued his political legacy. His tilt towards China during the 13th SAARC summit in Dhaka reinforced Nepal's policy of diluting its dependency on India. At the Dhaka Summit, he linked Nepal's support to the proposal of inclusion of Afghanistan in SAARC to China's status as an observer.[78] The Maoists too have been uninhibitedly expressing their fascination for China and have not allowed the Dalai Lama's representative to function from Kathmandu, explicitly affirming that they would not condone any action that could displease China.[79]

Can China Play a Decisive Role in Nepal?

Nepal has occupied a very important though a secondary position in China's policy regarding its external periphery ever since the two countries established diplomatic relations in 1955. Among several reasons for treating Nepal modestly in Chinese foreign policy, the most important one could be India's acceptance of the Tibet Autonomous Region as part of China and Chinese acknowledgement of the southern Himalayas as India's sphere of influence, in 1954-59 and during Rajiv Gandhi's visit to Beijing in 1988.[80] China, nevertheless, had continued to influence the domestic polity of Nepal whenever the situation demanded. Its role in Nepal was determined mostly to secure its internal periphery from external threats.

Despite its recent multi-layered engagement with Nepal, China still believes that India has better leverage in Nepal. China did not intervene when India played a role in the mainstreaming of the Maoists in 2005 and resignation of Prachanda in 2009. This was apparent during Prachanda's visit to China in October 2009 and 2010 when he tried to solicit the help of the Chinese leaders to forge a consensus between the major political parties of Nepal and support a Maoist-led national unity government in Kathmandu—and the Chinese reportedly refused to intervene. The Chinese leaders in turn suggested that Nepal should resolve its misunderstandings with India. Moreover, Prachanda himself proposed a triangular strategic dialogue between China, India and Nepal to ensure peace and stability in Nepal. The triangular strategic dialogue proposal was not even mentioned during the Chinese Premier's visit to India in December 2010. During 1989 Indo-Nepal transit problem, China had accepted its "own limitations in assuming India's role, especially in supplying essential commodities, etc."[81]

Nevertheless, with its growing multi-dimensional relationship in Nepal, China can influence policy decisions in Nepal in the future as it has substantial influence over the Left parties. China's budding leverage will be utilised diligently, while accommodating its relationship with India.[82] China may deepen its engagements in Nepal due to growing unrest in Tibet and presence of external powers in Nepal. However, China would still prefer an Indian-influenced Nepal rather than western countries presence in that country.

China's benign image in Nepal and the smooth relationship between the two countries reflects the success of its policy towards the latter despite the geographic and cultural constraints. Since 1950, China has successfully managed the security threats emanating from Tibetan refugees living in Nepal and India. Nepal's support to the one-China policy and acknowledgement of

TAR as an integral part of China is a landmark diplomatic victory for China. It has also successfully resisted Western forces from supporting the Tibetan refugees in Nepal. Media reports indicate that China bribed the Nepal Police to apprehend Tibetan refugees who wanted to cross the border to escape persecution.[83] According to *a New York Times* report of 13 April 2013, the number of Tibetan refugees crossing over to Nepal has gone down to 400 in 2013, as compared to 2011. Earlier, the United Nations High Commissioner for Refugees had observed that Tibetan influx into Nepal reduced "after the 2008 Beijing Olympic Games, from an average of some 2,000 a year before 2007 to about 800."[84]

Given that China has been able to acquire a visible presence and influence in other continents like Africa and South America, it would not be very difficult for it to play a decisive role in Nepal in the future. It seems, however, that China does not want to disturb its relationship with India. It knows that the Tibet issue can be managed in a different way. China wants to play a major role in South Asia without impacting the normal course of China-India relations. China's on-going economic engagement and cooperation policy in South Asia may be considered as a strategic investment to achieve a more active role in the region. Its entry into SAARC as observer in 2005 is another achievement for China's south of the Himalayas policy.[85]

Implications for India

India has been historically apprehensive about the major powers' involvement in Nepal for many reasons. First, due to its geographic, historical and cultural linkages with Nepal, India has to take note of the developments in that country. Though India seems to be following a non-intrusive foreign policy in South Asia, at no point would India like to concede its existing leverage over crucial neighbours like Nepal to any other external actors.

Second, Beijing has already qualitatively improved its relations with all of India's neighbours and has enhanced its political and strategic presence in the Indian Ocean Region. With this vulnerability already reflecting on India's South Asia policy, Nepal would be among the last few frontiers where India would compete with China to sustain its political sway.

Third, as the Maoists are known to have politically prospered because of their strong anti-India stance, New Delhi would like to ensure that no future dispensation in Nepal fosters negative sentiments towards India at government level. The presence of external forces in Nepalese territory means that they can have easy access to separatist and Maoist outfits operating within the Indian territory to foment anti-India activities.

Fourth, there is a concern in India that strong Chinese presence may reduce India's influence in Nepal. Moreover, Nepal may seek China's active engagement to balance India. While India has been coping with growing Chinese influence in Nepal, Pakistan's proven anti-India activities in Nepalese soil complicates the situation further. Although there is no explicit understanding between both the countries on working together in Nepal, India feels uncomfortable with the possibility of the presence of two traditional adversaries consolidating their strategic presence in its backyard. In recent years, Nepal is believed to have become a haven for terrorists, smugglers and anti-India elements sponsored by the ISI. For example, around 20 terrorists had entered India from Nepal and fake Indian currency worth almost INR 2 crore was seized from them in 2009.86 (for details see Chapter 3 and 7).[86]

In India's perception, a democratic, stable and peaceful Nepal will be in India's interest. As a result, India has played a major role in resolving the political deadlock and furthering the peace process since February 2005. Any external force acting as a spoiler of this process, would be unacceptable to India. Indian policy makers believe that its understanding on Nepal will be somewhat different from that of other countries because of India's comprehensive relationship with that country.[87]

Finally, China's growing influence in Nepal could come at the expense of India and key Western players, such as the United States and the United Kingdom.[88] Some Nepalese scholars argue that the UN's role in Nepal could promote Chinese influence in Nepal because most countries view the UN as an extension of US foreign policy.[89] The competition between the major powers for influence in South Asia in general and Nepal in particular may disturb regional peace and stability.

Conclusion

Historically, China has been seen as a hegemon in its dealings with its neighbours, especially when it believes that it cannot control peripheral developments. "Great powers suffer from survival anxieties no less than weak states, and it is this concern for survival that drives them toward regional hegemony. The result is the paradoxical logic of "expand to survive".[90] Of late, China is not quite comfortable with the developments in its external periphery. Although the Chinese Defense White Paper which was released in early 2013, does not mention Tibet and Xinjiang, those issues remain China's soft underbelly, and of late, it has been feeling insecure due to the absence of a credible political partner in Nepal. That was underscored by Prachanda's[91] official visit to Beijing in April 2013 and his meeting with top political leaders of China including President Xi Jinping. He was the first South Asian leader to meet President Jinping after he assumed office in March 2013.

One Chinese scholar has observed that: "China's new leadership decided to invite Dahal as the first guest from South Asia as per its policy to give priority to neighbouring and developing countries."[92] Moreover, China re-confirmed Nepal's importance to its internal security and stability in Tibet by sending the State Councilor of the People's Republic of China Yang Jiechi on a two-day official visit to Nepal from 25-26 June 2013. This was the first high ranking official visit to Nepal after leadership change in China in March 2013. During the visit, Jiechi discussed Nepal's support for the one-China policy with the new Chief Justice-led election government. To add to Chinese worries, the Tibetan refugees have taken advantage of the situation in Nepal and have held several protests against China. Most importantly, one Tibetan refugee immolated himself in Kathmandu on 13 February 2013. This was second incident after a monk set himself afire in November 2011. If the Nepalese political instability is prolonged, Chinese micro-management and intervention in Nepal might increase in future.

China is in favour of a powerful, stable and neutral government in Kathmandu no matter what its ideology, more so if it is sensitive to China's concerns. Given the economic and people-centric diplomacy in Nepal, it seems China does not want any confrontation at this moment in this region. For the time being, China would prefer to concentrate on developmental programmes in its western region.

In the short-term, China will continue its diplomatic engagement in Nepal as part of the comprehensive partnership policy at various levels to keep external forces away from the Tibetan refugees' issue. For its long-term benefit Beijing will expand its economic engagement and people-to-people relations with Nepal. Moreover, Chinese policy towards Nepal is expected to acquire greater importance in the coming days both because of the twin factors of Tibet and India, and its official emphasis on external periphery.

*

NOTES

1. Several important developments in South Asia (SA) might have influenced China to revamp its policy towards this region by late 1990s and early 2000. These include Pokhran-II (May 1998), US President Clinton's visit to India (March 2000), emergence of India as a favourite investment destination in the post-1991 economic reforms, implementation of its own Western Development Strategy, India-Pakistan border stand-off (December

2001) and the initial discussions on 2005-Indo-US civil nuclear deal.

2. "External Environment and Strategic Direction of the "Go Global" Strategy for Chinese Enterprises," Remarks by Vice Foreign Minister Song Tao at the 10th China Import and Export Enterprise Annual Conference, 11 January 2012. For details see at http://www.fmprc.gov.cn/eng/wjdt/zyjh/t898393.htm (accessed on 15 July 2013).
3. "The Rapid Development of China's Diplomacy in a Volatile World," address by Assistant Foreign Minister Le Yucheng at the seminar on *China's Diplomacy in 2011 and its Prospect*, 18 December 2011, at http://www.fmprc.gov.cn/eng/wjdt/zyjh/t890675.htm (accessed on 15 July 2013).
4. Rukmini Gupta, "National Interests and Threat Perceptions: Exploring the Chinese Discourse," IDSA Monograph Series no. 17, April 2013, p.17.
5. In the meanwhile, the *Chinese Defense White Paper* titled "The Diversified Employment of China's Armed Forces" released in early 2013, focused largely on Chinese preparedness to deal with broader issues of concern and assumed that the threats mentioned in earlier white papers continue to influence Chinese security policies. For details visit at http://www.china.org.cn/government/whitepaper/node_7181425.htm (accessed on 2 May 2013).
6. *China's National Defense in 2010*, Information Office of the State Council, The People's Republic of China, March 2011, Beijing, pp.4-5.
7. "Serving the Nation with Vigorous Steps: China's Diplomacy in 2011," by Yang Jiechi, Minister of Foreign Affairs of the People's Republic of China, 2 January 2012, at http://www.fmprc.gov.cn/eng/wjdt/zyjh/t896194.htm (accessed on 15 July 2013). This article appeared in the January 2012 edition of the *Seeking Truth* magazine.
8. Xiao Ren, *et al.*, "Chinese Foreign Policy and Domestic Decision-making," *Asian Policy*, No 10, July 2010, p. 46.
9. Ibid.
10. Ibid., p. 82.
11. Rukmini Gupta, "National Interests and Threat Perceptions: Exploring the Chinese Discourse," n.4, p.69.
12. B. Raman, "China's Strategic Influence in South Asia," *Maritime Affairs*, 7 (2), Winter 2011, p. 134.
13. Barry Buzan, "South Asia Moving Towards Transformation: Emergence of India as a Great Power," *International Studies*, 39 (1), January-March 2002, p.5.
14. Pan Zhenqiang, "China and South Asia," Occasional paper, No. 99, Konrad Adenauer Foundation Beijing, 2010, p. 5.
15. B. Raman, "China's Strategic Influence in South Asia," n. 12.
16. Nepalese Congress Central Committee member Shekhar Koirala on 10 June 2012 said "indigenous community have hyped [up] the issue of single ethnic based identity backed by [the] money poured [in] by Western countries." For details see *The Rising Nepal*, Kathmandu, 11 June 2012.
17. Jagannath P. Panda, "Dragon Looks South: Current Drives in China's South Asian Neighbourhood Policy," in Srikanth Kondapalli and Emi Mifune (eds), *China and its Neighbours*, Pentagon Press, New Delhi, 2010, pp. 181-183.
18. "Nepal likely to figure prominently in China's foreign policy", *Republica*, Kathmandu, 24 November 2012, at http://www.myrepublica.com/portal/index.php?action=news_details& news_id=45341 (accessed on 15 July 2013).

19. Zhang Li, "To manage conflict in South Asia: China's stakes, perceptions and inputs", Asia Paper, Institute for Security and Development Policy, Stockholm, October 2009, p.81.
20. "China concerns over Nepal", *The Red Star*, a publication of the then CPN (Maoist), Kathmandu, I (01), 8 November 2007, p.1, at http://www.bannedthought.net/Nepal/RedStar/TheRedStar-vol1-01.pdf (accessed on 12 February 2014). Also see, Sharad Adhikary, "Here's how Beijing is scanning Kathmandu", *Kathmandu Newsline*, 15 July 2008.
21. Zhang Li, "To manage conflict in South Asia: China's stakes, perceptions and inputs", n. 19, p.76.
22. Ibid., pp.77-78.
23. Kunda Dixit, "A New Himalayan Game", *The Fletcher Forum of World Affairs*, 34(1), Winter 2010, pp. 125–34.
24. "Nepal becomes Tibet's most important trading partner: Official", *Xinhua* (English), 15 July 2012, at http://news.xinhuanet.com/english/business/2012-07/15/c_131716978.htm (accessed on 17 July 2013).
25. B. Raman, "China's Strategic Influence in South Asia," n. 12, p. 136.
26. Prime Minister, Atal Bihari Vajpayee during his official visit to Beijing in June 2003, acknowledged: "The Indian side recognises that the Tibet Autonomous Region is an integral part of the People's Republic of China". For details see G. Parthasarathy, Editorial: "Vajpayee visit—Foreign policy lessons from China," *Business Line*, Delhi, 18 July 2003.
27. Rukmini Gupta, "National Interests and Threat Perceptions: Exploring the Chinese Discourse," n.4, p. 06.
28. Quoting Indian Government sources, *NDTV* reported that "three Chinese army officers had been denied visa after the [Lt Gen (Retd)] Jaswal incident and pointed out that J&K was as important to India as Tibet was to China," 27 August 2010, at http://www.ndtv.com/article/india/china-in-damage-control-mode-after-stopping-indian-general-s-visit-47573 (accessed on 16 July 2013).
29. Ross H. Munro, "China's Relations with its Neighbours", *International Journal*, Spring 2006, p. 323.
30. Interview of Ai Ping, Vice-Minister at the International Department of the Central Committee of the Communist Party of China, to *The Kathmandu Post*, 19 September 2011, at http://www.ekantipur.com/the-kathmandu-post/2011/09/18/oped/monday-interview/226470.html (accessed on 25 March 2012).
31. Zhang Li, "To manage conflict in South Asia: China's stakes, perceptions and inputs", n. 19, p. 75.
32. "Nepal and China have win-win ties", interview of Chinese ambassador to Nepal, Qiu Guohong, *Nepali Times*, Kathmandu, [weekly] Issue 448, 24–30 April 2009.
33. Zhang Li, "To manage conflict in South Asia: China's stakes, perceptions and inputs", n. 19, p. 85. Also see Sudeshna Sarkar, "China cements ties with Nepal Maoists," *Two Circles*, 3 December 2007, at http://twocircles.net/2007dec03/china_cements_ties_nepal_maoists.html (accessed on 16 July 2013). The news was originally reported in Indo-Asian News Service.
34. For more information about the US observations on post-February 2005 political developemtns in Nepal, see "United States Interests and Goals in Nepal", Principal Deputy Assistant Secretary Donald Camp's statement before the US House of Representatives

Committee on International Relations, Washington, DC, 2 March 2005, at http://www.state.gov (accessed on 13 July 2008).

35. Bruce Vaughn, "Nepal: Background and US Relations", Congressional Research Service (CRS) Report for Congress, The Library of Congress, 2 February 2006, p.08.
36. *White Paper on China's National Defense, 2008*, The Central People's Government of The People's Republic of China, at http://www.china.org.cn/government/whitepaper/node_7060059.htm (accessed on 17 July 2013). Also see *China's National Defense in 2006*, at http://www.china.org.cn/english/features/book/194421.htm (accessed on 12 February 2014).
37. Kunda Dixit, "A New Himalayan Game", n. 23.
38. Changhee Park, "Why China attacks: China's geo-strategic vulnerability and its military intervention", *The Korean Journal of Defence Analysis*, 20(3), September 2008, pp. 263-267.
39. Kunda Dixit, "A New Himalayan Game", n. 23, 127–08.
40. "US partnering with India to contain China", *Economic Times*, Delhi, 4 January 2011, at http://economictimes.indiatimes.com/news/politics/nation/us-partnering-with-india-to-contain-china/articleshow/7215341.cms (accessed on 17 July 2013).
41. Zhang Li, "To manage conflict in South Asia: China's stakes, perceptions and inputs", n. 19, p. 87.
42. Ibid., p. 81.
43. "We Will not tolerate any foreign interference in Nepal: China", *The Telegraph Weekly*, Kathmandu, 5 November 2008, at http://www.telegraphnepal.com (accessed on 10 November 2008). Liu Hong Chai made this statement during an interaction with some Nepalese journalists in Beijing on 4 November 2008.
44. "China uniting Nepal communists to get support on Tibet", *Express India*, Delhi, 25 June 2008, at http://www.expressindia.com/latest-news/China-uniting-Nepal-communists-to-get-support-on-Tibet/327258/ (accessed on 8 January 2011).
45. Ivan Campbell, *et al.*, "China and conflict-affected states: Between principle and pragmatism," Report, Saferworld, UK, January 2012.
46. "China and Nepal: Friendly Neighbours across Himalayas," Embassy of The People's Republic of China in The Federal Democratic Republic of Nepal, at http://np.china-embassy.org/eng/News/t895866.htm (accessed on 25 March 2012).
47. Zhang Li, "To manage conflict in South Asia: China's stakes, perceptions and inputs", n. 19, pp. 83-84.
48. Prime Minister Pushpa Kamal Dahal alias Prachanda and Madhav Kumar Nepal visited China in September 2008 and December 2009 respectively. Defence Ministers Ram Bahadur Thapa and Bidya Devi Bhandari visited China in September 2008 and March 2010 respectively. Home Minister Bhim Rawal visited China in February 2010. Deputy Prime Minister and Home Minister Bijaya Kumar Gachhadar and Deputy Prime Minister (DPM) and Minister for Foreign Affairs Narayan Kaji Shrestha under took official visit to Beijing in December 2011 and in November 2011 respectively. Prachanda undertook an official visit to Beijing in April 2013.
49. Abanti Bhattacharya, "China's Inroads into Nepal: India's concerns", IDSA Comment, 18 May 2009.
50. Nepalese top political leaders visit to China mostly take place at the invitation of either the CPC or the government with prior planning.

51. M.K. Bhadrakumar, "China courts Nepalese army leadership", *rediff* (blogs), 31 March 2011, at http://blogs.rediff.com/mkbhadrakumar/2011/03/31/china-courts-nepalese-army-leadership/ (accessed on 17 July 2013).
52. "Joint Statement of the People's Republic of China and the Federal Democratic Republic of Nepal", Ministry of Foreign Affairs of the People's Republic of China, 31 December 2009, at http://www.fmprc.gov.cn/eng/wjdt/2649/t649608.shtml (accessed on 1 March 2014).
53. Yongkang is member of the Standing Committee of the Political Bureau of the CPC Central Committee and Secretary of the Political and Legislative Affairs Committee.
54. Jainendra Jeevan, "Suspicious minds", *Republica*, 18 August 2011, at http://www.myrepublica.com/portal/index.php?action=news_details&news_id=34843 (accessed on 17 July 2013). Also see Prashant Jha, "China proposes cooperation with Nepal", *The Hindu*, 19 August 2011.
55. "China's topmost priority is Nepal-China relations: Envoy Wu", *The Himalayan Times*, 7 January 2014, at http://www.thehimalayantimes.com/fullNews.php?headline= China's+topmost+priority+is+Nepal-China+relations%3A+Envoy+Wu&NewsID= 402181 (accessed on 14 January 2014).
56. Kosh Raj Koirala, "China trying to match India in Nepal", *Republica*, 18 August 2009. Also see Prashant Jha, "China proposes cooperation with Nepal", *The Hindu*, 19 August 2011.
57. Kiran Chapagain, "Anti-Tibet activities in Nepal unacceptable: China", *Republica*, 28 July 2010, at http://www.myrepublica.com/portal/index.php?action=news_details&news_id=21528 (accessed on 8 January 2011).
58. According to *White Paper: China's Foreign Aid*, April 2011, China's foreign aid mainly falls into tree types: grants (aid gratis), interest free loans (tenure is 20 years-five years of use, five years of grace and 10 years of repayment) and concessional loans (Export-Import Bank of China). The data provided in the Table 4.2 are mainly development assistance.
59. A report by Ivan Campbell, *et al.*, notes that according to Government of Nepal statistics: It is possible to trace a steady increase in Chinese aid to Nepal from NR [s] 10 million ($128,200) in fiscal year 2005/6 to NR 2.55 billion ($32.5 million) in 2010/11. The increase in 2011 is particularly notable: China had reportedly pledged loans and grants worth more than NR 10 billion ($127.4 million) by August 2011. This included a sizeable concessional loan for the Trishuli hydro-power construction and $19 million for assistance to the Nepal Army. For details see Ivan Campbell, *et al.*, "China and conflict-affected states: Between principle and pragmatism," n. 45, p. 67.
60. Bikash Sangraula, "Projects for 105mw with Chinese funds", *ekantipur*, 6 March 2008, at http://www.ekantipur.com/the-kathmandu-post/2008/03/07/related_articles/projects-for-105mw-with-chinese-funds/139879.html (accessed on 13 January 2014).
61. "China agrees to provide assistance to Nepal for different projects," *People's Daily Online*, 1 March 2011, at http://english.peopledaily.com.cn/90001/90776/90883/7303824.html (accessed on 13 January 2014).
62. "China's Nepal engagement tempo steps up; neighbourhood a priority," *ekantipur*, 18 August 2011, at http://www.ekantipur.com/2011/08/18/editors-pick/chinas-nepal-engagement-tempo-steps-up-neighbourhood-a-priority/339285.html (accessed on 13 January 2014).

63. "Non-tariff barriers affect trade with China", *Republica*, 23 June 2013, at http://www.myrepublica.com/portal/index.php?action=news_details&news_id=56642 (accessed on 18 July 2013).
64. "Tibet's foreign trade up 63% in 2011", *People's Daily Online*, 1 February 2012, at http://english.people.com.cn/90778/7717054.html (accessed on 18 July 2013).
65. Also see "China surpasses India in JV projects", *Republica*, 16 September 2010, at http://www.myrepublica.com/portal/index.php?action=news_details&news_id=23356 (accessed on 1 August 2012).
66. For details see "China commits highest FDI in 2012-13: Nepal," *China Daily*, 21 August 2013, at http://www.chinadaily.com.cn/bizchina/chinadata/2013-08/21/content_16910101.htm (accessed on 05 March 2014).
67. "2009 Investment Climate Statement-Nepal", Bureau of Economic, Energy and Business Affairs, US Department of State, February 2009, at http://www.state.gov/e/eb/rls/othr/ics/2009/117847.htm (accessed on 28 July 2012).
68. Zhang Li, "To manage conflict in South Asia: China's stakes, perceptions and inputs", n. 19, p. 81. Also see Jagannath P. Panda, "Dragon Looks South: Current drives in China's South Asian neighbourhood policy", n. 17.
69. "Importers divert cargoes to Kolkata from Khasa," reported by Prabhakar Ghimire, *Republica*, 29 November 2010, at http://www.myrepublica.com/portal/index.php?action=news_ details&news_id=25668 (accessed on 18 July 2013).
70. "China will start construction of Larcha Dry Port this year", *Republica*, 31 August 2011.
71. "Customs infrastructures high on agenda", *Republica*, 4 May 2011, at http://archives.myrepublica.com/portal/index.php?action=news_details&news_id=30951 (accessed on 18 July 2013).
72. "Nepal, Chinese contractor to sign agreement for Pokhara airport," *Xinhua*, 31 May 2013, at http://news.xinhuanet.com/english/business/2013-05/31/c_132423005.htm (accessed on 18 July 2013).
73. "Chinese entrepreneurs meet PM Nepal", *Nepal News*, Kathmandu, 17 September 2010, at http://www.nepalnews.com/main/index.php/business-a-economy/9231-chinese-entrepreneurs-meet-pm-nepal.html (accessed on 18 July 2013).
74. China Study Centre, China Information Centre, Nepal-China Mutual Cooperation Society, Nepal-China Executive Council, Nepal-China Friendship Association, Nepal-China Youth Friendship Association, Nepal-China Investment Promotion Centre, Nepal-China Himalayan Friendship Society and Nepal-China Media Forum, China-South Asia Friendship Organisations' Forum.
75. Kosh Raj Koirala, "China trying to match India in Nepal", *Republica*, 18 August 2009, at http://www.myrepublica.com/portal/index.php/thweek/slc/?action=news_details&news_ id=8755 (accessed on 18 July 2013).
76. "Bilateral Relations (Nepal-China)," Ministry of Foreign Affairs, Government of Nepal.
77. Rajesh Joshi, "Why China's influence on Nepal worries India", *BBC* (Hindi), Kathmandu, 8 May 2013. For more information visit http://www.bbc.co.uk/news/world-asia-22365488 (accessed on 14 May 2013).
78. Siddharth Srivastava, "Delhi knocked out over China," *Asia Times*, Hong Kong, 16 November 2005, at http://www.atimes.com/atimes/South_Asia/GK16Df03.html (accessed on 9 January 2014).
79. See "Nepal Maoists start anti-Dalai Lama", *Hindustan Times*, 16 October 2007.

80. Sangeeta Thapliyal, "Mutual Security: The Case of India-Nepal," Lancer Publishers, New Delhi, 1998, p.63. See Kunda Dixit, "A New Himalayan Game", n. 23, p. 127. Also see C. Raja Mohan, "Tibet static in China," *The Hindu*, 22 June 2003.
81. T. Karki Hussain, "China's Role in Indo-Nepal Relations", in Lok Raj Baral (ed.), *Looking to the Future: Indo-Nepal relations in perspective,* Anmol Publications, New Delhi, 1996, p.147.
82. Ibid.
83. "China Pays Nepal Police to Catch Tibet Refugees", *AFP*, 20 December 2010, at http://www.google.com/hostednews/afp/article/ALeqM5gAcJ673go50URtzW2B9jl3owe10g (accessed on 18 July 2013).
84. Lin Meilian, "Nepal entrapped," *Global Times*, 7 March 2013, at http://www.globaltimes.cn/content/766645.shtml (accessed on 18 July 2013).
85. Jagannath P. Panda, "Dragon Looks South: Current drives in China's South Asian Neighbourhood Policy", n. 17.
86. "Nearly 20 terrorists entered India via Nepal: Indian envoy," *NDTV*, 29 April 2010, at http://www.ndtv.com/news/india/nearly-20-terrorists-entered-india-via-nepal-indian-envoy-21997.php (accessed on 18 July 2013).
87. Shyam Saran's interview on Dishanirdesh, *Nepal Television*, on 12 July 2004, www.south-asia.com (accessed on 26 October 2007).
88. David G. Wiencek, "China's geopolitical manoeuvring in the Himalayas", China Brief, 7 May 2005, Jamestown Foundation, www.asianresearch.org (accessed on 26 October 2007).
89. Suman Pradhan, "Long and Winding Road to UN Mediation", *South Asia Intelligence Review,* Weekly, 04(02), 25 July 2005, at http://www.satp.org/satporgtp/sair/Archives/4_2.htm#assessment1 (accessed on 12 February 2014).
90. Amitav Acharya, "Theoretical Perspectives on International Relations in Asia," in David Shambaugh and Michael Yhuda (eds), *International Relations Asia*, Rowman & Littlefield Publishers, Inc., Lanham, 2008, p. 63.
91. Dahal visited Beijing as Chairman of the UCPN (Maoist).
92. Interview of Wang Hongwei of the Institute of Asia-Pacific Studies to *Republica*, 22 April 2013. For details see http://www.myrepublica.com/portal/index.php?action=news_details&news_id=53519 (accessed on 18 July 2013).

CHAPTER 5

Return of the Super Power: The US in Nepal

Nepal's strategic location makes it natural for external powers to take interest in its domestic as well as foreign policy. Moreover, its sense of insecurity vis-à-vis its neighbours and occasional uneasy relations with them, the 10-year long spell of Maoist insurgency and the prolonged periods of political uncertainty have attracted the attention of external powers for many years. Nepal has assumed even greater salience for extra-regional powers—particularly the US, the UK, the European Union etc.—since the Jana Andolan-II of 2006 which initiated the difficult process of political transition in Nepal—from monarchy to democratic republic.

Amidst tumultuous political developments in Nepal, these powers have made efforts to secure their strategic objectives, which might have also, directly or indirectly, influenced the political transition. However, their interests in Nepal do not make their engagement a one-sided affair. It is also true that Nepal needed their support to overcome its economic challenges, particularly when India—as a dominant partner in Nepalese economy—was not in a position to deliver by itself. At a strategic level also, Nepal has been seeking the support of external powers to neutralise the interference of its neighbours in its internal affairs ever since its formation as a sovereign entity. Some observers in Nepal note that for Kathmandu, "US influence could be used to counter undue outside influence on the part of India and China."[1] Such policy measures are deemed natural in the case of smaller countries to secure their sovereignty and territorial integrity. According to Amitav Acharya:

> Since weak powers are structurally incapable of maintaining order and achieving security and prosperity on their own terms and within their own means (there can be no such thing as a "regional solution to regional problems"), the best way to manage the security dilemma is to keep all

> the relevant great powers involved in the regional arena so that they can balance each other's influence.[2]

This approach is generally successful if the small state has a strong political and economic base and is not completely dependent on its bigger neighbours. However, in the case of Nepal, it is overly dependent on India and has limited access to its northern neighbour—China. Against this setting, the engagement of external powers with their divergent interests in Nepal has complicated matters even further. The political forces are also divided in terms of their links or association with external powers who are furthering their own interests. Both China and India have been concerned about the proactive involvement of Western forces in the domestic politics of Nepal. In this context, this chapter examines the US engagement with Nepal.

Strategic Relevance of Nepal for US

While the reasons for Chinese engagement with Nepal are obvious, the involvement of major powers like the US is driven by divergent political and strategic objectives. Since 1950, US policy towards Nepal has been determined by Nepal's strategic location, containing the domino effect of Chinese communism in South Asia,[3] and the emergence of China and India as economic and military powers. From a Nepalese point of view:

> The US policy towards Nepal appears to have been shaped by three fundamental objectives, i.e., (a) support for peace and stability in South Asia, (b) support for Nepal's independence and territorial integrity, and (c) support for one of the world's least developed countries in its development efforts through selected programmes of economic aid and technical assistance.[4]

Nevertheless, a cursory analysis of US aid to Nepal since 1951 indicates that the US was more interested in preventing Nepal from coming under the Communist/Maoist influence and used aid as a foreign policy tool. Since the Maoists were targeting the peasantry and Nepal's agricultural sector was vulnerable due to poor infrastructure, the US initially directed a large portion of its aid into agriculture. In fact, the 'Peace Corps Programme'[5] was designed to support the US containment policy against Communism.[6]

Washington also considered Nepal to be the ideal window for monitoring the relationship between India and China and their influence in South Asia. While the containment policy towards China and the Tibet factor dominated American policy towards South Asia in general and the Himalayan region in particular, until the early 1970s, monitoring of India-China relations may also have been an important objective of its Nepal policy. From mid-1970s, US interest in Nepal diminished due to its engagements in other regions. However, in post-9/11 period, US concerns regarding political instability in Nepal increased. When the Maoist movement gained momentum, the US reframed its Nepal policy. Bruce Vaughn observed that "American foreign policy interests in Nepal seek to prevent the collapse of Nepal which, should it become a failed state, could provide operational or support territory for terrorists."[7] American aid to Nepal was reduced between 1970 and 2001, but was increased when the Maoist movement gained traction and began to target US citizens in Nepal. The United States declared that: "...it has a strong interest in helping the people of that country overcome the serious political problems they face, and the developmental problems from which much of their current political crisis derives."[8]

Nepal and US Containment Policy

During the Cold War, the US identified that entire South Asian region was vulnerable to communism due to massive poverty and underdevelopment. Nepal was the bridge between China and South Asia, where a political vacuum had been created following the departure of the British from India. Nepal established diplomatic relations with the US in 1947, and the two countries entered into an agreement for economic and technical assistance in January 1951. The purported US agenda was to use aid as a means to achieve its foreign policy goals. After the communist revolution in China, the US took a significant geostrategic interest in Nepal as a potential outpost to monitor China. The fear of communist expansion to third world countries also motivated the US to provide aid to Nepal.[9] Interestingly, while the US had used its diplomatic levers to prevent the spread of communism into Nepal, two Left ideologies—Communism and Maoism—made their way into the country from the south.

But behind these political and strategic interests, there was also an economic interest. Initially, the US was more interested in the mineral resources of the Himalayas. For example, "the first project to be undertaken involved a survey of Nepal's mineral resources by Robert S. Sanford of the US Bureau of Mines."[10]

China's occupation of Tibet during 1950-51 prompted the US to support the Rana regime in Kathmandu on the assumption that the regime would provide a stable administration in Nepal. In 1959, the US Ambassador to Nepal Henry E. Stebbins opined that "Nepal as being within the US defence perimeter, [required] protection against communist imperialism".[11] The US increased its military assistance to Nepal in 1965-66 to US$1.8 million. Some analysts believed that the objective of this arms assistance was to help the Tibetan rebels based in Khampa.[12] From 1952 to 1986, the United States provided "more than $368 million in bilateral development assistance."[13]

The US remained an influential donor throughout the period when the demand for restoration of multiparty democracy was the strongest, in the 1970s and 1980s. By 1990, American aid to Nepal was to the tune of $475 million.[14] This level of economic assistance continued until the collapse of the Soviet Union in 1991. However, such aid to Nepal began to decline by early 1970 on account of Nixon's landmark visit to China, which significantly changed the US-China equation. Economic assistance from West European countries, Japan, etc., increased and the Nepal Aid Group was formed, which had, to some extent, replaced the US aid to Nepal.[15] Although the US supported the nascent democratic movements, it continued to tacitly back the monarchy as well as political parties after 1996, to counter the rise of the Maoists.

Nepal and the US War Against Terror

The palace massacre in June 2001 and the CPN (Maoist) party's declaration that its movement was shifting gears from the 'strategic defensive' to the 'strategic equilibrium' phase in the later part of the year drew the immediate attention of the US. Meanwhile, the Bush administration sent Christina Rocca, Assistant Secretary of State, to make an assessment of the situation. The deployment of the Royal Nepal Army (RNA) escalated the violence in remote areas. The terrorist attacks of 11 September 2001 on US home territory had serious implications for the Maoist insurgency in Nepal. As part of its so-called the Global War on Terrorism, US military intervention in Nepal became imminent following the increasingly anti-US statements made by the Maoists. In 2001, the US also appointed a military attaché at its Kathmandu mission.

The US Secretary of State Colin Powell's visit to Nepal in January 2002 was the first high-level diplomatic trip by a US official in 30 years, and signalled the mounting concerns in the US regarding the emerging political changes in Nepal. These concerns prompted the renewed political and military support to suppress the Maoist-led armed conflict. By mid 2002, the Nepal government had committed its strong support to US counter-terrorism activities and action against international terrorism. In response, the Maoists in their press statements threatened foreign missions, including the US embassy, for supporting the government of Nepal. The Maoists also targeted US properties, business establishments, including Coca Cola and Pepsi, and US embassy staff in Nepal.[16] Despite these developments, the US did not formally designate Maoists as terrorists but it seriously considered doing so.[17] In 2002, as part of the counter terrorism cooperation, it announced a US$20 million aid package along with 12,000 M-16 submachine guns and military training support for the Nepalese security forces. The US also provided military advisers to King Gyanendra to aid him in fighting terrorism. One scholar observed that:

> In mid-2001, Washington anticipated spending some $225,000 the following fiscal year (October 2001-September 2002). After September 11, $20 million was added in a supplemental allocation. In fiscal [year] 2003, Nepal received $3.15 million from the Foreign Military Funding program and $500,000 under another program. The US had allocated $45 million in aid for Nepal in the year to September 2004, 10% of which was reportedly for security. For fiscal 2005, $44 million has been set aside with only one-third for security-related activities.[18]

The Republican Party's policy of the Global War on Terrorism had a serious impact on political conflicts in Nepal. The Himalayan country witnessed an increase in violence after India and the US declared the CPN (Maoist) as a terrorist outfit. As the Table 5.1 indicates, the number of fatalities went up around 10 times between 2000 and 2005. However, other factors like the failure of negotiations between Maoists and King Gyanendra, the Maoists declaration of their movement entering into the strategic equilibrium phase and the entry of RNA into the counter insurgency operations had influenced

Table 5.1: Maoist Violence in Nepal from 2000 to 2010

Years	*Civilians*	*SFP*	*Maoists*	*Total*
2000*	18	113	44	175
2001	50	198	803	1051
2002	238	666	3992	4896
2003	214	307	1584	2105
2004	380	481	1590	2451
2005	231	309	1305	1845
2006	61	181	238	480
2007	59	00	40	99
2008	55	01	25	81
2009	35	01	14	50
2010**	12	01	25	38

* Data since March 26, 2000.

** Data till December 2010. *SFP-Security Force Personnel*

Source: South Asia Terrorism Portal.

the conflict. The US support for the monarchy could have been one of the major reasons for the Maoists deviating from their traditional political line from 2002 onwards and entering into negotiations with India and some communist parties of Nepal, which resulted in the 12-point agreement in November 2005 and a comprehensive peace agreement in November 2006. The number of fatalities came down in 2007 after the CPN (Maoist) entered into a comprehensive peace agreement.

As the US-led Global War on Terrorism intensified, the nature of conflict changed in Nepal. Kathmandu's policy of "internal militarisation with US support did not yield the intended results; instead, the [conflict] spread rapidly to districts previously unaffected."[19] The US opposed the peace talks between the Maoists and government in January 2003. Despite that, the peace talk began and collapsed in August 2003. The civil society groups in Nepal held the US responsible for the failure of the peace talks in August by instigating the army not to cooperate with the government.[20] Since the Maoists vowed to continue their political and military campaign after the collapse of the peace talks, the US included the Maoists in its terrorist list in October 2003. US Department of State on 31 October 2003, under "Determination Pursuant to Section 1(b) of Executive Order 13224 Relating to the Communist Party of Nepal (Maoist)", proscribed "the Communist Party of Nepal (Maoist), also known as the United Revolutionary People's Council, also known as the People's Liberation Army of Nepal, also known as CPN(M)", which "committed, or poses a significant risk of committing, acts of terrorism that threaten the security of U.S. nationals or the national security, foreign policy, or economy of the United States."

Not only the August 2003 peace talks but also several attempts subsequently to initiate peace talks between the Maoists and the state were supposedly sabotaged by the US, which wanted to suppress the movement by undertaking military action with the support of the then RNA.[21] In this regard, the US supplied sophisticated arms and equipment to the RNA under the anti-terrorist agreement signed with Nepal on 25 April 2003. Around 50 US special forces trainers were providing training to 20 battalions of 700-800 men each through a 12-week counterinsurgency programme. Washington had supplied the then RNA with 5,000 M-16 sub-machine guns, (to be followed by another 5,000); Belgium sold 5,500 machine guns to Nepal while Britain and India helped them by sending military advisers.[22]

The Maoists blamed the US for the failure of the peace talks in August 2003. Top Maoist leaders like Baburam Bhattarai, Ram Bahadur Thapa alias

Badal and Prachanda criticised US activities against the Maoists in Nepal and determined to drive the US away from Nepalese soil.[23] During this period the Maoists, in fact, sought support from China and India as both the countries would be affected by the US military support to the RNA.[24] With no options left, the Maoists sought to exploit India's anxieties regarding the US presence in Nepal. As S.D. Muni observes: "India has been very sensitive to the strategic presence in Nepal of intraregional powers like the United States and of its known adversaries like China and Pakistan"[25] given the misuse of the open border between both countries. Interestingly, this was a period when China remained neutral regarding the US military assistance to Nepal while India to some extent endorsed the US policy against Maoists because of its own domestic experience. However, later India realised the implications of the US presence in Nepal and tried to resolve the conflict by bringing the Maoists and the political parties together. Given Nepal's geostrategic location and the uneasy state of US-China relations, Beijing was concerned about growing US interest in Nepal. It was perhaps India's belief that the extended presence of the US might force China to readjust its policy across the south of Himalayas.

The EU was divided over US approach to the conflict resolution. While some EU members, including the UK, supported US military intervention as long as it did not lead to serious human rights violation, others became critical of US policy when the Nepal government tried to set up "Village Defence Volunteers", modeled on the Latin American paramilitary "Death Squads".[26] After the February 2005 political change, in which the king assumed absolute power, India, and the US along with its Western allies suspended arms supplies to the RNA. The king then looked to China for supply of arms and ammunition. China agreed to king's request in exchange for strong action against Tibetans.

The US opposed the 12-point agreement between the Maoists and seven political parties in November 2005. Although the US admonished King Gyanendra for his February 2005 action, it suggested the king to initiate dialogue with major parties. With no progress in negotiation between the king and major political parties after making repeated suggestions, in the aftermath of the 12-point agreement, Washington worked with New Delhi and other powers to counter-balance the king by supporting other political parties against him.[27] After the king abdicated power in April 2006, the US Ambassador to Nepal, James Moriarty, told the media that the king had no choice but to give in to the opposition's demand for a return to democratic rule.[28] Contrary to Moriarty's position on the 12-point agreement, Secretary of State Condoleezza Rice acknowledged that the US was working "very closely with the Indian government" to resolve the crisis in Nepal. However, wary of American manipulation, the Maoists observed that this maneuvering was not about bringing democracy to Nepal. Rather, it was about trying to ensure that the "resolution of the current crisis" would be in the interest of the US and India and that would not translate into any gains for the Maoists.[29]

Moriarty had repeatedly urged the king and the parliamentary parties to work together to defeat the People's War, while criticising the opposition parties for working in tandem with the Maoists. Before the monarchy withdrew from power, Assistant Secretary of State for Central and South Asian Affairs, Richard Boucher, remarked:

> We need to work as much as we can to pressure the king to restore democracy, to encourage the parties to stay together and to come up with a workable, functioning democracy. And be able to expunge the Maoists from Nepali society. What the US cannot accept is a revolution that takes up arms in order to overthrow a regime that serves US interests. What the US cannot allow is a revolution which aims to fundamentally change the current economic, political, and social relations under which the masses of Nepalese people are oppressed.[30]

Interestingly, while the entire US administration was against peace talks with the Maoists, the Carter Center, an Atlanta-based NGO, was supporting the peace initiative with the Maoists. The Center's attempts to establish linkages with the Maoists and mediate, contrary to the US policy, made policy-makers in India and Nepal suspicious.[31] Barring the initial phase of the democratic movement in Nepal in the 1950s, the US had supported the monarchy against communism. In fact, after the dissolution of the first democratically elected government in December 1960, the US believed that monarchy would be a much stronger bulwark against communist uprising in Nepal.[32]

An analysis of US relationship with Nepal in the initial phase of conflict indicates that it adopted multi-pronged strategy to resolve the civil conflict in the Himalayan country of which, four strategies were most significant. First, like other Western countries, the US also initially perceived the conflict as an ideological movement arising from underdevelopment and bad governance. The Maoists wanted to capture power by military means and set up a single party communist state by exploiting these issues. On this the US initially increased its development assistance to Nepal to counter the ideological movement in rural areas. Second, it encouraged mainstream political parties to come together to strengthen democracy. The US was worried about the frequent change of prime ministers and lack of consensus between the political parties and the king for countering the radical Maoist movement. After the collapse of two rounds of truce and negotiations in the later part of 2001, the US found that the Maoists had been using the ceasefire for regrouping and to re-coup. The US concerns depended further with the Maoists policy of upgrading the movement by adopting Khmer Rouge tactics to achieve their political objective in 2003. The US gathered that Nepal could quite easily turn into a failed state which could become a potential haven for terrorists like Afghanistan.[33] As a third strategy to contain the Maoists militarily, the Bush administration supported the RNA by increasing security aid. Lastly, the US gathered global support and mobilised international community against the Maoists by regular consultations with other missions in Kathmandu, including India and the UK to "prevent the Maoists from attaining [military] victory".[34]

Post-2006: Looking at Nepal through an Independent Prism?

The US remained sceptical about Maoists' commitment to the peace process and multiparty democracy. It closely monitored the Maoist leaders' statements and behaviour. The US revived its interest in Nepal in 2006, and especially with the success of Jana Andolan-II, and people's support to the seven-party-led anti-monarchy movement. During this period, the US extended all possible support to the then interim government for the successful conduct of the CA elections.[35] The Carter Center played an important role as an observer in the CA elections. The Centre deployed short-term delegations of around 62 observers from more than 20 countries for the purpose. In the post-election period, the Carter Center has been active in monitoring the peace process and Constitution-drafting process.[36]

The Maoists' victory in the 2008 CA elections came as a surprise for the US. Some actions of the Maoists in the post-election period that included anti-US resolutions and their eagerness to improve relations with China only strengthened US suspicions about the Maoists. Immediately after the elections, the US declared that its policy towards the new government would "depend on the attitude of the new government towards both our [humanitarian] programmes and maintenance of democratic norms."[37] The US did not remove the Maoists from its terrorist list and the Deputy State Department Spokesman Tom Casey, on 14 May 2008 reiterated that the Maoists were on the terrorist exclusion list, which bars their members or associates from entering the United States.[38] In the post-election period, the US was reportedly making a case for the Nepali Congress to lead the new government. The then US Ambassador in Kathmandu, Nancy Powell, was "actively pushing" the idea that Girija Prasad Koirala should continue as the prime minister.[39]

There was a marked change in the US policy towards Nepal after the Democrats came to power under the leadership of Barack Obama in January 2008. Although the Obama administration continued the Global War on Terrorism, it perhaps analysed the global conflicts on the basis of local dynamics. Therefore, the administration probably decided not to pay heed to conflicts in Nepal because of the active peace process and also since the Maoists were not posing any serious threat to the US. It also probably did not want to interfere in the India-led peace initiative. Moreover, one of the key features of the Obama administration has been to engage the rebels in negotiations. These US policy changes were immediately reflected in the appointment of Scott H. DeLisi as the new ambassador to Nepal in November 2009. Instead of looking at Nepal through the Indian perspective, the US decided to extend its engagement with Nepal. In fact, by 2009, the US had to some extent changed its views on the Maoists commitment to peace and democracy. In a discussion with the Vice-Chairman of the UCPN(Maoist) party Narayan Kaji Shrestha, DeLisi said that the "US was positive towards formation of a National Unity Government under the leadership of [the Maoists]."[40] The US appeared to be convinced that a major section of the top Maoist leadership, except for the Mohan Baidya faction, were committed to multi-party democracy and were willing to institutionalise the peace process.

While articulating US policy towards Nepal, the then US Ambassador to Nepal, Scott DeLisi, said that US policy goals in Nepal include: successful completion of the peace process; the acceptance of a democratic Constitution; security sector reform; enhancing the rule of law and human rights; development; economic growth; and disaster preparedness in the post-conflict period.[41]

The effect of the restructured US foreign policy as articulated by the Democrats, became visible with the diversion of its annual aid assistance to the social sector and consolidation of the peace process in the post-conflict period. Earlier the military capacity building programmes dominated. Table 5.2 details the US aid to Nepal during the fiscal years 2001-2010. Since 2006, a major portion of the US assistance has been for health, economic support, military education and training, and food aid programmes. US funding for the Nepalese Army and security forces was reduced drastically. Until February 2005, the US provided Nepal Government(s) with light weaponry and other military assistance to fight against the Maoists.[42] Surprisingly, in 2011, the US announced a 'peace process support' of US$2 million while clarifying that: "this amount is an additional Foreign Military Financing (FMF) and International Military Education and Training (IMET) funding made available

Table 5.2: US Assistance to Nepal, FY2001-FY2010

(In US$ '000)

Account	*2001*	*2002*	*2003*	*2004*	*2005 est.*	*2006*	*2007*	*2008*	*2009 est.*	*2010 request*
CSH	9,250	20,000	19,899	24,840	23,540	18,613	18,090	19,891	22,200	24,400
DA	11,858	7,597	10,247	8,874	10,000	8,393	10,447	9,136	—	—
ESF	0	3,000	4000	4,971	4,960	4,950	11,250	16,423	22,151	26,015
FMF	0	2,000*	2,950	3,975	1,488	-	-	—	—	1,100
IMET	237	377	500	546	650	644	793	869	800	1,200
INCLE	-	-	-	-	-	0	0	30	330	3,700
NADR	-	-	-	-	-	0	840	1,242	700	1,300
P.L. 480 Title II	0	2,352	0	0	1,000	1,213	6,056	18,833	—	—
Total	21,345	32,974	37,596	43,206	40,638	33,813	47,476	66,424	46,181	57,715

*Supplemental Appropriation $12,000/-

Note: See CRS Report RL31362, US Foreign Aid to East and South Asia: Selected Recipients, by Thomas Lum. (CSH) Child Survival and Health, (DA) Development Assistance, (ESF) Economic Support Fund, (FMF) Foreign military Financing, (IMET) International Military Education and Training, (INCLE) International Narcotics Control and Law Enforcement, (NADR) Non-proliferation, Antiterrorism, Demining, and Related Programs, PL 480 (food aid programme). US Department of State, South and Central Asia, Budget Justification Document, FY2008.

Source: Bruce Vaughn, 'Nepal: Political Developments and Bilateral Relations with the United States', Congressional Research Service, 07 April 2011, p. 12 and CRS (2006 and 2008).

specifically to provide technical and training support for the new Nepal [ese] Army directorate,"[43] and that its policy on the army remained unchanged. The US also enhanced its annual financial assistance to $80 million in 2011 from the earlier average of $54 million since 1951.[44]

Defining US policy objectives and interests in Nepal, the CRS Report 2011 indicated that the US wanted "promotion of democracy and regional stability in Nepal."[45] The same Report also spoke of the radical transformation underway in Nepal and of the substantial progress made in the ongoing peace process. The Maoists' commitment to their previous political line (one-party Republic) was not clear. Therefore, Nepal's peace process might have to overcome multiple challenges.[46]

Nepal however remains a vital part of the US policy towards the region, given its proximity to Tibet. The US wants to maintain psychological pressure on China by remaining engaged in Nepal. Having a friendly regime in Kathmandu is therefore a priority for any US administration. The CRS Reports since 2005 consistently mentions that China's key interests in Nepal revolve around anti-China activities organised by the Tibetan refugees. It further observed that China has made "significant inroads in developing ties with South Asian states."[47] Therefore, the US also seems to have understood that the Maoists (reformed) are the future of Nepal. As Walter Andersen observes, it is, "almost certain that the United States would not refuse to deal with Maoists ... because they have gained power in democratic elections."[48]

It seems the US policy towards Tibet has changed and it has renewed its economic engagement with Nepal to justify its presence. After keeping a low profile in Nepal affairs for around three years—2007-2010, it [US] has begun to consolidate its presence in Nepal by leveraging its soft power. Over the past one-and-a-half years the US has taken some significant steps such as: enhancing its annual assistance to $80 million; signing a Trade and Investment Framework Agreement; withdrawing the travel advisory issued in January 2011; selecting Nepal for Millennium Challenge Corporation (MCC); reviving Peace Corps operations after nearly eight years; sanctioning $2 million for a new directorate in the Nepalese Army; and setting up a disaster management cell with support of the NA and the US Pacific Command. The US interest in Tibet is reflected by its proposed investments in Tatopani, the border town between Nepal and China, where China is already developing infrastructure. According to US embassy sources in Kathmandu the US wants to invest in the construction, agriculture, and hydropower sectors in the (Tatopani) area.[49]

The exchange of high-level political visits is also increased during Obama Administration. Secretary of State Hillary Clinton was supposed to visit Nepal in April 2012, but instead the Under Secretary of State for Political Affairs Wendy R. Sherman undertook the visit. She discussed issues relating to US-Nepal cooperation, trade and Tibetan refugees, among others.[50] Earlier, US Congressman Steve Chabot expressed concerns regarding Tibetan refugees but praised Nepal for the effective handling of the issue.[51] Assistant Secretary of State for South and Central Asian Affairs, Robert O. Blake Jr., visited Nepal on 25 April 2010. He was followed by the Commander of the Pacific Command of the US Navy, Admiral Robert F. Willard on 27 April 2010, at the invitation of the then Chief of Army Staff, Chhatraman Singh Gurung.

The US continues to persuade Nepal to deal with Tibetan refugee issue sensibly. According to Nepalese media reports, Robert O. Blake Jr., during his two official visits—April 2010 and September 2012—stated that the Tibetan refugee issue was a 'high profile' agenda for US foreign policy. During his meeting with former Foreign Minister Narayan Kaji Shrestha, Blake urged Nepal to respect the 'gentlemen's agreement', as per which Nepal needs to treat the refugees humanely and provide them passage to India.[52] This issue was also discussed during the visit of the US Under Secretary of State for Democracy and Global Affairs, Maria Otero, to Nepal in November 2012. Given the Chinese sensitivities on this issue, the US position on the Tibetan refugees may exacerbate the suspicions between China and the US.

Trade and Business

Trade relations could also prove to be of significance for the two countries. Currently, the US is the second-largest export partner of Nepal. While readymade garments, Pashmina and woollen carpets are the major items exported to the US; Nepal imports aircrafts, machinery and medical instruments from the US. Nepal's exports to the US have declined since 2006 on account of intense competition from other countries and the economic recession in the US (see Table 5.3).[53]

Table 5.3: Nepal's Trade with US

(in US$ million)

	2005	*2006*	*2007*	*2008*	*2009*	*2010*	*2011*	*2012*	*2013*
Export	111.2	99.4	89.94	84.9	54.7	60.5	77.4	83.5	77.7
Import	24.7	16.6	29.0	28.5	31.0	28.3	40.3	37.0	32.7

Source: Census Bureau, U.S. Department of Commerce.

In the post-conflict period, the US administration went beyond its traditional thinking on Nepal as a conflict-ridden society and looked upon it as an unexploited area for investment. Therefore, investments from the US increased in the post-conflict period. According to the US report on the Investment climate in Nepal 2011, the US was the second largest investor in Nepal until 2010. China has replaced the US since then. In the year 2011, the US was ranked as third largest investor in Nepal with 174 joint ventures (accounting for 7.28 per cent of total foreign investment) after India and China. The US feels that Nepal-US Trade and Investment Framework Agreement (TIFA) would expand economic ties further. After the TIFA agreement a nine-member business delegation from the US visited Nepal in June 2011 to study the investment environment and potential in the country. The members of the delegation expressed their interest in investing in hydropower, health, information technology, trade, aviation, infrastructure and agriculture. However, the US observes that despite liberal investment polices are being followed, investment risks are high due to poor basic infrastructure in Nepal.[54]

Maoists and the US Rebalance to Asia

After nine years of observation, interpretation and analysis, the US was convinced that the Maoists were willing to accept multi-party democracy, and do not pose any threat to US foreign policy and its citizens. On 6 September 2012 it ceased to term the Communist Party of Nepal (Maoist)—CPN (Maoist)—and its front organisations as a Specially Designated Global Terrorist Entity under Executive Order 13224, and took it off the Terrorist Exclusion List (TEL) under the Immigration and Nationality Act (INA).[55]

The decision to mend relations was taken after 27 May 2012, when Nepal was passing through a constitutional crisis which had hamstrung the performance of the caretaker government and adversely affected the economy. So much so that around the world, there has been a growing perception that Nepal may soon figure on the list of failed states. The people of Nepal believe that currently there is no legitimate government or legislature in the country. Since the US is interested in peace and development in Nepal, it was thought that this change of policy could hasten the reconciliation and peace-building process in Nepal. Further, the UCPN (Maoist) itself has split into two factions—the new faction being the CPN-Maoist. The nomenclature of the CPN (Maoist) was changed to UCPN (Maoist) after the merger with a fringe Communist party in 2009. Therefore, the listing of CPN (Maoist) became extraneous since the outfit was non-existent. Also, the central committee of the CPN-Maoist on 5 September 2012 resolved that it will begin another armed struggle if its peaceful struggle does not help it to come to power. It decided to form people's governments both at the local and central levels. Moreover, the US felt that the major political parties in Nepal have failed to institutionalise the peace process after four years of debate and negotiations on the contentious political issues. Most importantly, the decision coincided with the resumption of PLA integration into the Nepal Army. The statement from the US State Department reads:

> After a thorough review, the Department has determined that the CPN (M) is no longer engaged in terrorist activity that threatens the security of US nationals or US foreign policy. Additionally, in recent years, the Maoist party has been elected as the head of Nepal's coalition government, has taken steps to dismantle its apparatus for the conduct of terrorist operations, and has demonstrated a credible commitment to pursuing the peace and reconciliation process in Nepal.

The improvement in the US–Maoist relations would benefit both sides. The Maoists can now travel freely to the US and raise funds for the party because the stigma of being a terrorist organisation has been removed. "The [then] CPN (Maoist)'s property and interests in property in the US or within the possession or control of US persons will no longer be blocked."[56] The US and other countries will not object to any former Maoist party members being sent as ambassadors to their countries. The party can have linkages with democratic forces in any country. Technically, it was bit difficult for the US to deal with the Maoists in the post-2008 CA election period. The executive order would enable the US agencies to directly deal with the Maoists. The formation of two Maoist governments since the 2008 CA elections might have brought the realisation in the US establishment about the importance of Maoists' in Nepal's future polity and that it could be nurtured as a dependable ally.

In fact, the two Maoist-led governments (2008-09 and 2011-2013) did not attach much importance to the US demand for the humane treatment of Tibetan refugees and providing them safe passage to India. It was officially declared that Nepal would prioritise "geo-political sensitivity' and 'national interest' while dealing with the Tibetan refugee issue."[57] In view of the geopolitical changes in Asia and especially in the sub-Himalayan region,—again from the US point of view—China and India-related issues are much more important than the Maoists of Nepal; therefore, antagonising the Maoists would affect its long term interests in the sub-Himalayan region. Moreover, even if the US endorses India's role in Nepal, it is not sure about India's capacity to face Chinese competition on its own.[58] Within a month of delisting the Maoists, some media reports and senior politicians observed that around 65 American soldiers were sent on a humanitarian mission to assess the healthcare services available in Kaski, Manang and Mustang districts of Nepal. Security analysts in Nepal have linked US health mission in these three border districts and reported the construction of the 'Lily Pad' in the Gorkha districts with US strategic interests in the region.[59]

The delisting of the Maoists was also followed by the visit of Robert O. Blake Jr. to Kathmandu on 10 September 2012. The visit coincided with a number of US activities[60] in the sub-Himalayan region, including the first ever joint-humanitarian assistance operations in the Himalayas, conducted by the Nepalese Army and the US Pacific Air Forces. 'Operation Pacific Angel Nepal' began on 10 September 2012 at Pokhara and lasted for six days.[61]

Nepal's Perception of the US

Like other South Asian countries, most of the regimes in Nepal, except the Maoists, consider the US to be a balancing factor with regard to China and India. After the 12-point agreement between the Maoists and seven political parties in November 2005, the royalists were of the view that 'the US views Nepal through the Indian prism'. This impression was natural because despite its opposition to the agreement, the US to some extent came around to endorsing India's policy of accommodating the Maoists. One Nepalese scholar observed that "The US, despite Moriarty's opposition to the 12-point programme, came to support India's lead role in Nepal eventually, which meant accepting the Maoists' leading role in politics."[62] This Nepalese perception was contradicted by US officials.

There are both positive and negative aspects to the US presence in Nepal. While Nepal has benefited both politically and economically, it has also paid a heavy price. Being a small and landlocked country it has been struggling to balance the interests of the US and regional powers. For example, each country has its views on Tibet. While the issue is of concern to China, the US interprets it as an international refugee issue and want Nepal to hand over the Tibetan refugees to the UN agencies concerned. On the other hand, for China it is an internal security issue and it wants Nepal to continue with its one-China policy and does not want Nepalese territory to be used by Tibetan refugees for anti-China activities. While both these major powers compete for strategic space and increased presence in Nepal, India perceives it as interference in its natural sphere of influence. Therefore, the US presence would force the two neighbours to increase their presence in Nepal.

Nepalese policymakers and intellectuals have historically linked US policy goals in Nepal, with Nepal's safety, security and territorial integrity. Some policymakers, especially the anti-India elements in Nepal, maintain that the US presence could serve as a deterrent for Nepal's immediate neighbours, especially India. This group criticised the US when it silently supported India's efforts to bring the democratic forces together in November 2005. They saw this as a US policy preference for "working with a major regional power rather than dealing with all the smaller states individually."[63] Another group believes that the US presence will create security concerns for both of Nepal's neighbours. Nepal should keep the sensitivities of its neighbours in mind and the US should understand Nepal's limitations as a landlocked country.

In the post-monarchy period, Nepal's political leaders have again realised that the country's peace, prosperity, political stability and economic development depend more on India and China than any other countries. There is a perception in Nepal that all the major political transformations have taken place since 1950 in the country with the active or passive endorsement of its powerful neighbours. More importantly, given the geographical contiguity and economic prosperity of its two neighbours, Nepal feels that investments from these countries—in exchange for protecting their security concerns—will be of greater benefit than investment from other countries.

Conclusion

In the absence of any serious conflict in Nepal, the US policy towards South Asia seems to be pre-occupied with Afghanistan, Pakistan and India. For the rest of the South Asian countries, the US has to some extent relied on India's regional leadership. Interestingly, this was reflected at the 6th IISS-NESA South Asia Security Conference held in Muscat, Oman, on 1 December 2012 on "US-South Asia Relations: A Vision for the Future." During the conference, Geoffrey Pyatt, Principal Deputy Assistant Secretary, Bureau of South and Central Asian Affairs, spoke about US engagements in the region. There was no mention of Nepal or sub-Himalayan region in the presentation although Pyatt touched upon Bangladesh, Pakistan, Afghanistan and India. He in fact mentioned that US bilateral relations with each country in South Asia are "intended to strengthen our [US] respective ties, address impediments, and increase security and prosperity". Surprisingly, Nepal did not figure in the US-proposed India linked 'New Silk Road' and the Indo-Pacific economic connectivity agenda.[64]

Despite that Nepal still continues to be an important strategic country for US in South Asia. Nepal-US bilateral relationship has remained cordial, friendly and without any tension since 1947. Given the US's fragile relations with Pakistan and Afghanistan, tensions with Sri Lanka over the principle of Human Rights the US has, and periodical differences with India over many global and regional issues, Nepal could be an important country to follow developments in South Asia. The US has started a new news channel called *Khabar South Asia*, which provides information in English, Bengali and Urdu on developments affecting the stability and security of the South Asian region. Given its growing interests in this region, it is believed that the US might deepen its engagements in Nepal. One Nepalese scholar observed that "It is inappropriate for a military behemoth to run a news-and-analysis portal [allegedly sponsored by the US Pacific command] aimed at the South Asian public, for it can only be a masquerade".[65]

After the visit of Assistant Secretary for South and Central Asian Affairs Robert O. Blake in September 2012, and the disagreements over the Tibetan refugees issue during discussions with the then Deputy Prime Minister and Foreign Minister Narayan Kaji Shrestha, the US seem to be seriously rethinking its relationship with Nepal in view of the changing geopolitical situation in the sub-Himalayan region. Future US policy towards Nepal would be determined on the basis of the political situation in the country in the coming years as well as India-Nepal and India-US relations.

*

NOTES

1. Narayan Khadka, "US Aid to Nepal in the Cold War Period: Lessons for the Future", *Pacific Affairs*, 73(1), Spring 2000, p. 78. Also see Narayan Khadka, *Foreign Aid and Foreign Policy: Major Powers and Nepal*, Vikas Publishing House Pvt. Ltd, New Delhi, 1997.
2. Amitav Acharya, "Theoretical Perspectives on International Relations in Asia," in David Shambaugh and Michael Yhuda (eds), *International Relations Asia*, Rowman & Littlefield Publishers, Inc., Lanham, 2008, p. 64.
3. It should be mentioned here that the US had supported the Khampa resistance movement against China in 1959 and later the Tibetan rebels were trained by the CIA during 1959-64.
4. Madhab P. Khanal, "Nepal-U.S. Relations: A Historical Overview", in *Nepal's Relations with United States of America*, Policy Study Series-4, Institute of Foreign Affairs, Kathmandu, 2004, p. 2.
5. The Peace Corps members were mostly working in the rural areas of Nepal. Their primary task was to provide technical assistance to peasants and promote education in rural areas. They also tried to understand the local culture and familiarise the people with American

culture. Moreover, the information provided by the Peace Corps members greatly helped the US in shaping its foreign policy towards the country. Since 1962, over 4,000 Americans have served as Peace Corps Volunteers in Nepal. The Peace Corps was established on 1 March 1961.

6. Eugene B. Mihaly, *Foreign Aid and Politics in Nepal: A Case Study*, Himal Books, Kathmandu, 2009, pp. 30-31. Also see Joel M. Isaacson, *et al.*, *Half-a-Century of Development: The History of U.S. Assistance to Nepal 1951-2001*, published by the United States Agency for International Development (USAID) in Kathmandu, Nepal, 2001.
7. Bruce Vaughn, "Nepal: Background and U.S. Relations", Report for Congress, Congressional Research Service Report, The Library of Congress, 2 February 2006, p. 17.
8. Donald Camp, Principal Deputy Assistant Secretary, "United States Interests and Goals in Nepal", statement before the US House of Representatives Committee on International Relations, Washington, DC, 2 March 2005, at http://www.state.gov (accessed on 13 July 2008).
9. Narayan Khadka, "US Aid to Nepal in the Cold War Period: Lessons for the Future", n. 1.
10. Evan M. Duncan, "Chronology of relations between the United States and Nepal, 1947-87", at http://findarticles.com/p/articles/mi_m1079/is_v87/ai_5278931/ (accessed on 29 July 2013).
11. Vinod Kumar, "Great Powers and Nepal", in S.D. Muni (ed.), *Nepal: An Assertive Monarchy*, Chetana Publications, New Delhi, 1977, p. 152.
12. Narayan Khadka, "US Aid to Nepal in the Cold War Period: Lessons for the Future", n.1, p. 82.
13. Evan M. Duncan, "Chronology of relations between the United States and Nepal, 1947-87", n. 10.
14. *Country Studies, Nepal*, available at http://countrystudies.us/nepal/70.htm (accessed on 24 October 2007).
15. Narayan Khadka, "US Aid to Nepal in the Cold War Period: Lessons for the Future", n.1, pp. 84-86.
16. *Patterns of Global Terrorism 2002 - April 2003,* Office of the Coordinator for Counter-terrorism, US Department of State p.10.
17. Peter Burleigh, "Nepal: Western Views of the Maoist Insurgency and the Royal Takeover," Working Paper, 9 July 2005, Institute of Governmental Studies, University of California, Berkeley.
18. Ramtanu Maitra, "US jittery over Nepal", *Asia Times*, Hong Kong, 16 March 2005, at http://www.atimes.com/atimes/South_Asia/GC16Df01.html (accessed on 29 July 2013).
19. John Mage, "The Nepali Revolution and International Relations", *Monthly Review*, 59 (1), 1 May 2007, at http://monthlyreview.org/commentary/the-nepali-revolution-and-internationalrelations (accessed on 29 July 2013). This also appeared in *Economic and Political Weekly*, Mumbai, 19 May 2007 issue.
20. Ibid.
21. In an interview to *Janadesh Weekly*, Kathmandu, on 2 June 2006 the then CPN (Maoist) Chairman, Prachanda, alleged "attempts by America to sabotage the historic 12-point agreement between the Maoists and Seven Party Alliances (SPA). Also see Baburam Bhattarai, "On Moriarty's Pontification" *The Kathmandu Post*, 23 February 2006, at

http://www.bannedthought.net/Nepal/MIB/MIB-Nepal-14.htm (accessed on 29 July 2013).

22. Alex Perry, "Living on the Brink", *Time*, 8 September 2003, at http://www.time.com/time/printout/0,8816,483345,00.html# (accessed on 2 August 2012). Also see Prakash A Raj, "Recent Trends of U.S. Interest in Nepal", in *Nepal's Relations with United States of America*, Policy Study Series-4, Institute of Foreign Affairs, Kathmandu, 2004, p. 62.
23. Their anti-US statements were carried in *Nepal Samacharpatra* on 11 June 2003 and *The Himalayan Times* on 16 August 2003. For more details see Prakash A Raj, "Recent Trends of U.S. Interest in Nepal", n. 22, p. 61.
24. Prakash A Raj, "Recent Trends of U.S. Interest in Nepal", Ibid.
25. S.D. Muni, "Bringing the Maoists down from the Hills: India's Role", in Sebastian v. Einsiedel, *et al.* (eds), *Nepal in Transition: From People's War to Fragile Peace*, Cambridge University Press, Cambridge, 2012, p.356.
26. John Mage, "The Nepali Revolution and International Relations," n. 19.
27. Monalisha Adhikari, "Renewed American Engagement with Nepal's Maoists," Issue Brief, 27 November 2012, Institute for Defence Studies and Analyses, New Delhi.
28. Nihar Nayak, "Involvement of Major Powers in Nepal since the 1990s: Implications for India", *Strategic Analysis*, 33 (1), January 2009.
29. Li Onesto, "Upsurge Continues in Nepal: US interests, Plots and Intrigues," *Revolution*, Chicago, Issue 45, 1 May 2006, at http://www.revcom.us/a/045/nepal-upsurge-continues.html (accessed on 12 February, 2014).
30. Ibid, Boucher quoted by Li Onesto.
31. Teresa Whitfield, "Nepal's Masala Peacemaking", in Sebastian v. Einsiedel, *et al.* (eds), *Nepal in Transition: From People's war to Fragile Peace*, n.25, p. 164.
32. Narayan Khadka, "US Aid to Nepal in the Cold War Period: Lessons for the Future", n. 1, p. 82.
33. "Statement on Nepal," Donald Camp, Deputy Assistant Secretary for South Asian Affairs, US Department of State, Washington DC, 3 March 2003.
34. Peter Burleigh, "Nepal: Western Views of the Maoist Insurgency and the Royal Takeover," n. 17.
35. Jason Miklian, "Nepal—The View from the US", *Nepal News*, 23 July 2007 (accessed on 24 April 2008).
36. "Waging Peace: Nepal", The Carter Center, Nepal. For more information on Carter Center reports see at http://www.cartercenter.org/countries/nepal-peace.html (accessed on 18 May 2013).
37. Stephen Kaufman, "Maoist Rule in Nepal Marks Potential Turning Point for Group," *IIP Digital* (United States of America Embassy), 27 May 2008, at http://iipdigital.usembassy.gov/st/english/article/2008/05/20080527173119esnamfuak0.6162378.html#axzz2ri2BIPUr (accessed on 28 January 2014).
38. Ibid.
39. Siddharth Varadarajan, "U.S. subverting Nepal poll mandate", *The Hindu*, 26 April 2008 (accessed on 30 April 2008).
40. "US envoy changes stance, says unity govt under Maoist command positive", *The Telegraph Weekly*, Kathmandu, 14 May 2010, at http://www.telegraphnepal.com/news_det.php?news_id=7680 (accessed on 29 2013).
41. Remarks of Ambassador Scott H. DeLisi on "U.S. Partnership for a Transforming Nepal,"

at Tribhuvan University, 18 November 2010. For details, see http://nepal.usembassy.gov/pr-11-18-2010.html (accessed on 29 July 2013).
42. Bruce Vaughn, "Nepal: Political Developments and Bilateral Relations with the United States", Congressional Research Service Report for Congress, Library of Congress, Washington DC, 23 October 2008, p. 11.
43. "US announces aid; policy on NA remains unchanged", *ekantipur*, 8 February 2012, at http://www.ekantipur.com/2012/02/08/editors-pick/us-announces-aid-policy-on-na-remains-unchanged/348570.html (accessed on 2 August 2012).
44. "US pledges $80m to Nepal to support dev initiatives", *Republica*, 26 January 2012, at http://www.myrepublica.com/portal/index.php?action=news_details&news_ id=41307 (accessed on 2 August 2012).
45. Bruce Vaughn, "Nepal: Political Developments and Bilateral Relations with the United States", Congressional Research Service Report for Congress, Library of Congress, Washington DC, 7 April 2011, p. 11.
46. Ibid.
47. ibid., p. 14.
48. "U.S.-Nepal Relations Complicated After Terror Group Wins Elections", *Fox News*, 24 April 2008, at http://www.foxnews.com/story/0,2933,352432,00.html (accessed on 29 July 2013). Walter Andersen is professor of South Asia studies at the Johns Hopkins University School of International Studies.
49. "US keen to develop Nepal-China border", *ekantipur*, 24 January 2012, at http://www.ekantipur.com/2012/01/24/top-story/us-keen-to-develop-nepal-china-border/347782.html (accessed on 2 August 2012).
50. "US sending highest official in a decade", *Republica*, 27 March 2012, at http://www.myrepublica.com/portal/index.php?action=news_details&news_id=33257 (accessed on 2 August 2012.
51. "US lauds Nepal's handling of Tibetan refugees", *ekantipur*, 30 September 2011, at http://www.ekantipur.com/2011/09/30/top-story/us-lauds-nepals-handling-of-tibetan-refugees/341644.html (accessed on 2 August 2012).
52. "Govt clears stance on Tibetan refugee issue", *The Himalayan Times*, 11 September 2012, at http://www.thehimalayantimes.com/fullNews.php?headline=Govt+clears+stance+on++Tibetan+refugee+issue&NewsID=346942 (accessed on 29 July 2013).
53. "NEPAL, US sign TIFA", *ekantipur*, 17 April 2011, at http://www.ekantipur.com/the-kathmandu-post/2011/04/16/money/nepal-us-sign-tifa/220684.html (accessed on 2 August 2012).
54. "2012 Investment Climate Statement – Nepal", Report, June 2012, Bureau of Economic and Business Affairs, US Department of State, at http://www.state.gov/e/eb/rls/othr/ics/2012/191206.htm (accessed on 13 February 2014).
55. "Delisting of the Communist Party of Nepal (Maoist)", Press Release, Embassy of the United States, Kathmandu, Nepal, 7 September 2012, at http://nepal.usembassy.gov//pr-09-07-2012.html. Also see http://www.state.gov/r/pa/prs/ps/2012/09/197411.htm (accessed on 29 July 2013).
56. Ibid.
57. Deputy Prime Minister and Foreign Minister of Nepal Narayan Kaji Shrestha's discussion with the visiting US Assistant Secretary for South and Central Asian Affairs, Robert O. Blake, on 11 September 2012. For details, see "Govt clears stance on Tibetan refugee

issue", *The Himalayan Times*, 11 September 2012, at http://www.thehimalayantimes.com/fullNews.php?headline=Govt+clears+stance+on++Tibetan+refugee+issue &NewsID=346942 (accessed on 29 July 2013).

58. Author's interview with S.D. Muni by email on 13 September 2012.
59. Arun Shrivastava, "US soldiers in Nepal on China's Tibet border, on a reconnaissance "humanitarian mission", *The Weekly Mirror*, Kathmandu, September 2012, at http://weeklymirror.com.np/index.php?action=news&id=2742 (accessed on 25 November 2012). Also see former Foreign Minister of Nepal and NC leader Sujata Koirala's observation on the issue at "Nepal: US Soldiers sneak into Mustang in civilian dress, Sujata reveals", *The Telegraph Weekly*, Kathmandu, http://www.telegraphnepal.com/headline/2012-09-30/nepal:-us-soldiers-sneak-into-mustang-in-civilian-dress-sujata-reveals.html (accessed on 25 November 2012).
60. The 60,000th Bhutanese refugee departed for the US from Nepal on 04 September 2012. The US removed the CPN (Maoist) and its front organisations from the terrorist exclusion list on 6 September. The new Ambassador Peter Bodde arrived in Nepal on 8 September. Twenty Peace Corps volunteers arrived in Nepal on 9 September. Also see Kanak Mani Dixit, "The Americans amidst us", *ekantipur*, 14 September 2012, at http://www.ekantipur.com/2012/09/14/opinion/the-americans-amidst-us/360213.html (accessed on 29 July 2013).
61. "U.S. Military and Nepal Army Working Together On 'Pacific Angel Nepal' ", Press Release, 9 September 2012, Embassy of The United States, Kathmandu, Nepal.
62. Yubaraj Ghimire, "Bridging the divide", *The Indian Express*, New Delhi, 11 September 2012.
63. Jayaraj Acharya, "USA and South Asia: Before and After 9/11, 2001", *Today*, Kathmandu, 26 (2), July-September, 2008, p. 13. Acharya was Nepal's Ambassador to the US.
64. Geoffrey Pyatt, "US-South Asia Relations: A Vision for the Future", US Department of State. For details see at http://www.state.gov/p/sca/rls/rmks/2012/201398.htm (accessed on 17 May 2013).
65. Kanak Mani Dixit, "The Pentagon's Southasia", *Himal Southasian*, 2 April 2012, see at http://www.himalmag.com/component/content/article/5043-.html (accessed on 17 May 2013).

CHAPTER 6

Institutionalise Peace and Democracy: Role of the EU and Major European Countries in Nepal

Nepal's diplomatic relations with the European Union (EU)[1] and European countries are at regional, bilateral and multilateral levels. At the multilateral level many international organisations including the EU and the UN have played important roles to further the peace process. Since the EU and the UN have been involved in the various stages of the peace process in Nepal, the book discusses the role of these two multilateral bodies separately. While the role of the UN in Nepal peace process has been discussed in Chapter 2, the role of EU is covered in detail in this chapter. The role and influence of individual European countries have also been discussed separately in this chapter.

European countries have contributed to Nepal's socio-economic development as part of the EU's framework and also at the bilateral level in various ways. The role of the four most significant of these countries namely, the UK, Norway, Switzerland and Germany (hereinafter referred to as 'major European countries') has been taken up for discussion in this chapter. These countries are important because of the quantum of financial aid, their support for the peace building process and conflict resolution efforts, and their enduring interest in Nepal. Although some other European countries—Denmark, Finland, Sweden, France and Belgium—are part of the conflict resolution process in Nepal, their involvement has not been discussed in this chapter.

As Key Development Partners

The EU began its engagement with Nepal in 1973 as a development partner and is represented in Nepal by the European Commission (EC). The EU's establishment of diplomatic relations both complemented and strengthened Nepal's engagement with Western countries. In the late 1940s, the US replaced the UK as a major international power with a growing interest in South Asia. It was natural therefore, that the relationship with the US would subsequently be of greater significance for Nepal, compared to other Western countries. Against this backdrop, in the early 1970s, when the US shifted its aid diplomacy to East Asia after its rapprochement with China, the EU and other European countries made their presence felt in Nepal and focused on democracy, governance and development-related issues. By the end of the Cold War, when Nepal ceased to be of much significance, especially for the US and the former Soviet Union, the EU emerged as the new source of foreign funds for Nepal.

In the 1990s, differences emerged between the EU member countries and some other major European countries over the nature of the political system and governance in Nepal. It is believed that as social democrats, the Scandinavian countries supported the Nepalese communists. During this period, the CPN-UML reportedly received much support from these countries. Some Scandinavian countries shifted their support from the CPN-UML to Maoist movement in 1996 to understand the nature of conflict. On the other hand, other Western European countries supported the constitutional monarchy. The UK especially played a role of proxy-super power in the Himalayan sub-region because of its long association with Gorkha soldiers and as a trusted ally of the US. The UK along with the US supported the monarchy for stability. This support continued until the Maoists joined mainstream politics in 2008.

Unlike the US, most EU member countries, at the individual level, have been actively engaged in conflict resolution and restoration of democracy in Nepal and have acquired a "distinct image as development partners of Nepal."[2] Norway, as a non-EU member country, has been contributing liberally to the United Nations Peace Fund for Nepal (UNPFN) and has also been working with EU member countries in other development and peace building programmes in Nepal. Collectively, the EU provided Nepal with a total of €240 million as aid from 1977 to 2006 mainly for irrigation, watershed management, livestock, reproductive health, primary education, refugees and institutional capacity-building. During the period 2007-2013, the EU provided assistance of €120 million to Nepal for: education, stability and peace building, trade facilitation and economic capacity building. The EU is also engaged in human rights assistance (energy, food, and elections) and has been supporting civil liberty and democratic movements since 2001. The EU has also taken an interest in resolving the problems of Bhutanese refugees living in the two eastern districts of Nepal.[3]

According to the EU Country Strategy Paper, EU funding to Nepal fluctuated after the commencement of the internal conflict between the Maoists and the state in 2001. The EC allocated €70 million aid for the period 2002–2006. The aid did not achieve its developmental objectives due to some technical problems. As protests against the royal takeover in February 2005 ensued, many important programmes initiated by the EU were kept on hold. In the post-conflict period, however, at the request of the government, the EC prioritised education, peace building, capacity development, governance issues, trade facilitation and economic capacity building as areas of intervention.[4]

As part of the process of institutionalisation of peace and democracy, the EC contributed to conflict mitigation through its support to core legal institutions, and worked towards improving peace research capacities and assistance programmes aimed at the victims of Maoist insurgency.[5] The EC also supported the Office of the High Commissioner for Human Rights (OHCHR) with a contribution of €5 million (around 30 per cent of budget). The first EU Troika led by Dutch presidency, the European Commission, and other high representatives of EU countries had visited Nepal on 13-15 December 2004. It was mandated to offer EU support for all efforts aimed at promoting multi-party democracy within the framework of a constitutional monarchy and human rights.[6] In September 2007, the European Parliament (EP) launched the "Friends of Nepal Group", a political campaign to improve parliamentary dialogue between the EP and the Nepalese Parliament. The EP also undertook several missions to Nepal over the next two years to support the new democratic reconstruction efforts.[7]

Strategic Interests of EU Member Countries

There is a perception in Nepal and China that some of the EU member countries are part of the US strategy of encircling China; that they use Nepal as a strategic base to support the anti-China movement led by the Tibetan refugees living in Nepal and Dharamshala in India. Some facts on the ground that prompt such speculations are that Nepal serves as a nodal point for monitoring China's activities in the Tibetan Autonomous Region (TAR). Moreover, both the US and EU member countries are putting pressure on the Nepalese government to treat the Tibetan refugees, who are crossing TAR border into Nepal and heading for Dharamshala, as international refugees and hand them over to the UN bodies in Nepal. Therefore, China has been very suspicious of the presence of international NGOs and their support to the ethnic groups in Nepal.

There were also economic and security interests behind Western aid assistance to Nepal. The western donors including EU members "since the late 1970s started making their aid programme conditional behind the veil of good governance and structural adjustment policies. Their objectives were to carry out market oriented neo-liberal policies that would promote their economy and shape their long-term political interests."[8] The Nepal government, therefore, initiated policy changes as instructed by the donors. In fact, there have been occasions when Western donors[9] have financed projects directly without channelising the funds through the government mechanism.[10] Some Nepalese analysts shared with this author that these funds might have been utilised for empowering Tibetan refugees and other ethnic groups. Interestingly, Thomas Gass, Ambassador of Switzerland to Nepal and co-chair of the 13 Basic Operating Guidelines (BOG) signatories and Robert Piper, UN Resident and Humanitarian Coordinator, another co-chair of the 13 BOG group, during a media interaction on 23 November 2012 accepted that some 60-70 per cent of the aid is routed through government channels.[11] In the post-9/11 period, aid was leveraged to co-opt countries into the Global War on Terrorism.[12] As part of their security concerns, some European countries had reformulated their aid assistance policy in line with Nepal's counter insurgency policy against the Maoists.

Until the king's takeover, the international community was mostly divided over the root cause and nature of the conflict. For example, while some European countries analysed the conflict as a structural problem and appealed to both parties to stop human rights violations and resolve the conflict through negotiations, others, including, the UK, Germany, Belgium, in tandem with US policy, supplied arms and ammunition to the Nepalese Army as part of their commitment to the Global War on Terrorism. Since the onset of the Maoist insurgency, the donor agencies believed that "an effective development strategy would mitigate and ultimately resolve a conflict that was fundamentally political in nature."[13] Though the donors' generosity with funds supposedly aggravated the conflict (because some donors are regarded as 'conflict-insensitive', a term used in some UN documents), on the positive side, they "prevented major displacement of people and kept the social fabric of villages and rural communities largely intact"[14] and also checked human rights violations. Since most of the development aid from India, China and the US were invested in locations strategically important to these countries, the EU funding penetrated into areas neglected not only by these countries but also by the state agencies. The EU countries continued their activities in these areas, either by paying security money or by taking both the conflicting groups into confidence. For example, in 2003, the Maoists decided to allow the NGOs funded by European countries to operate in the districts under their control in an effort to seek their support. At the same time, they prevented US funded NGOs from operating in remote areas because the US was supporting the Nepalese Army in its counter insurgency strategy against the Maoists. Interestingly, for smooth operations in the conflict zones, "all bilateral Western aid agencies—with the exception of USAID—and the UN agencies adopted basic operating guidelines (BOG)[15] in October 2003."[16]

Role in Negotiations

Throughout the Maoist insurgency period, the parties to the conflict maintained Track II channels for communicating with each other. Before the palace massacre in June 2001, the Maoists were in touch with King Birendra. In fact, there was some information that the king wanted the Maoists to counter the democratic forces. The conflict took a new turn with the killing of King Birendra and assumption of power by King Gyanendra. Sensing an external design to quell the movement and given their disagreements with King Gyanendra, the Maoists intensified their armed struggle. King Gyanendra deployed the army to suppress the movement. But when this did not bring results, Prime Minister Sher Bahadur Deuba offered peace talks. After three rounds of talks, the negotiation process collapsed in November 2001. The negotiations started again in January 2003 and collapsed in August 2003. During this period, some European countries, especially Switzerland and Norway, tried separately to mediate by using their contacts with civil society groups. European Union member countries like Denmark, Finland, Germany, Sweden and the UK organised workshops for comparing these peace initiatives with those in other conflict theatres in the world.[17] The EU delegation representative in Nepal, the EC, was not involved directly in any negotiations. It condemned human rights violations by both parties to the conflict and appealed to them to resolve the conflict through peaceful negotiations. In the post-conflict period, the EC was concerned about the delay in the completion of the peace process and promulgation of the new Constitution. As part of the peace-building strategy, the EC along with EU member countries was also anxious about the delay in the establishment of a Truth and Reconciliation Commission (TRC).

Organisations like the Centre for Humanitarian Dialogue (CHD)[18] and Department for International Development (DFID) were actively involved in the first round of peace negotiations and the intervening period between 2001 and 2003. The DFID organised several meetings between Nepalese scholars and many experienced Western peace negotiators, who were brought in for initiating dialogue between the warring factions.[19] The CHD's mediation efforts did not, however, yield much result due to its poor understanding of the conflict and the reluctance of both India and the king to get involved. Some Western countries were of the view that India believed that third-party involvement would complicate matters further.

After the fall of the royal regime in April 2006, Nepal needed a mediator to drive the peace process forward. The UN expressed its interest, but India opposed it. Many Indian analysts felt that UN officials did not have sufficient knowledge of the conflict in Nepal. Moreover, India could not trust foreign countries to mediate a peace deal for its immediate neighbour.[20] Despite India's cold response on the UN involvement, many EU member countries supported the UN proposal indirectly and expressed their interests in funding separately for this cause. In fact, some EU member countries unofficially lobbied for UN Secretary General's office to be utilised to resolve the conflicts.

As Trading Partners

Apart from being a dependable development partner, the EU has also proved to be a reliable trade partner of Nepal. It is the largest importer of Nepalese goods. According to the data available with the European Economic Community, the EU exported €84,056,326 worth of goods and services and imported €73,116,955 during 2003-04. According to government sources:

> Around 37 per cent of the total overseas exports of Nepal are with the EU, whereas the imports are to the tune of 10.27 per cent. Nepal's total trade with EU in the fiscal year 2007/2008 was worth €150 million, of which exports were worth €62 million and imports worth €88 million.[21]

Germany is the largest exporter (mechanical tools) among the EU countries to Nepal. Nepal's exports include woollen carpets, readymade garments, hides and goatskin, woollen and Pashmina goods.[22] Nepal's balance-of-trade deficit with the EU is much less than that with India and China. However, Nepal receives very little FDI from the EU region compared to what it gets from India, China and the US. Out of a total 619 joint venture companies operating in Nepal, only around 48 joint venture industries or firms have their origins in the EU.[23]

Dilemma of Conflict Prevention

Nepal has been receiving human development-related funds since the 1950s from a large number of countries. In fact, in some years Nepal received more foreign aid than FDI. Even so, Nepal's Human Development Index is not very impressive. The country has already witnessed a few rounds of armed struggles because of the inequalities in Nepalese society. This indicates that the development aid had not reached the needy people for lack of planning and implementation, poor administrative support and, most importantly, because the aid was linked to strategy. Some in Nepal feel that large amount of the development-related funds go back to the donor countries as consultancy, remuneration and technical support. A country in need of funds becomes an economic parasite if it receives more foreign aid than FDI. That is why some argue that Nepal needs FDI, not aid, for its economic growth and steady development. Switzerland is also a landlocked country, with many topographical similarities with Nepal, but Switzerland has never depended upon foreign aid.

Some critics argue that foreign donors, especially from Europe, target soft projects in Nepal. Krishna Hachhethu argues that "frustrated by political instability, the poor state of accountability and responsibility of the political society (i.e., political parties, parliament and government) and more so the absence of local elected bodies since 2002",[24] the donor agencies have diverted their funds to soft projects from infrastructure-related projects. This interpretation may not correspond with the reality on ground. For example, until 2002, there was political stability,[25] but distribution of aid in the country was unequal. As a result, the country was reeling under poverty and underdevelopment, which was exploited by the Maoists. It would be pertinent to mention that from the beginning, the European countries were committed to provide aid mostly for the social and political development sectors.[26]

Within the EU, there were differences of opinion on how to deal with the Maoists. While the Scandinavian countries were sympathetic to the social transformation agenda put forward by the Maoists, the UK, France and Belgium were in favour of resolving the conflict by military means. Going ahead with their peace and development agenda at the regional level, some European countries like the UK, mostly influenced by the US, also provided the Nepalese government with arms and ammunition to quell the Maoists. According to an EU document:

> The EU upholds the Government of Nepal's right to defend the country's newly established democracy in countering this terrorist insurgency. The

> EU notes that the democratic state has the sole right to use legitimate force to preserve the rights and security of its citizens. The EU believes that the authorities in Nepal must seek to establish basic security and an environment in which developmental efforts to overcome poverty can be pursued, and that the insurgency hinders the development process.[27]

Other EU members condemned the supply of arms, alleging that these might possibly be responsible for killing thousands of innocent Nepalese caught in the crossfire. However, the EU in general endorsed such transfers on grounds that "Nepal was a democratic state fighting an illegal Maoist rebellion, not a country engaged in civil war."[28] It also upheld Nepal's right to defend its newly established democracy in countering terrorist insurgency.[29] In fact, the EU remained silent while Belgium tried to supply 5,500 automatic rifles to Nepal. This led to confusion in international community about EU's role in the peace building process in Nepal. Commenting on this state of affairs [during the conflict phase], Kanwal Sibal, the then foreign secretary of India, noted that "Europe [was] unified economically but not in the defence domain."[30] But despite this, EU member countries were known to be exchanging their views on political developments and consulted each other regularly on peace building in Nepal.

Post-Conflict Approach

In the post-conflict period, the EU and some of its member countries supported the peace process, the 2008 CA elections and the Constitution-drafting process by providing technical and financial assistance. EU member countries were the largest donors for the integration and rehabilitation of the former Maoist combatants. As part of the conflict resolution programme, they had put pressure on the then interim government(s) for the setting up of a Truth and Reconciliation Commission (TRC) and Commission for the Investigation of Disappeared Persons (CIDP) in accordance with international norms in order to deliver justice to the Maoist insurgency (13 February 1996 to 21 November 2006) victims. Despite the setting up of the TRC through an ordinance on 14 March 2013, the EU member countries found that the Nepal government had failed to implement the main objectives of the TRC as per international standards due to the vested interests of the political class of Nepal. The bill was perceived to be heavily focused on amnesty. The Nepal Peace Trust Fund (NPTF),[31] which was established in January 2007, also did not conform to international standards as claimed by the then government. They also felt that some provisions of the bill in fact were in violation of international law. Therefore, the EU decided not to fund the TRC and CIDP.[32]

Similarly, the UN Resident and Humanitarian Coordinator Robert Piper identified some practical problems in the process of translating the government's commitment to human rights into action.[33] Many suspected criminals, including Nepalese Army officials, political leaders and Maoist cadres, were moving about openly despite being guilty of serious crimes during the Maoist insurgency. Earlier, in response to delay in the formation of the TRC, the UK had arrested Colonel Kumar Lama of the NA on 3 January 2013, under a British law that allows prosecution for alleged war crimes.[34] This led to a diplomatic tussle between Nepal and the UK government. The Nepalese media and political parties also condemned the arrest of NA officer.

Apart from that, EU supported the formation of women and *Janajati* caucuses in the 2008 Constituent Assembly. They also funded research and activism on identity issues. Although some EU member countries have been supporting these issues for a long time, their support to these causes was criticised when the 2008 CA was finally dissolved without drafting a new Constitution and the demand for ethnicity-based federalism remained unresolved. This controversy led to divisions among the EU members. While Switzerland, Sweden and Denmark supported ethnicity-based federalism for bringing about justice and equality in Nepal; the UK stopped funding that cause, because of serious ethnic polarisation and especially after ethnic conflicts in the far-western districts in 2012. In fact, the HLPC, which was formed to help the CJ-led government to resolve differences between political parties, suspected the intentions of some EU countries because of their continuing support to some *Janajati* organisations, who were demanding ethnicity-based federalism. However, EU countries welcomed the second CA election of November 19 and announced additional financial support for the NPTF[35] with a view to support elections. There was a perception in Nepal that EU support for ethnicity-based federalism might scuttle the election process. None other than the UCPN (Maoist) Vice-Chairman, Baburam Bhattarai, a one-time favourite of Scandinavian countries, observed that "European countries are lobbying hard against CA elections."[36] Although Bhattarai did not specify these anti-election activities, many Nepalese believed that the newly-formed Federal Socialist Party of Ashok Rai was supported by some European countries.

Approach of Major Countries to the Peace Process

The UK

Among the European countries, the UK has the oldest association with Nepal in terms of employing Gorkha soldiers, whose remittances have contributed to socio-economic development of Nepal. The UK shared US concerns over the internal security situation in Nepal and provided military assistance to fight the Maoists during the conflict. While the other EU members more or less described the Maoist insurgency as a political movement that had its origins in social grievances, the UK treated the Maoists as terrorists. According to Peter Burleigh:

> There appear to be two fundamental goals in both the US and UK policies: (a) help Nepal become a peaceful, more prosperous, and democratic nation and (b) in the process, prevent the Maoists from attaining victory. By and large, the US/UK reaction has been multi-faceted, and has thus included both increasing development assistance to the government, especially since 2001, and increasing military assistance, both equipment and training.[37]

Table 6.1: US, UK and EU Countries' Understanding of the Maoist Insurgency in Nepal

	Understanding on Maoists	*Development Assistance*	*Arms supply*	*Human Rights Violations*
US	Terrorists	Increased	Yes	Maoists and Security Forces
UK	Terrorists	Increased	Yes	Maoists and Security Forces
EU	Divided: condemned violence; Maoists are social transformation agents	Traditional development aid	Some member countries	Maoists and Security Forces

Source: English media; Peter Burleigh, "Nepal: Western Views of the Maoist Insurgency and the Royal Takeover," Working Paper, 9 July 2005, Institute of Governmental Studies, University of California, Berkley.

Like the US, the UK was a leading arms supplier to Nepal and a strong supporter of the monarchy. The military assistance increased after the terrorist attack on the US mainland on 11 September 2001 and deployment of the NA against the Maoists in November 2001. Military assistance from both the US and the UK was initially in the form of training for security forces and logistical support, and was a "gift".[38] Peter Burleigh observed that both "publicly and privately the US (and UK) strongly advised the Government of Nepal that there [had] to be a political solution to the Maoist challenge; a solution that would include the Maoists, the democratic political parties, and the king."[39] Despite that the UK supplied 6780 assault rifles in 2001; two MI-17 helicopters in 2003; and two Islander short-takeoff-and-landing aircraft in 2004. According to Whitehall's official export figures, Britain exported

£110,000 worth of military equipment to Nepal between 2001 and 2003. It also noted that a number of senior Nepalese Army officers, including the then Chief of Army Staff, were trained at Sandhurst in the UK.

However, the UK suspended military assistance to Nepal after the king captured power in February 2005. After the king lifted the state of emergency in April 2006, Foreign Secretary Jack Straw announced a review of security assistance to Nepal, while condemning the human rights record of the then RNA, which created some controversy.[40] In the post-conflict period, when Nepal was struggling to complete the integration of the Maoist combatants into the NA, the UK offered help for the modernisation of the NA. The issue was discussed during British Army Chief General Sir David Julian Richards's visit to Kathmandu in February 2010. General Richards had also emphasised the strengthening of relations between the armies of the two countries. Surprisingly, while the international community was busy consolidating the peace process, the UK's offer of military aid created further distrust between the then ruling party CPN-UML and the Maoists.

The UK's policy on Nepal has thus been different from that of the EU, which places greater emphasis on a negotiated settlement. The UK is nevertheless the second-largest bilateral donor to Nepal after Japan, and comes fourth among all donors after the World Bank and the ADB. The UK had committed around £331 million official development assistance (ODA) during the period 2011-2015 for peace building and development in Nepal. DFID had disbursed £55.9 million of bilateral development assistance for the year 2012/13 and more than 50 per cent of the total ODA was spent for governance and security, wealth creation and climate change programmes.[41] The UK had also invested significant political and financial resources in conflict prevention and resolution.[42]

After the dissolution of the first CA, the UK continues to focus on peace-building, disaster management and justice for victims of the war. A further US$26 million funding support was announced for earthquake preparedness in Nepal during the official visit of the Minister of State for International Development, Alan Duncan, in June 2012.[43] However, its continuing stand on violation of human rights by the Maoists and the state agencies in the conflict phase is believed to have had an adverse effect on the democratic transition process. For example, shortly after Duncan's visit, the British Embassy in a press release (issued on 30 August 2012), on behalf of EU member countries and others, appealed to the Nepal government to expedite the establishment of a TRC to investigate the cases of human rights violations and facilitate reconciliation.[44]

Norway

Norway, which is a non-EU country, is the fourth-largest bilateral donor to Nepal. The bilateral relationship was established in 1973. Before the Maoist insurgency, Norway was engaged in community development and capacity building programmes in the rural areas. Most of the projects were prioritised according to the requirements of the Nepalese government. Contrary to the UK's perspective, Norway was open to negotiations with the Maoists and has consistently maintained that the Maoists were the agents of social transformation in Nepal. It criticised both the government and the Maoists for human rights violations and appealed for resolution of the conflict through political dialogue.

Given its experience in conflict theatres across the globe and its engagement in the Sri Lankan conflict, Norway had indicated during the conflict period that it was willing to be a mediator in Nepal in case the government required its services. In 2003, the Norwegian Ambassador to Nepal, Ingrid Ronnaug Ofstad had stated: "Norway would mediate peace talks in Nepal if both parties showed genuine interest in its involvement."[45] The initiative was not, however, taken further because of India's strong objections on third-party extra-regional mediation in its neighbourhood, and also because of the lack of support from the US and the UK.

After the king took over in February 2005, the Norwegian Government reduced its financial aid to Nepal and declared that it would re-start it when democracy was restored in that country. The Norwegian Ambassador played a leading role in raising the issue of delay in the completion of the peace process and lack of consensus on the contentious issues. Norway supported peace-building programmes initiated by multilateral agencies like the UNMIN and other UN agencies and also appointed its former Ambassador to Nepal, Tore Toreng, as a special envoy for the peace process in Nepal. It has been reported that Toreng was sympathetic towards the Maoists and facilitated meetings between US embassy officials and Maoist leaders. He also coordinated a dialogue between the international community and the political leaders of Nepal in 2010.[46] The Norwegian Minister for Development Cooperation, Erik Solhem, also undertook several visits to Kathmandu between 2006-2012 to end the political stalemate and to ensure the establishment of peace.

Switzerland

Switzerland offered to mediate in the peace process in Nepal in early 2000. This offer was generally related to four factors: (1) the Swiss experience in mediation in other conflict areas; (2) its reputation and acceptance as a neutral actor by warring parties; (3) its experience of managing ethnically diverse populations in its own territory and (4) its geographical similarities with Nepal. Even before it established normal diplomatic relations with Nepal, some Swiss NGOs were operating there as far back as 1956. Nepal has been one of the priority countries for Swiss state development aid since the end of the 1960s. The Swiss government has also been involved in many community development programmes, promotion of good governance and human rights, and natural resources management. Switzerland has also supported infrastructure development like roads and bridges in remote areas.[47] The first Swiss Ambassador to Nepal, Thomas Gass, observed that:

> Switzerland and Nepal are both landlocked, they both have a strong rural history and both had to bring together a culturally and linguistically diverse population. These are some of the reasons why Switzerland started its work in Nepal, first through non-governmental organizations and then officially through the SDC [Swiss Agency for Development and Cooperation].[48]

With the onset of the Maoist insurgency in 1996, Switzerland changed its aid strategy and focused more on peace promotion and strengthening of governance. In the post-conflict period, Switzerland has prioritised the promotion of peace and rule of law, rural infrastructure, vocational training, sustainable management of natural resources and healthcare. In addition, the Swiss Development Cooperation (SDC) has undertaken a comprehensive Conflict Sensitive Programme Management in coordination with other donor agencies. It was also a major donor for the various conflict resolution programmes undertaken by the UNMIN.[49]

During the period of armed conflict some Switzerland-based independent organisations such as the Centre for Humanitarian Dialogue (CHD) took some initiatives to facilitate talks between the warring parties and continued their peace effort even after 2006. From the beginning of the first phase of peace talks in 2001 and again in 2003, the CHD made indirect offers of mediation by engaging civil society representatives of Nepal.[50] The CHD dialogue initiative, in fact, continued even after the dissolution of the Constituent Assembly on 27 May 2012. It engaged civil society members for initiating a dialogue between major political parties for early resolution of the political stalemate.

Germany

Bilateral relations between Nepal and Germany were established in 1967. As mentioned earlier, Germany is Nepal's largest trading partner from the

European region. Around 24 joint ventures with Germany are currently operating in Nepal. Around 50 NGOs from Germany are also working in various fields such as: human rights, rural development, education and health in various parts of Nepal. The country's official donor—GTZ—has been funding many peace-building programmes. During the period of conflict, many Germany-based NGOs wound up their projects in the rural areas fearing Maoist attacks. Although Germany-based NGOs were not directly involved in any peace dialogues like those from Switzerland and Norway, they opposed the human rights violations by both parties. Both German NGOs and the government followed the EU line of conflict resolution through dialogue and negotiation.[51]

Nevertheless, despite its declared stance of adhering to the EU Code of Conduct of 1998 on supplying small arms to conflict-ridden countries, Germany did supply arms to the Nepalese Army. According to an Amnesty International report, a consignment of ammunition allegedly arrived at the Tribhuvan International Airport from Germany on 23 May 2005, when India, the US and the UK stopped supplying arms to Nepal. The report also stated that Belgium, another EU member, supplied around 3000 Minimi LMGs to Nepal after the German Government refused to supply arms in 2002.[52]

Major European Countries and UNPFN

Some European countries have also been consistently providing funds, technical human resources support, election observers and consultancy for UN programmes in Nepal like OHCHR, United Nations Peace Fund for Nepal (UNPFN) and Transition Support Strategy, etc. The UK, Norway, Denmark and Switzerland are regular donors to these UN programmes. As of 2 March 2012, the UNPFN had received a total of US$24,273,364 in contributions from the UK ($11,075,308), Norway ($8,819,691), Denmark ($4,178,390) and Switzerland ($199,975) out of a total of $44,494,663.[53] These contributions account for more than half of the total funds received by the UNPFN. Earlier, the EU countries had agreed on the BOG on aid assistance at a meeting in Paris. Surprisingly, except for the Nepal Peace Development Programme, the US does not support any major programmes in Nepal. Nepal's immediate neighbours, India and China, too are not listed in these UN programmes.

Despite the differences between European countries, their contribution to Nepal's peace process from the beginning of the conflict has been largely helpful in conflict prevention. After the dissolution of the Constituent

Assembly on 27 May 2012, the UN peace-building fund released $8 million for consolidation of peace. The UN has already allocated a total of $19 million for peace-building in Nepal since 2010.[54] This funding has worked as an alternative to the state-sponsored development programmes when both the state and the government of Nepal are passing through a period of critical transition.

Besides, the European Initiative for Democracy and Human Rights (EIDHR) has been funding community-based awareness campaigns and conflict mediation, which have become mired in controversy since the *Janajatis* and *Madhesis* launched their demand for ethnicity-based federalism in Nepal. Since then the foreign ministry has asked the donor countries to focus on infrastructure and development projects. Many scholars have observed that this state regulation of the INGOs in the absence of a credible and stable political system may create social tensions in future.

The UNPFN donors from the EU member countries are concerned about the delay in the drafting of the new Constitution and political instability in Nepal. They have made several attempts to forge a consensus between the major political parties to form a national unity government, but these efforts have been termed by both the government and some political parties as interference in the internal affairs of Nepal. Non-Maoist parties have alleged that some European countries are sympathetic to the Maoists. There is a perception in Kathmandu that some Europe-based INGOs are also engaged in religious conversion.[55]

European Aid and Federalism

The European countries' support to the development programmes in Nepal is not free from controversy. There is a growing perception in Nepal that aid from European countries has encouraged ethnic movements, and increased the possibility of violent ethnic conflict. During the visit of ministers from Norway and the UK after the dissolution of the CA on 27 May 2012, the Nepalese media raised questions regarding the social tensions in Nepal being aggravated by funds being pumped into the country by various NGOs. During a media interaction programme in Birgunj on 22 May 2010, Kamal Thapa, chairman of the Rastriya Prajatantra Party-Nepal, said: "They [the European countries] have been pouring in huge sums of money in the conversion drive that they are carrying out in Nepal."[56] He also alleged that religious conversions have increased in the post-conflict period. According to K.B. Rokaya, there were around 800 Christians in Nepal in 1978. In comparison, he said:

> It was estimated that by the year 2000, the number of Christians in Nepal crossed 800,000. The growth rate of Christians in Nepal has been rising sharply after Nepal became a republic and a secular state. There are unverified reports that in the recently conducted population census, the number of Christians is between 1.5 and 2 million which is more than 5 [per cent] of the total population.[57]

Interestingly, there have been conflicting reports about the rise in the numbers of the Christian population in Nepal. Since the Christian population was not included in the 2001 Census, the exact percentage of its increase in the last ten years has been ambiguous. While the ultra-rightist groups argue that the number of Christians is between 1.5 and 02 million, according to the 2011 Census, the Christian population in Nepal is 3,75,699, which is 1.4 per cent of the total population of 26,444,504.[58] Interestingly, one private source indicated that the Christians constituted 0.4 per cent of the total population in 2007.[59] In fact, challenging the 2011Census, the Federation of National Christians-Nepal (FNCN) claimed that "there are more than 8,500 churches and over 2.5 million Christians across the country [Nepal]."[60] Yubaraj Ghimire, a journalist and security analyst observed that since donor countries such as "Denmark, Norway, Switzerland and Britain have provided assistance to ethnic organisations that espouse extreme views in the name of ethnic empowerment. Such assistance has increased the danger of social and ethnic tension and social violence."[61] Similarly, Dirgha Raj Prasai argued: "There is increasing concern among foreigners in promoting ethnic federalism."[62]

In an effort to curb external support to the armed groups, in May 2010, the government of Nepal objected to a meeting planned between visiting European parliamentarians and the armed Limbuwan and Khumbuwan groups. In a statement, the Ministry of Foreign Affairs (MoFA) said: "The EU parliamentarians should abstain from meeting the armed groups as they were illegal and they did not represent any social or political groups."[63] Moreover, on many occasions, China has expressed concerns about the EU-supported INGOs allegedly extending support to Tibetan refugees.

Although these allegations are unsubstantiated, on 23 November 2012, the UN Resident and Humanitarian Coordinator and 13 signatories of BOG, issued a statement reiterating their impartiality and gave the assurance that aid would not be misused by any civil society organisations to support activities that would lead to violence during the election period.[64]

The hyperactivity of the EC and other European countries for establishing the TRC in the post-CA dissolution period and their meetings with political leaders have been criticised by the government of Nepal. The MoFA criticised such activities as "foreign interference into Nepal's internal affairs. This is against diplomatic decorum and has been perceived as an attempt to drag the constitutional head of state into political issues."[65] This reaction came after representatives of the EC and the ambassadors of some European countries met President Ram Baran Yadav on 7 September 2012 despite MoFA disallowing such a meeting. There is a perception in the Nepalese media that the CA was dissolved due to the external support for the *Janajatis* and *Madhesis* on the federalism issue.

Conclusion

Although there has been a consistent effort and support by the international community to complete the peace and Constitution-drafting process in Nepal, the community is divided over the means to be adopted to achieve the goal. There are three distinct approaches—Western, Indian and Nepalese–for resolving the political stalemate. The Western approach is further divided between the US and Europe and the latter is again divided between Scandinavians and non-Scandinavian countries.

Despite the comprehensive peace agreement of November 2006, the completion of integration programme and formation of a new government after the second CA elections in an attempt to draft the Constitution, uncertainty prevails in Nepal. Furthermore, external interventions and conflicting political interests have also added to these uncertainties. Since Nepal is heavily dependent on European countries for the development budget, they can influence the Constitution-making process in future. The continuous engagement of the US, the UK and other Western powers and their support for the Tibetan movement would convert Nepal into a conflict region. Therefore, instead of promoting individual country formulas for conflict resolution, an effort needs to be made to evolve a homegrown solution.

*

NOTES

1. The EU has 28 member-countries including Germany and United Kingdom as on 31 December 2013. The EU and European Commission (EC) is used interchangeably in this chapter.
2. Krishna Hachhethu, "The European Union's Role in Democracy Building in Nepal", 2009, International Institute for Democracy and Electoral Assistance, Stockholm, p. 6.
3. "Nepal: Country Strategy Paper," 2007–2013, European Union, pp. 01-04, at http://eeas.europa.eu/nepal/docs/07_13_en.pdf (accessed on 12 August 2013). There is no

separate data available about how much of this assistance was provided during the establishment of the EU (1993). Also see "The EU's relations with Nepal – An Overview," at www.ec.europa.eu.

4. Ibid., p.02. For more information, see http://eeas.europa.eu/nepal/docs/07_13_en.pdf (accessed on 12 August 2013).
5. "European Initiative for Democracy and Human Rights/Non-Governmental Organisations," European Union, at www.ec.europa.eu. (accessed on 9 March 2014).
6. "The EU's relations with Nepal—An Overview," at www.ec.europa.eu. Also see "Nepal: EU Troika," Press Release, Kathmandu, 15 December 2004, .Council of the European Union, at http://www.consilium.europa.eu/uedocs/cms_data/docs/pressdata/en/er/83197.pdf (accessed on 12 August 2013).
7. "MEPs Give Nepal a Helping Hand", *New Europe*, at http://www.neurope.eu/article/meps-give-nepal-helping-hand (accessed on 12 August 2013).
8. Yam Prasad Chaulagain, "Official Development Assistance in Nepal: A Development Perspective", *e-International Relations*, 28 August 2012, at http://www.e-ir.info/2012/08/28/official-development-assistance-in-nepal-a-development-perspective/ (accessed on 24 November 2012). Also see "A little help from our friends", *ekantipur*, 20 November 2012, at http://www.ekantipur.com/2012/11/20/opinion/a-little-help-from-our-friends/362949.html (accessed on 24 November 2012).
9. Media reports indicated that three donor agencies—Department for International Development (DFID), Swiss Agency for Development and Cooperation (SDC) and Finnish International Development Agency (FINNIDA)—had pledged a sum of US$61.8 million for the four-year multi-stakeholder forestry programme. For details see "Submit documents on foreign aid, forest ministry told", *Republica*, Kathmandu, 25 March 2012, at http://www.myrepublica.com/portal/index.php?action=news_details&news_id=33221 (accessed on 24 November 2012).
10. Yam Prasad Chaulagain, "Official Development Assistance in Nepal: A Development perspective", n.8.
11. "Donors not to allow use of aid for violence, political gains", *Republica*, 23 November 2012, at http://www.myrepublica.com/portal/index.php?action=news_details&news_id=45260 (accessed on 24 November 2012).
12. Bishwambher Pyakuryal, "What is aid for?" *Republica*, 26 January 2011.
13. Jorg Frieden, "A Donor's Perspective on Aid and Conflict", in Sebastian v. Einsiedel, *et al.*(eds), *Nepal in Transition: From People's War to Fragile Peace*, Cambridge University Press, Cambridge, 2012, p. 101.
14. Ibid., p. 108.
15. For details, see Appendix-V.
16. Jorg Frieden, "A Donor's Perspective on Aid and Conflict", n. 13, p. 103.
17. Teresa Whitefield, "Nepal's Masala Peacemaking", in Sebastian v. Einsiedel, *et al.*(eds), n. 13, p. 161.
18. CHD is a Switzerland-based mediation organisation mostly engaged in peace process in conflict-ridden countries.
19. Teresa Whitfield, "Nepal's Masala Peacemaking", n. 17, pp. 158-9.
20. Author's interaction with one senior Government of India official, who was closely associated with Nepal affairs in 2006, in October 2012 in New Delhi.
21. "Nepal-EU Relationships in Brief," Embassy of Nepal, Brussels, at http://

winweb10.ovh.net/specicom.net/www/nepal/NewEU.asp (accessed on 12 August 2013).

22. For more information, see "EU-Nepal Relations," European Economic Chamber (EEC), at http://www.eec-nepal.org.np/eec/ (accessed on 29 January 2014).
23. Research and Information Division of FNCCI, Department of Industries, Government of Nepal, as on April 2008.
24. Krishna Hachhethu, "The European Union's Role in Democracy Building in Nepal", n.2.
25. Despite frequent changes in the executive head, there was a functioning parliamentary democracy till October 2002. The system became dysfunctional when Gyanendra sacked the democratically elected executive head.
26. Education, health, community development, infrastructure development and empowerment of marginalised groups, etc.
27. "Declaration by the Presidency on behalf of the European Union on Human Rights in Nepal," Press Release, at http://www.consilium.europa.eu/uedocs/cms_data/docs/pressdata/en/cfsp/P-078-EN.doc.html (accessed on 12 August 2013). Also see "EU calls for peace in Nepal", *BBC News*, 3 June 2000, at http://news.bbc.co.uk/2/hi/south_asia/775889.stm (accessed on 12 August 2013).
28. "Belgium arms sale row deepens", *BBC News*, 27 August 2002, at http://news.bbc.co.uk/2/hi/europe/2220116.stm (accessed on 12 August 2013).
29. "Nepal-EU Relations," Bilateral Relations, Ministry of Foreign Affairs, Governmental Nepal, at http://www.mofa.gov.np/bilateral/nepal-eu.php (accessed on 12 August 2013).
30. Kanwal Sibal, "Arms and the Country", Vivekananda International Foundation, 29 July 2012, at http://www.vifindia.org/article/2012/july/29/arms-and-the-country (accessed on 12 August 2013).
31. The NPTF was formed after contributions from the UK, Norway, Finland, Denmark, Switzerland, European Commission and Germany in January 2007 with an objective of providing technical and financial support for the implementation of the Comprehensive Peace a Agreement. The NPTF also agreed to support the formation of the TRC and CIDP. For more information visit www.nptf.gov.np
32. "Donors against funding TRC under existing law", *ekantipur*, 5 May 2013, at http://www.ekantipur.com/the-kathmandu-post/2013/05/04/top-story/donors-against-funding-trc-under-existing-law/248347.html (accessed on 12 August 2013).
33. "Let's not reopen old wounds: PM", *ekantipur*, 11 December 2012, at http://www.ekantipur.com/2011/12/11/top-story/lets-not-reopen-old-wounds-pm/345327.html (accessed on 12 August 2013).
34. "Nepal's Colonel Kumar Lama charged in UK with torture," *BBC News*, 5 January 2013, at http://www.bbc.co.uk/news/world-asia-20914282 (accessed on 12 August 2013).
35. Switzerland (NPR 450 million), Finland (€2.5 million), Denmark (DKK 10 million), Norway (NOK 20 million), European Union (€9.5 million) and UK (£7.5 million). Apart from that the EU members have also offered the election related technical support to UN agencies.
36. "Bhattarai cautions UK on anti-poll initiatives", *The Himalayan Times*, Kathmandu, 7 June 2013. In fact, both the Nepali Congress and the CPN-UML share similar views regarding some European countries' supporting the ethnicity based federalism. While the Nepali Congress had been opposing ethnicity-based federalism from the very beginning, the formation of the Federal Socialist Party by Ashok Rai, who was earlier

with the CPN-UML, made the CPN-UML critical of external support to the federalism issue.

37. Peter Burleigh, "Nepal: Western Views of the Maoist Insurgency and the Royal Takeover," Working Paper, 9 July 2005, Institute of Governmental Studies, University of California, Berkeley, p. 1.
38. UK government's reply to the questions raised in the UK Parliament concerning arms supplies to Nepal. For more information, see "Nepal: Military assistance contributing to grave Human Rights violations," *Amnesty International Report* 2005.
39. Peter Burleigh, "Nepal: Western Views of the Maoist Insurgency and the Royal Takeover," n.37, p. 4.
40. Richard Norton-Taylor, "British arms supplies fuelling abuses in Nepal, says Amnesty", *The Guardian*, 15 June 2005, at www.politics.guardian.co.uk. For more information, also see "Nepal: Military assistance contributing to grave Human Rights violations," n.38.
41. "DFID Nepal Portfolio Review 2012/13", DFID, British Embassy Kathmandu, at https://www.gov.uk/government/uploads/system/uploads/attachment_data/file/237274/Nepal-portfolio-review-2012-13.pdf (accessed on 31 January 2014).
42. International Crisis Group, "Nepal Crisis: Mobilising International influence," Crisis Group Briefing, 19 April 2006, p. 5.
43. "UK announces $26 mn support for Nepal quake preparedness", *Zee News*, 28 June 2012, at http://zeenews.india.com/news/south-asia/uk-announces-26-mn-support-for-nepal-quake-preparedness_784418.html (accessed on 12 August 2013).
44. British Embassy, Kathmandu, Press Release, 30 August 2012.
45. "Norway offers to mediate in Nepal", *The Hindu*, 30 January 2003, at http://hindu.com/2003/01/30/stories/2003013001811200.htm (accessed on 12 August 2013).
46. "Nepal: Norway appoints Special Envoy", *Cablegatesearch, confidential Kathmandu 000077*, E.O. 12958: DECL: 01/26/2020, charge d'Affaires, a.i., John M. Ordway 1.4 (b/d), released on 30 August 2011, at http://www.cablegatesearch.net/cable.php?id=10KATHMANDU77 (accessed on 12 August 2013).
47. "Bilateral relations between Switzerland and Nepal", Federal Department of Foreign Affairs, Switzerland, at http://www.eda.admin.ch/eda/en/home/reps/asia/nnpl/bilnep.html (accessed on 12 August 2013).
48. "Switzerland establishes closer ties with Nepal", *swissinfo.ch*, 17 August 2009, at http://www.swissinfo.ch/eng/politics/foreign_affairs/Switzerland_establishes_closer_ties_with_Nepal.html?cid=983622 (accessed on 12 August, 2013).
49. Swiss Agency for Development and Cooperation, Swiss Embassy in Kathmandu. For more information, see http://www.swiss-cooperation.admin.ch/nepal/en/Home/Swiss_Cooperation_in_Nepal/The_Swiss_Embassy_in_Nepal (accessed on 12 August 2013).
50. Teresa Whitfield, "Nepal's Masala Peacemaking", n. 17, pp. 155-74.
51. Ram Pratap Thapa, *German NGOs and Political Strife in Nepal*, Friedrich Ebert Stiftung, December 2003.
52. "Nepal: Military assistance contributing to grave Human Rights violations", n. 38.
53. United Nations Development Group. For more information, see http://mptf.undp.org/factsheet/fund/npf00 (accessed on 2 March 2013).
54. UN Office of the Resident and Humanitarian Coordinator Nepal, Press Release, 29

June 2012. For details see "Nepal receives $8 million from UN peacebuilding fund", *UN News Centre*, 29 June 2012, at http://www.un.org/apps/news/story.asp/html/www.unicef.org/story.asp?NewsID=42362&Cr=nepal&Cr1=#.UvxSIGJ6WtE (accessed on 13 February 2014).

55. Author's interaction with political leaders, civil society activists and media personnel in Kathmandu in June 2011 and November 2013.
56. "EU Nations funding for Religious Conversion in Nepal: Kamal Thapa", *The Telegraph Weekly*, Kathmandu, 23 May 2010, at http://www.telegraphnepal.com/news_det.php?news_id=7720& PHPSESSID= 8e2636e8c32b7e8bff63c389bd244d9d (accessed on 12 August 2013).
57. K.B. Rokaya, "Nepal: Christmas and Christianity", *The Telegraph Weekly*, Kathmandu, 1 February 2012, at http://www.telegraphnepal.com/views/2012-01-02/nepal:-christmas-and-christianity.html (accessed on 12 August 2013). Rokaya is General Secretary of the National Council of Churches of Nepal (NCCN), Executive Committee member of United Christian Alliance of Nepal (UCAN), Founding Vice-President of Inter-Religious Council of Nepal (IRCN), President of Nepal Intellectuals Forum and member of the National Human Rights Commission of Nepal (NHRC).
58. National Population and Housing Census 2011, *National Report, Volume 01*, Central Bureau of Statistics, Government of Nepal.
59. "Nepal's First-Ever Census Reveals Good News for Christians", *Christianity Today*, 30 November 2012, at http://www.christianitytoday.com/gleanings/2012/november/nepals-first-ever-census-reveals-good-news-for-christians.html (accessed on 19 August 2013).
60. "FNCN: Christian population below actual size," *The Kathmandu Post*, 6 December 2012, at http://www.ekantipur.com/the-kathmandu-post/2012/12/05/metro/fncn-christian-population-below-actual-size/242499.html (accessed on 19 August 2013).
61. Prakash A. Raj, "Money for nothing", *The Kathmandu Post*, 5 March 2012, at http://www.ekantipur.com/the-kathmandu-post/2012/03/05/oped/money-for-nothing/232309.html (accessed on 12 August 2013).
62. Ibid.
63. "There was no plan to meet armed groups: EU", *Republica*, 5 May 2010, at http://www.myrepublica.com/portal/index.php?action=news_details&news_id=19227 (accessed on 12 August 2013).
64. "Donors not to allow use of aid for violence, political gains," *Republica*, 23 November 2012.
65. "Diplomatic headache as envoys try to reach President", *The Himalayan Times*, 7 September 2012, at http://www.thehimalayantimes.com/fullNews.php?headline=Diplomatic+headache+as+ envoys+try+to+reach+prez&NewsID=346480 (accessed on 12 August 2013).

CHAPTER 7

Pakistan's Engagement with Nepal

Nepal figured prominently in Pakistan's foreign policy since the late 1950s. Especially during the monarchy period, India was a major factor in the consolidation of this relationship. After deciding to diversify Nepal's foreign policy, King Mahendra was also seeking international and regional support for his regime to reduce Nepal's dependence on India. Pakistan took advantage of King Mahendra's unhappiness over India's support to the democratic forces in Nepal and his craving for international recognition. The monarchy perceived India as the greatest challenge to its power and legitimacy. Pakistan, taking advantage of India-Nepal tension and also because of its enduring rivalry and strategic competition with India, sought a new ally in the neighbourhood. For Pakistan, no other country could have been more attractive in the region than Nepal, with whom India shares an open border. Apart from these factors, the two countries had many other commonalities—asymmetry vis-à-vis India in terms of territory, economy and military power, and similar apprehension regarding New Delhi's intentions. The anti-India stance of the elites in both the countries led to a deepening of relationship through high-level visits and discussions relating to their common concerns in South Asia.

Compared to other countries like India, China, the US and European countries, Pakistan's presence[1] in Nepal as a development partner, has been low key; but its diplomatic success rate in Nepal has been disproportionate to its presence. In spite of its limited contribution to the socio-economic development and also despite having played almost no role in the post-conflict period in Nepal, Pakistan has continued to be one of Nepal's friendliest neighbours. It is considered to be a benign neighbour by Nepal. On many occasions people in Nepal express their anti-India feelings by praising Pakistan. Most importantly, Pakistan has also managed to keep India's repeated allegations regarding its nefarious anti-India operations from Nepalese territory off the agenda of its bilateral meetings with Nepal. This is because some Pakistani leaders, in the past, have maintained good relations with the power centers—including the monarchy—in Nepal and have thus managed to achieve their limited strategic objectives. Since 1961, Pakistan has been asking Nepal to support its regional initiatives to limit India's influence both regionally and globally. One scholar wrote that Zulfikar Ali Bhutto, former prime minister of Pakistan, had equated Nepal with Afghanistan by saying:

> Nepal is to Pakistan what Afghanistan is to India–Nepal's proximity to East Pakistan and the vital states of Sikkim and Bhutan and the province of Assam with its Naga and Mizo freedom fighters give Nepal a high place in the calculations of Pakistan's foreign policy.[2]

Therefore, after India, Pakistan is the second South Asian country that considers Nepal to be of strategic importance. While for India the concern is cross border linkages, which can be easily penetrated by elements inimical to India's security; for Pakistan, Nepal is important because of its proximity to China and conflict theatres in the north-eastern flank of India. In fact, the open border between Nepal and India has been used to launch a proxy war against India by Pakistan.

Nepal is also much more comfortable with Pakistan and other smaller SAARC neighbours because it does not have any problems arising from identity, security and geographic proximity with them as it has with India. And the most important factor has been that Nepal does not share a border with any other South Asian country except with India. These countries are not engaged with Nepal on a day-to-day basis. In terms of people-to-people contact, India has the largest Nepalese Diaspora among SAARC countries. Since the 1960s, to counter India's influence, Nepal engaged with some external powers, who had adversarial relations with India.

In the post-monarchy period, Pakistan has been trying to readjust and expand its constituency in Nepal, especially among the Terai-based minority groups. Media reports indicated that during November 2013 CA elections some Terai based political parties' claimed having support from Muslims.[3] From field visits in Nepal, one gathers that Pakistan has established links with many Muslim groups in the region and even funded some of the candidates during elections. Therefore, Pakistan's links with other political groupings among the Terai-based minority groups cannot be ruled out. Moreover, Pakistan has also been reportedly funding some NGOs operating in southern Nepal for the recruitment and training of anti-India fundamentalist groups.[4]

Pakistan's Strategic Perspective on Nepal

As discussed earlier, the strategic importance of Nepal for Pakistan may not be the same as it is for other countries. To begin with, the first diplomatic contacts between them were made during their participation within the Non-Aligned Movement (NAM) forum and the Colombo plan. Since then, Pakistan has sought to engage Nepal to weaken India-Nepal relationship. Pakistan has succeeded to some extent because certain groups and regimes in Nepal perceive India to be an interventionist power and have been eager to court Pakistan as a pressure tactic. Moreover, certain sections in Nepal feel Pakistan is another South Asian country with similar grievances against India.

Pakistan's evolving relationship with Nepal has been shaped mostly by the geopolitical changes in South Asia in general and India's relationship with Pakistan in particular. Nepal's geographic location has been strategic for Pakistan. Virtually, it is India's northern front. For Pakistan, Nepal can be used as a strategic ally to counterbalance India in South Asia. Until the formation of Bangladesh, from Pakistan's point of view, Nepal did not matter much in its overall strategic calculus. The two countries had plans to utilise the ports in eastern Pakistan for trade and commerce purposes. Nepal's geographical proximity to India's disturbed northeastern region, which is affected by the presence of both Maoists and other separatist groups, might have attracted the attention of the Pakistani intelligence seeking to stoke the fire in the region. But matters changed after 1971 when Pakistan was truncated and Bangladesh was formed, which increased Nepal's importance for Pakistan as a launching pad for subversive activities directed against India. In the post-1971 period, Nepal continued to remain important for Pakistan both because of India's north-eastern conflict theatre, and as a corridor for easy infiltration of subversive elements through open border between India and Nepal. Thus "[i]n view of [India's] strategic location in the sub-continent, Pakistan and Nepal [royal administration] felt a need to develop close relations with each other."[5]

Anti-Democratic Front against India

During King Mahendra's regime, Nepal's relations with India were tepid. At that time Pakistan interpreted its relationship with Nepal as my-enemy's-enemy-is-my-friend. Also, Pakistan was comfortable with the lack of democracy in Nepal in keeping with its own political situation at that time. Pakistani leaders were also equally apprehensive about India's role in supporting democratic movement in its neighbourhood. Thus the Pakistani military leadership thought it prudent to support the monarchy in Nepal. Even prior to that, "[d]uring the times of President Ayub in Pakistan and King Mahendra in Nepal, both the rulers adopted a narrow based political system of 'basic' and 'Panchayat' democracy respectively. Both the rulers believed that the western type of democracy was not fit for their countries."[6] Even after the introduction of multiparty democracy in 1990, Pakistan stoked the anti-India sentiment in Nepal.

In response, Nepal, to some extent, was in accord with Pakistan's views with regard to deepening their relationship to counter India's influence in South Asia. Apart from other factors "political motivation to resist external interference...brought Nepal and Pakistan closer."[7] Being a small state, the monarchy was apprehensive of China's policy towards the Himalayan region as well as India's support for the democratic forces. Therefore, Nepalese leaders might have thought that strong bilateral relations with Pakistan, an all weather friend of China, worked in two different ways to their advantage—both to mellow down the Chinese, and spite the Indians.

In the early 1970s, Zulfikar Ali Bhutto, the then prime minister of Pakistan, said: "We [Nepal and Pakistan] share the same neighbours [India] and face identical problems. We should be sympathetic with each other in times of difficulty so that we can protect our freedom and achieve adequate progress."[8] He said this when India-Nepal relations had hit a rough patch over Nepal's decision to declare its territory a Zone of Peace (ZoP). Pakistan was the first country to recognise the ZoP proposal. As reciprocation, Nepal endorsed Pakistan's proposal to make South Asia a nuclear weapon-free zone in 1974. Pakistan's intention during this period was to create further distrust between Nepal and India by branding India as an interfering power in the region and to mobilise small countries against India.

Liberal Visa Regime of Nepal

Since tourism is a major revenue earner in Nepal, it has been following a liberal visa regime for quite some time. It offers visa-on-arrival for all except 11 countries in the world. Pakistani citizens are granted visa-on-arrival for 60 days, a facility that has been abused by many Pakistan-backed terrorists to reach Nepal and infiltrate into India using the open border. Pakistan took advantage of that when India tightened its border security in the north-western sector and the eastern sector.

With the declaration of the rehabilitation policy by the Jammu and Kashmir government, a large number of Kashmiri dissidents and local insurgents, who had crossed over to Pakistan occupied Kashmir (PoK) in the early 1990s with the objective of fighting to liberate Kashmir, returned to India via Nepal. In September 2012, for example, some Kashmiri dissidents, while returning from PoK, disclosed that after arriving in Kathmandu they destroyed their Pakistani passports and crossed the Nepal border to go to Kashmir.[9] As per media reports—based on intelligence sources—around 107 men and 43 women, the highest number in last five years, have crossed into India through the Nepal-India border till October 2012. The sources also reportedly said that between 2007 and 2011, around 188 men and 20 women, all Kashmiris, who had been living in PoK for over 15 years, had crossed over to India from Nepal. Indian security agencies suspect that there is a grand ISI design to carry out subversive activities in India through such easy movement of people and materials through the porous India-Nepal border.[10]

Muslims Presence in Terai

There is a strong Muslim presence in Nepal's Terai region, along the India-Nepal border. Islam is the third-largest religion in Nepal, accounting for 4.27 per cent of the population. Muslims have a strong presence in Banke (20 per cent), Kapilbastu (19.4 per cent), Parsa (15.4 per cent), Bara (13.4 per cent), Mahottari (19.4 per cent), Sunsari (10.9 per cent) and Rautahat (19.5 per cent) districts. These seven districts, which share a border with either Uttar Pradesh or Bihar, together account for 95.3 per cent of the Muslim population in Nepal.[11]

The Muslim dominated Terai region has become a major strategic location for the ISI operations in Nepal. Available documents indicate that the Islam followers, who had been largely quiet in Nepal, became politically active and began to raise their voice against Hindu extremism in the areas with the introduction of multi-party democracy in Nepal in 1990. The Muslims contested both the 1991 and 1994 parliamentary elections. The differences between the Hindus and Muslims in the Terai region increased further in the aftermath of the Ayodhya incident in Uttar Pradesh of India in 1992. The ISI, which had begun anti-India operation in 1989 in Nepal, took advantage of the situation. This was when bilateral relations between India and Nepal were at its lowest ebb due to economic blockade by India. The ISI reportedly established networks in Terai and was in touch with Mirza Dilshad Beg, who contested and won the Parliament seat from Kapilabastu-4 on the Rastriya Prajatantrik Party (RPP) ticket in the 1994 elections.[12] The Indian and Nepalese security agencies had confirmed that Beg was working for Dawood Ibrahim, who is still living in Karachi under ISI protection.[13] Quoting intelligence reports, the *Outlook* said that "apart from his [Beg] role in patronising international criminals and providing them logistical support, the don [Beg was] also associated with ISI activities in a big way."[14]

Moreover, ISI operations in Nepal have not been confined to the Terai region only. It has spread its tentacles across Nepal. For example, on 9 January 1994, the Nepalese police had conducted a raid at Hotel Karnali, Kathmandu, and seized many secret documents relating to ISI operations (Operation Tufail) against India from Nepalese territory.[15] Despite that raid, the ISI operations revived from the same hotel in 1996. Further, on 12 April 2001, Nepalese Police seized a large quantity of RDX explosive from the house of Muhammad Arshad Cheema, first secretary in the Pakistan embassy in Kathmandu. Besides, the mosques in Nepal are reportedly used by Islamist terrorists as shelter. For example, the NA had shot dead two Muslims inside a mosque at Mahalwari in Nawalparasi district of Nepal on 5 May 2008. An unspecified amount of explosives were seized from the mosque during the operation. Several interactions during a fieldtrip and media reports, also indicated that LeT and IM members take shelter in Mosques located in western and central districts of Nepal.[16]

Some media reports have indicated that the ISI has been regularly funding madarsas[17] in these districts (Terai, western and central) and providing training to IM, LeT activists and other terrorist groups. The activities of these groups have increased due to political instability in Nepal since 2006. The ISI reportedly prints counterfeit Indian and Bangladeshi currencies in Pakistan, and circulates it through its organised networks in Nepal and Bangladesh. A major portion of the money received from this business is used to fund terrorist and jehadi outfits like LeT, IM, Hizbut Tahrir, Hizbut Towhid and separatist movements in Jammu and Kashmir.[18]

India expressed its concerns over the operations of Islamist fundamentalist groups in the border regions at the home secretary-level bilateral talks in January 2012 and also in June 2013. During the 2013 meeting, Indian officials raised the issue of jehadis using Nepal as a new route for infiltration into India through the porous border between two countries. India also informed Nepal that madarsas located in the border region have been receiving illegal funding and that there has been an increase in the smuggling of fake Indian currency notes by Pakistani nationals through Nepal to India.[19] Within seven months of this meeting the Nepalese Police arrested three persons, two of them Pakistani nationals, and seized INR 29 lakh in counterfeit Indian currency from them. According to the police, the currency was brought to Kathmandu from Karachi by the two Pakistani nationals.[20]

Source of Strategic Information

Nepal is the only country from where Pakistan can easily collect information about the deployment of various Indian Army regiments/formations. Every year, a large number of Gorkha soldiers are recruited by the Indian Army from the Pokhara region. A large number (around 85 per cent) of retired Gorkha soldiers also live there. Pakistan's presence in this area came to light when a large number of Gorkhas protested against India deploying the Gorkha battalion during the Kargil conflict. Moreover, in 1994, the Pakistan-based Sachal Engineering Works (Private) Limited secured a road repairing contract from the Government of Nepal in the Marshyangdi-Kairenitar sector. The company recruited some retired Gorkha soldiers and their relatives for the purpose and had also submitted tenders to extend and renovate the Biratnagar Airport.[21]

Presence of Kashmiri Diaspora

There is a large presence of Kashmiri businessmen in Nepal—mostly in Kathmandu and they frequently visit Kashmir. Some media reports and interrogation of arrested Kashmir-based terrorists have revealed that the ISI is in touch with them. Quoting the US official sources, WikiLeaks reported that:

> To dispatch men and material and to execute explosions in India, Kathmandu was invariably made the nodal point and JKIF (Jammu and Kashmir Islamic Front) exploited the vulnerable Kathmandu-based Kashmiri businessmen for such activities since they had a readymade and clean past. JKIF kingpin Javed Krawah himself used to run a carpet business in Kathmandu.[22]

The involvement of Pakistani agencies with Kashmiris living in Nepal is indicated by the celebration of Kashmir Solidarity Day by the Pakistani embassy in Kathmandu every year on 5 February with lot of pomp and fanfare. Pakistan's material support to Jammu and Kashmir militants through Nepal has also been confirmed by many arrested terrorists. Quoting the interrogation report of two arrested militants, Mushtaq Ahmed Dar and Shamima alias Shazia alias Bitti, media reports indicated that they had received money from Altaf Qadri, executive member of the All Parties Hurriyat Conference (APHC), presently in Pakistan, from Kathmandu in March 2002, at the instance of Jammu Kashmir Liberation Front (JKLF) chief Mohammad Yasin Malik.[23]

Bilateral Relations (1950 to 1990)

The Pakistan-Nepal relationship was formalised in March 1960. It is based on the five principles of peaceful coexistence. Earlier, the two countries used to discuss bilateral issues on the sidelines of the preparatory meetings of the Colombo Plan and NAM. In fact, Pakistan wanted to establish formal relations with Nepal in 1947.[24] Since Nepal's foreign policy was India-centric and India had a wide ranging influence on its foreign, defence and economic affairs until 1955,[25] Pakistan's proposal for establishing formal relations with Nepal did not materialise. Moreover, given the regional turmoil during that time, Nepal had a close and special relationship with India. M.D. Dharamdasani has observed:

> Pakistan tried to woo the Nepalese by alleging that India had undermined the independence and sovereignty of its small neighbours and pursued aggressive policies towards them. But Nepal [King Tribhuvan] reacted sharply to Pakistani attempts by sending a strong protest to Pakistan.[26]

Apart from that, the Nepal Government was busy settling its internal political squabbles and managing the impending threats to Nepal's territorial integrity, especially those emanating from China's claims over the Himalayas. It was only after King Mahendra dissolved parliament in December 1960, the diplomatic relationship took momentum as part of his anti-India policy.

Mahendra enunciated Nepal's new foreign policy of maintaining an equidistance with India and China and diversified the foreign policy to reduce dependence on neighbouring countries. That policy consolidated Nepal's bilateral diplomatic relationship with Pakistan. Mahendra was the first head of state and government to visit Pakistan in September 1961. During this visit Pakistan conferred the "Nishan-i-Pakistan", its highest civilian decoration, on him. In response, King Mahendra conferred the "Ojaswi Rajan", Nepal's highest civilian decoration, on President Ayub Khan during his 12-day visit to Kathmandu in May 1963. It may be noted that India and Nepal have never exchanged such decorations.[27]

The domestic political situation brought the ruling regimes in both the countries even closer. When India criticised King Mahendra's action against democracy, Pakistan supported him, and justified it, because it was on the lines of Ayub's coup in 1958. During Mahendra's visit to Pakistan in 1961, Ayub Khan was reported to have had advised him "to go ahead with his new scheme [party-less Panchayat System] without worrying about what somebody else from outside said."[28] India's change of policy in 1962 towards the monarchy was evident when it formally recognised the establishment of Panchayat system,

Table 7.1: Pakistan-Nepal Official Visits (1961-2010)

Nepal			Pakistan		
Date	*Visiting Official*	*Issues Agreed upon*	*Date*	*Visiting Official*	*Issues agreed upon*
Sept 1961	King Mahendra	NA	May 1963	Ayub Khan	Resident Diplomatic Mission
Nov 1980	King Birendra	NA	Sep 1970	Yahya Khan	Transit and port facilities, scholarships to Nepal students
1975	PM, Nagendra P. Rijal	NA	Feb 1975	Faizal I. Chandhuri	Supported ZoP
Feb 1983	PM, Surya B. Thapa	NA	May 1983	Zia-ul-Haq	Joint Economic Commission
Aug 1988	PM, Marich M.S. Shrestha/ King Birendra*	NA	May 1994	PM, Benazir Bhutto	MoU on cultural exchange
—	—	NA	Jan 2002	Pervez Musharaf*	
Nov 1996	PM, Sher B. Deuba	FS level consultation mechanism, Joint Business Council	Nov 2004	PM, Shaukat Aziz*	Offered military training and equipment
			Apr 2010	PM, Yousaf R. Gilani	Prospects of investments

*Led SAARC delegation and also discussed bilateral issues. NA—Not available, PM—Prime Minister, FS—Foreign Secretary.
Source: Hiranya Lal Shrestha, *Golden Jubilee-Nepal-Pakistan Relations*, Janamaitri Prakashan, Kathmandu, December 2010.

which brought the two countries together again. This, to some extent, led to a slump in Pakistan-Nepal relationship.[29] Pakistan also insisted that Nepal openly support it on the Kashmir issue, condemn India during its wars with Pakistan and not allow the Gorkhas to fight against Pakistan. Pakistan did not like Nepal's neutrality on these issues. The emergence of Bangladesh altered the geopolitical calculations in South Asia and both Pakistan and Nepal realised the limited scope for external forces, including China and the US, to play a role in the subcontinent.[30] India's image in Nepal changed after this development. The leadership in Nepal felt that India was more influential than other countries in the region, and therefore it was not wise on their part to antagonise India by supporting Pakistan on the Kashmir issue.

The relationship was consolidated further by the visits of President Yahya Khan and Zia-ul-Haq in September 1970 and May 1983 respectively. Yahya Khan offered transit and port facilities to Nepal. The officials of the two countries also discussed cooperation in trade and economic matters. Pakistan increased the number of scholarships for Nepalese students for higher and professional studies in Pakistan. Zia-ul-Haq signed an agreement for the setting up of a Joint Nepal-Pakistan Economic Commission (JEC). The 5th minister-level meeting of the JEC was held in Kathmandu in March 2005. The two countries signed a Free Trade Agreement (FTA) at the end of the meeting. Nepal became the second country in South Asia to enter into an FTA with Pakistan after Sri Lanka. Pakistan also offered a US$5 million credit facility to Nepal for furthering bilateral and economic relations.[31]

Many official meetings also took place during this period on the sidelines of the SAARC summit and *en route* to other countries via Pakistan. For example, King Mahendra undertook an unofficial visit to Pakistan in 1967. King Birendra attended the fourth SAARC summit in Islamabad in December 1988. During the 1960s and 1970s, the kings of Nepal used Pakistan airports to visit other countries, thus proclaiming their independence from India.[32]

Relations During Democratic Regimes

Over the years, the relationship has acquired a dynamic of its own. Initially, the contacts were between the heads-of-the states; however, gradually it has led to regular government-to-government and people-to-people interaction. With the introduction of multiparty democracy in Nepal, Pakistan may now seek to appeal to the popular sentiments more proactively to deepen bilateral relations to further its strategic interests vis-à-vis India. Both the countries have so far diversified their relationship by encouraging Track-II level visits, business and media delegations, tourism, increasing educational scholarships and training programmes for government officials, especially those offered by Pakistan to Nepal. During Prime Minister Benazir Bhutto's official visit to Kathmandu in May 1994, the two countries signed an MoU on cultural exchange.

With the onset of the Maoist insurgency in Nepal in 1996, Pakistan wanted to exploit the anti-India feeling and political instability in Nepal to its own advantage. In this regard, the ISI contacted the Maoists for supplying them with arms and ammunition to fight against India. The chairman of then CPN (Maoist), Prachanda, has said on record: "It was not a direct offer. The ISI wanted to know whether we wanted any kind of help, especially outside Nepal."[33] However, given the warm relationship the royalty shared with Pakistan, it is difficult to imagine that the ISI wanted to enable the Maoists against the king. Perhaps there was a move by Pakistani intelligence to use the Maoists to reach out to similar forces in India to fuel subversion in different parts of India beyond Kashmir. Another reason for Pakistan's offer to the Maoists could be to discredit the democratic forces in Nepal who were pro-India in their approach.

Interestingly, Pakistan's pro-monarch stance became very clear later, during the visit of Shaukat Aziz, former prime minister of Pakistan, to Kathmandu in November 2004, when he openly offered to equip and train the Nepalese Army to fight the Maoists. Nepal did not consider the offer seriously then because it was already getting military support from India, the US and the UK.

After the royal takeover in February 2005, when these countries stopped the supply of arms, King Gyanendra approached Pakistan and China for arms. Justifying the king's action, President Pervez Musharraf said "a nation is not made for democracy, democracy is made for the nation. If the nation is suffering, something has to be done."[34] Pakistan's second round of attempts to bolster an authoritarian anti-India regime proved unsustainable due to India's timely support to the democratic forces in the latter part of 2005.

Since top Nepalese Maoist leaders were reportedly living in India at that time, King Gyanendra and some of his advisers grew suspicious that India had been supporting the Maoists to increase its leverage in Nepal by abolishing the monarchy. To get even with India, Gyanendra overlooked India's security concerns, may be with the intention of keeping India focused on its internal security issues. It has been observed that district level officials (specially from security agencies) sympathetic to ultra-nationalist and royalist forces deliberately ignored the ISI operations in their jurisdictions since India did not act upon their intelligence input to arrest Maoist leaders during their stay in India. Gyanendra perhaps wanted to follow in his father's footsteps by bringing foreign powers in Nepal to neutralise India's influence. Pakistan took advantage of this opportunity to regain lost ground by reactivating ISI stations and supporting the opening of new madarsas in the Terai region of Nepal to target India.

Nepal-Pakistan Relations in Post-Conflict Period

In the post-conflict period, Pakistan has been looking to diversify its relations with Nepal by investing in water resources development, banking and tourism sectors as stated by then Prime Minister Yousaf Raza Gilani during his one day visit to Kathmandu on 27 April 2010 on his way to attend the SAARC summit in Thimpu.[35] He was the first Pakistani prime minister to visit Kathmandu after five years. Despite its limited resources, Pakistan provided development assistance to Nepal. Moreover, Pakistan has shown a greater interest in developing cultural ties with Nepal. Table 7.2 indicates that there has also been a steady increase in the number of Pakistani tourists coming to Nepal since 2004. It increased further after the signing of the tourism cooperation agreement on 7 February 2009 by the two countries. However, the number of tourists from Pakistan to Nepal is less than ten per cent of the total tourist-arrival in Nepal in a year. Therefore, both the countries have agreed to increase the number of daily flights to facilitate people-to-people contacts and promote tourism.

Table 7.2: Pakistani Tourists to Nepal

Year	*Tourists from Pakistan*	*Total number of tourists visited Nepal*	*% share of Pakistani in total tourist*
2001	2319	361237	0.6
2002	1231	275468	0.4
2003	761	338132	0.2
2004	2020	385297	0.5
2005	1753	375398	0.5
2006	1861	383926	0.5
2007	2587	526000	0.5
2008	3248	500277	0.6
2009	3918	509752	0.8
2010	4342	602867	0.7
2011	4889	736215	0.6

Source: Hiranya Lal Shrestha, Golden Jubilee-Nepal-Pakistan Relations, Janamaitri Prakashan, Kathmandu, December 2010. Ministry of Culture, Tourism and Civil Aviation, Government of Nepal.

The new democratically elected government in Pakistan under the leadership of Nawaz Sharif revived its bilateral relations with Nepal. Both the countries had discussed the FTA in the Joint Technical Committee meeting held in Kathmandu in July 2013. Further, after a gap of eight years, the 6th Pakistan-Nepal Joint Economic Commission (JEC) met in Islamabad from 19-20 August 2013. During the meeting, both the countries discussed the diversification of bilateral relations in trade and commerce; in banking and finance; agriculture, energy, information technology and telecommunication, health, tourism, education, postal services and civil aviation sectors.[36] Speaking at the meeting the Finance Minister of Pakistan Muhammad Ishaq Dar stated that since the new government wants to strengthen relationship with South Asian countries, and Nepal remains an important neighbour for Pakistan, and therefore, it was "keen to enhance its existing friendly relations with Nepal for exploiting new avenues for cooperation in commercial and economic fields for mutual benefit of the two countries."[37]

After that statement, Pakistani media observed that Nepal has been formally part of Pakistan's 'look east policy' and the government should pursue the policy vigorously.[38] Earlier, China and some East Asian countries formed part of Pakistan's look east policy. The objective of the look east policy was to counter India's 'look west policy', especially with regard to Afghanistan. It is important to mention that after the JEC meeting Ishaq Dar proposed that "Pakistan should receive transit permission from India for Pakistan-Nepal trade as a *quid pro quo* for India-Afghanistan trade transiting through Pakistan, as sought by India."[39]

Implications of Pakistan's 'Look East Policy'

This policy-shift of including Nepal in its 'look east policy' indicates that Pakistan wants to have a long-term presence in Nepal by using soft diplomacy. Its move to expand the scope of bilateral relations and its eagerness to invest in infrastructure developments in the border regions, close to Pokhara and Terai, could strengthen its tactical presence in Nepal to undertake nefarious activities against India, and to justify the presence of extra manpower in its Kathmandu mission. Thus, India might witness more subversive activities directed against it by Pakistan-sponsored militants in future.

Nepal assumed a new place in Pakistan's foreign policy by late 1980s, especially after the Soviet withdrawal from Afghanistan and failure of its overall policy on Kashmir. So far it had resorted to war, anti-India propaganda and raising of the Kashmir issue at international fora, etc, without much effect.

With the success of insurgency in Afghanistan, the Pakistan Government wanted to replicate this experience in Jammu and Kashmir. The ISI diverted the attention of some of the Mujahideen groups towards Kashmir and provided training and logistical support to them. The post-Zia-ul-Haq civilian government also considered it a favourable option. For example, some reports suggest that Benazir Bhutto, then prime minister of Pakistan, had reportedly advised the ISI to destabilise India by waging a "proxy war strategy rather than resort to conventional war."[40] Apart from infiltrating insurgents through the Line of Control (LoC), Pakistan seemed to use the India-Nepal border for movement of insurgents and materials. The hijack of Indian Plane from Kathmandu in December 1999 indicated that the ISI had spread its tentacles well inside Nepal by the turn of the century.

In the post-9/11 period, when Pakistan was forced to stop infiltration through LoC in Kashmir, Nepal remained important as a country of passage for insurgents pushed by Pakistan into India. Nepal even assumed greater significance in ISI calculations, in the wake of fencing of International Border (IB) and LoC by India as well as Awami League's coming to power in Bangladesh, since 2008, known for its sensitivity to Indian concerns. ISI must be now much more dependent on the Nepal route than ever before. This may explain Pakistani efforts to retain its warm relations with Nepal in recent years.

Over the years, Pakistan has undertaken several development programmes to woo the Nepalese, especially in the Terai region. The Pakistan embassy has been working as the nodal agency for this purpose. The embassy, "besides performing other functions also keeps close contacts with Muslims"[41] in the Terai region. After India opened a Consulate at Biratnagar, Pakistan also applied to open a similar office there. The Nepal government rejected the proposal because Pakistan could give no good reason for doing so. The Indian Government also opposed the proposal of establishment of a Pakistani Consulate in Biratnagar, given its proximity to India-Nepal border. The objective may have been to cultivate Muslims in the Terai region, and set up new networks in the border region to supply fake Indian currency into India and extend support to Islamist fundamentalist groups operating in India.

Despite the arrests of Pakistan-based terrorists at the India-Nepal border, the sharing of intelligence reports and Nepal's assurance not to allow any external forces to use Nepalese territory for anti-India activities, Pakistan-sponsored terrorists continue to use Nepalese territory for training, recruitment, fund raising and as a shelter. The arrest of Mehrajuddin alias Javed Ahmad in September 2012, Abdul Karim Tunda[42] on 16 August 2013 and the arrest of IM founder Yasin Bhatkal on 28 August 2013 from the Nepal-India border are glaring examples of Pakistan using Nepalese territory for anti-India activities. During his interrogation by the Indian police on 12 September 2012, Mehrajuddin admitted that he had returned from Pakistan via Nepal and was "recruiting youth for militant attacks". He was allegedly involved in the hijack of Indian aircraft IC-814 in 1999 from Kathmandu.[43] He disclosed that a diplomat of an unspecified embassy (in Nepal) was closely involved in the plot. Police suspect that he was involved in smuggling weapons, ammunition and fake currency into India with the help of the diplomat.[44]

The ISI operation against India from Nepalese soil was further confirmed by David Coleman Headly, the American terror mastermind. He disclosed to the National Investigation Agency (NIA) in June 2010 that apart from a 'Karachi set up' the ISI also has a 'Nepal set up', which manages ISI networks in India. Abdur Rehman (retired Major of the Pakistan Army) had set up the Nepal station in the eastern part of the country and both Karachi and Nepal stations work closely.[45]

Anti-India Campaigning on Regional Issues

Pakistan has been constantly lobbying to convince Nepal to support China's attempts to have a major say in South Asian affairs. It has also tried to convince Nepal that their problems are identical and they have to work together to ward off the Indian influence. In addition, Pakistan also needs the support of Nepal in SAARC and other international fora to neutralise India's position on regional issues. During an interaction with a Nepalese media delegation in May 2008 in Islamabad, a senior official of the Ministry of Foreign Affairs of Pakistan, said "Pakistan accorded great priority to the relations with Nepal as both the countries share similar views and feelings on several regional and international forums, including SAARC and the United Nations".[46]

It was a major diplomatic victory for Pakistan when King Gyanendra linked the inclusion of Afghanistan as member to China's application to be associated as dialogue partner/observer with SAARC at the 13th SAARC summit in Dhaka in November 2005.[47] Pakistan opposed this because it did not want India to have a mutually beneficial relationship with Afghanistan. Nepal supported Pakistan's proposal for granting observer status to China to counter-balance India's role in South Asia and to gain Chinese support for the monarchy. Therefore, Nepal, in fact, did not accept the proposals made by several delegations that "SAARC sign a memorandum of association with China while admitting Afghanistan as a member."[48]

Pakistan has always linked regional political and economic instability with the resolution of the Jammu and Kashmir issue to pressurise India. Pakistani officials in bilateral meetings and other functions point out that: "The biggest impediment, however, on the path of lasting peace in South Asia is the Kashmir dispute. The Kashmir dispute has not only remained a stumbling block in the friendly relations between Pakistan and India but it has also forestalled the greater intra-regional economic and social interface".[49] Although Pakistan did raise the Kashmir issue at the 17th SAARC summit in Maldives, other SAARC member-countries are of opinion that India-Pakistan relations have been affecting the implementation of resolutions passed in the SAARC summits.

Cross Border Terrorism: Implication for India-Nepal Relations

On the security front, Nepal has its own concerns about the open border. Prior to 2006, the Nepalese Government was worried about the misuse of the open border by the Maoists. Nepal expected India to treat Nepalese Maoists as terrorists and take strong action against them just as India expected Nepal to take action against the LeT and IM.[50] In the post-conflict period, Nepal is worried about the misuse of the open border by criminal elements and Terai based armed groups. Therefore, Nepal expects reciprocity from India to take action against recalcitrant elements of the Maoist factions, Terai-based armed groups and criminals, who often take shelter in the Indian border districts.

The growing Islamic radicalism in the Terai region is another concern for Nepal. A report of the Home Ministry of Nepal in August 2013 identified seventeen types of crimes committed including involvement of international criminal and terrorist groups on its border with India. In this regard, the Ministry prepared a Cross-Border Crime Control Action Plan 2013 to prevent misuse of the border. Some analysts are of opinion that in the post-monarchy period, "the Pakistanis, through their military intelligence agency, may be inclined to seek additional ways to cause internal problems in India, and Nepal has always had that potential".[51] Media reports also suggest that several terrorist outfits have been operating clandestinely from Nepal. Some of these organisations have been identified as "Nepal Islamic Yuva Sangh, Kashmir Jama Masjid Democratic Muslim Association and Nepal World Islamic Council."[52]

While growing Chinese influence in Nepal remains a strategic challenge for India, the new look east policy of Pakistan to deepen its engagement with Nepal may add to India's security concerns. There is a perception in Nepal that India is involved in that country because of its concern relating to anti-India elements, especially Pakistan-sponsored terrorists. India feels that Pakistani sponsored terrorists would take advantage of prolong political instability and weak public order in Nepal. The continued use of Nepalese territory as a safe haven by anti-India elements may affect bilateral relations between the two countries. As a well-known Nepalese analyst would observe:

> India assumes that Pakistan's presence in Nepal takes many forms. The indicators include growth of *madrasas* and a Muslim population, the presence of Kashmiri Muslims, floating of fake Indian currency, underworld investment and a "visible negative attitude" against Indians in Nepal.[53]

Aid and Trade

Pakistan's economic assistance to Nepal is designed to support its clandestine operations there whose target is India. Under the JEC programme, most of the sectors identified for bilateral economic cooperation relate to southern Nepal.[54] Earlier, Pakistan had shown its keenness to invest in textile and cotton production, irrigation and livestock development in Nepal. All these sectors are based in the Terai region.[55] Pakistan has hardly undertaken any major socio-economic development programme in the relatively poorer mountainous districts of Nepal. Despite itself being heavily dependent on foreign aid, Pakistan has given development assistance, soft loans and made commercial investments in Nepal. It is interesting to note that Pakistan provided raw material for the Chinese-funded textile factory at Hetauda, most of which were transported by air from Pakistan.[56]

Trade

Pakistan and Nepal signed a trade agreement in October 1962, which provided for most-favoured-nation (MFN) status. Until December 1971, Pakistan was Nepal's second-largest trade partner after India. Pakistan exempted customs duty and other charges on goods transiting through East Pakistan. After the formation of Bangladesh, bilateral trade declined due to absence of any direct physical trade route.[57] Table 7.3 presents the status of current trade levels.

Table 7.3: Nepal-Pakistan Trade (2001-2002 to 2010-2011)

(*Value in '000 NPR*)

Year	*Nepal Export to Pakistan*	*Import from Pakistan*	*Trade Balance*
2001/2	61,558	133,130	–71572
2002/3	73,981	153,411	–79430
2003/4	277,840	191,415	+86425
2004/5	229,369	166,847	+62522
2005/6	186,228	191,380	–15152
2006/7	126,944	171,455	–44511
2007/8	80,681	179,766	–99085
2008/9	86,003	248,893	–162890
2009/10	78,971	281,240	–202269
2010/11	142,338	293,747	–151409

Source: Trade and Export Promotion Centre, Ministry of Commerce and Supplies, Government of Nepal.

The Table shows that the trade relationship between Nepal and Pakistan is hardly impressive. Except in 2003/4 and 2004/5, the trade balance has been in favour of Pakistan. Amongst the SAARC countries, Pakistan is the third largest trading partner of Nepal after India and Bangladesh. Nepal imports surgical equipment, salt, cotton, leather goods, and sports items and exports cardamom, mustard seed, tea, Pashmina, raw hides and skins and handicrafts. The absence of direct trade and transit routes is a major factor limiting the scope of trade between two countries. They have been seeking alternative trade routes like highway linkages through the Karakoram-Tibetan Autonomous Region. Therefore, both support the role of China in developing trade connectivity in South Asia. Both countries have also been supporting SAARC trade routes for uninterrupted trade.[58] Speaking at the Lahore Chamber of Commerce and Industry (LCCI) on 21 June 2012, then Nepalese Ambassador to Islamabad, Bharat Raj Paudyal, indicated that economic cooperation between both the countries should be further enhanced because Nepalese businessmen feel comfortable in dealing with Pakistani traders.[59]

Commenting on Pakistan-Nepal trade relations, one Pakistani scholar observed that there are two major hindrances affecting the free flow of trade between Nepal and Pakistan. The first constraint is the landlocked territory of Nepal and second is Nepal's dependence on India. Therefore, Pakistan's efforts since the 1960s have been to reduce Nepal's heavy dependence on India and to help Nepal find alternative trade routes.[60] However, Pakistan's strategy did not work after the formation of Bangladesh. While continuing its effort, Pakistan has been asking Nepal to look for alternative routes either in the north (through TAR) or explore SAARC trade routes.

Conclusion

Pakistan's relationship with Nepal is mainly driven by its strategic interests rather than any genuine inclination to forge close ties with the people of Nepal. It is clear from the discussion above that Pakistan backed the authoritarian regimes in Nepal and sought to secure its interests. While the international community supported peace and reconciliation in Nepal through mainstreaming of the Maoists in 2005, Pakistan chose to supply weapons to the king, who was rather looking for a military solution. While India was sympathetic to the democratic forces in Nepal, Pakistan sought to negate India's efforts and tarnish its image among the region's smaller countries. In the post-conflict period, Pakistan has tried to make amends and it is seen to be expanding its political and economic engagements with Nepal. In the absence of the monarchy, it is seeking to strengthen its engagement by building relations with like-minded political groups and adopting a wait-and-watch policy to consolidate its strategic interests in Nepal.

*

NOTES

1. Primary and secondary data in this area is scarce. Given this fact, the author has had to depend heavily on a single publication of the Pakistan Embassy in Kathmandu. A future study on this area would require consultation of detailed archives.
2. M.D. Dharamdasani, "India as a Factor in Pakistan-Nepal Relations", in Ramakant, *et al.*, (eds), *Contemporary Pakistan: Trends and Issues, Vol. II*, Kalinga Publications, Delhi, 2001, p. 244. Z.A. Bhutto was prime minister of Pakistan from 1973 to 1977.
3. "Analysis: Mushrooming blocs on which 'politics will revolve", *ekantipur,* Kathmandu, 3 October 2012.
4. Author's interactions with Madhesi leaders and common people during a research trip to Nepal in June 2011 and November 2013.
5. M. D. Dharamdasani, "India as a Factor in Pakistan-Nepal Relations", n. 2, p. 243.
6. Ibid.
7. Hiranya Lal Shrestha, *Golden Jubilee-Nepal-Pakistan Relations*, Janamaitri Prakashan, Kathmandu, December 2010, p. 2.
8. Zulfikar Ali Bhutto's interview to the media in April 1975. For more details, see Hiranya Lal Shrestha, *Golden Jubilee-Nepal-Pakistan Relations*, n.7.
9. "Rebuilding lives in Kashmir", *BBC News* (India), 12 August 2012. Abdul Rashid Khan in an interview to BBC said "We traveled on Pakistani passports to Nepal. The first day we checked into a hotel in Kathmandu as Pakistani citizens. The next day, we destroyed our passports and drove up to the Indian border near Gorakhpur in Uttar Pradesh state".

Another group also did the same thing before crossing over to India. For more information see "40 flee Pak-Occupied Kashmir for Dubai, enter India via Nepal", *The Indian Express,* 11 May 2012.

10. "Pak infiltration through Nepal border increases alarmingly", *The Times of India*, 25 October 2012.
11. Pitamber Sharma, *Unravelling the Mosaic*, Himal Books, Kathmandu, 2008, p. 18.
12. Mollica Dastidar, *Understanding Nepal: Muslims in Plural Society*, Har-Anand publications Pvt. Ltd, New Delhi, 2007, p.168.
13. LeT senior member Tunda disclosed this to Indian security agencies after he was held from India-Nepal border on 16 August 2013. For details see "Dawood in Karachi under ISI protection, says Tunda," *Hindustan Times*, 18 August 2013, at http://www.hindustantimes.com/India-news/NewDelhi/Dawood-in-Karachi-under-ISI-protection-says-Tunda/Article1-1109417.aspx (accessed on 25 August 2013).
14. Rajesh Joshi, "Dawood's Man In Nepal", *Outlook India*, New Delhi, 15 June 1998, at http://www.outlookindia.com/article.aspx?205702 (accessed on 25 August 2013). For more details about the ISI operations in Nepal see Josy Joseph, "Twilight zone", *rediff*, at http://www.rediff.com/news/2000/jan/18jos.htm (accessed on 25 August 2013).
15. Josy Joseph, "Twilight zone," n. 14. Also see Srikanta Ghosh, *Pakistan's ISI: Network of Terror in India*, APH Publishing Corporation, New Delhi, 2000, p.148.
16. Ravi Sharma, India and Nepal: "The playground of the spies," *Frontline*, Delhi, 18 (09), 28 April - 11 May 2001. See "Nepal army kills two people inside mosque," *Yahoo.com*, 6 May 2002, at https://groups.yahoo.com/neo/groups/ProletarianNews/conversations/messages/5905. Also see "Two Muslims killed in Nepal Army attack on mosque", *Muslim Population*, at http://www.muslimpopulation.com/asia/Nepal/Two%20Muslims%20killed%20in%20Nepal%20Army%20attack%20on%20mosque.php (accessed on 6 May 2014).
17. For detailed information about madarsas, see "Intelligence alarm as Bihar govt soft on SIMI", *The Times of India*, 6 October 2001, at http://articles.timesofindia.indiatimes.com/2001-10-06/patna/27253191_1_madarsa-saudi-arabia-simi (accessed on 13 January 2014).
18. Kartikeya Sharma, "Pakistan officially printing fake Indian currency notes," *India Today*, New Delhi, 6 November 2013, at http://indiatoday.intoday.in/story/nia-fake-indian-currency-notes-pakistan/1/321768.html (accessed on 13 January 2014). Also see "Pakistani ISI circulating counterfeit currency in India and Bangladesh", *Weekly Blitz*, Dhaka, 3 November 2012, at http://www.weeklyblitz.net/2720/pakistani-isi-circulating-counterfeit-currency-in (accessed on 24 November 2012).
19. "Nepal-India security summit: 'Criminals using Nepal to push fake notes to India' ", *The Kathmandu Post*, 17 January 2012.
20. "Fake IC note smugglers made public", *The Himalayan Times*, Kathmandu, 8 August 2012.
21. Josy Joseph, "Working on the Gurkhas", *rediff*, at http://www.rediff.com/news/2000/jan/19jos.htm (accessed on 20 January 2014). IM operative Yasin Bhatkal disclosed to Indian Police that Pokhara has been the major shelter zone of the IM and the ISI as Kathmandu has come under the surveillance of international intelligence agencies. For details, see Ramashankar, "Nepal casino city turns jihadi hub", *The Telegraph*, Kolkata,, 31 August 2013.

22. The cable was signed off by the US Ambassador to India, Frank Wisner. For more information, see "ISI used Nepal as a hub for terror inside India: WikiLeaks", *The Indian Express*, New Delhi, 7 September 2011.
23. "JKLF chief appears before court", *Daily Excelsior*, 11 March 2005, at http://www.dailyexcelsior.com/web1/11mar05/news1.htm (accessed on 13 January 2014).
24. Hiranya Lal Shrestha, *Golden Jubilee-Nepal-Pakistan Relations*, n. 7.
25. S.D. Muni, "The Dynamics of Foreign Policy", in S.D. Muni (ed.), *Nepal: An Assertive Monarchy*, Chetana Publications, New Delhi, pp.131-132. Also see S.K. Jha, "Policy Towards India: Quest for Independence," in S.D. Muni (ed.), *Nepal: An Assertive Monarchy*, Chetana Publications, New Delhi, p.206.
26. M. D. Dharamdasani, "India as a Factor in Pakistan-Nepal Relations", n. 2, p. 245.
27. Hiranya Lal Shrestha, *Golden Jubilee-Nepal-Pakistan Relations*, n. 7.
28. M. D. Dharamdasani, "India as a Factor in Pakistan-Nepal Relations", n. 2, p.248.
29. India was critical of King Mahendra's taking over of government by dissolving democratically elected government in December 1960 and introduction of Panchayat system. Government of India softened its policy towards him with the onset of War with China in October 1962. A series of diplomatic exchanges between both the countries took place at India's initiatives. During these visits India tried to appease the king by recognising the Panchayat system, giving an assurance that it would not allow Indian territory for anti-king activities and also offered aid for economic and infrastructure development in Nepal. For details see S.D. Muni, *Foreign Policy of Nepal*, National Publishing House, Delhi, 1973, pp.124-128.
30. M. D. Dharamdasani, "India as a Factor in Pakistan-Nepal Relations", n. 2.
31. Hiranya Lal Shrestha, *Golden Jubilee-Nepal-Pakistan Relations*, n. 7.
32. Ibid.
33. Anirban Roy, *Prachanda: The Unknown Revolutionary*, Mandala Book Point, Kathmandu, 2008, p. 96.
34. "Musharraf gives tacit backing to Nepal King's power grab", *Outlook India*, New Delhi, 21 May 2005, at http://news.outlookindia.com/items.aspx?artid=299582 (accessed on 20 January 2014).
35. Hiranya Lal Shrestha, *Golden Jubilee-Nepal-Pakistan Relations*, n. 7.
36. "Preconditions for IMF loan fulfilled, says Dar," *The Nation*, Islamabad, 21 August 2013, at http://www.nation.com.pk/pakistan-news-newspaper-daily-english-online/editors-picks/21-Aug-2013/preconditions-for-imf-loan-fulfilled-says-dar (accessed on 25 August 2013).
37. "Nepal for trade concessions", *Dawn*, Karachi, 20 August 2013, at http://dawn.com/news/1036979/nepal-for-trade-concessions (accessed on 25 August 2013).
38. "Pakistan rightly looks towards East," *Pakistan Observer*, Islamabad, 21 August 2013, at http://pakobserver.net/detailnews.asp?id=215914 (accessed on 25 August 2013).
39. "Pakistan seeks Indian cooperation on transit trade with Nepal," *Global Post*, 20 August 2013, at http://www.globalpost.com/dispatch/news/kyodo-news-international/130820/pakistan-seeks-indian-cooperation-transit-trade-nepal (accessed on 25August 2013).
40. Bidanda M. Chengappa, *Pakistan, Islamisation, Army and Foreign Policy*, APH Publishing Corporation, New Delhi, 2004, pp. 115-32. For more information, see B. Raman, "A Terrorist State as a Frontline Ally (Lancer Paper 7)", *Indian Defence Review*, New Delhi, 2002.

41. S.D. Muni, *India and Nepal: A Changing Relationship*, Konark Publishers, Delhi, 1992, pp. 24-25.
42. Tunda alias Abdul Quddooss has allegedly been a member of the banned Pakistan-based Lashkar-e-Taiba (LeT) militant outfit. He was involved in the 1993 Mumbai blasts and over 40 other deadly bomb blasts across India. He is a well known LeT explosive expert/terrorist. For more information see "LeT terrorist Abdul Karim Tunda held by Delhi Police," *The Hindu*, 17 August 2013.
43. "Arrest in Kashmir in India IC-814 hijack case", *BBC News* (India), 13 September 2012, at http://www.bbc.co.uk/news/world-asia-india-19582592 (accessed on 13 February 2014). For more information, see "Kashmir militants give up fight and head home," *BBC News* (Asia), 31 May 2012.
44. "Diplomat involved in 1999 hijack: Terrorist", *The Times of India*, 14 September 2012, at http://timesofindia.indiatimes.com/india/Diplomat-involved-in-1999-hijack-Terrorist/articleshow/16389121.cms (accessed on 13 January 2014).
45. "ISI even has a 'Nepal set-up': Headley", *The Times of India*, 27 October 2010, at http://timesofindia.indiatimes.com/india/ISI-even-has-a-Nepal-set-up-Headley/articleshow/6817126.cms#ixzz13eDihsLN (accessed on 13 January 2014).
46. Yuba Nath Lamsal, "Steady Growth of Nepal-Pakistan Ties", *The Rising Nepal*, Kathmandu, 21 May 2008.
47. Siddharth Srivastava, "Delhi knocked out over China" *Asia Times*, 16 November 2005, at http://www.atimes.com/atimes/South_Asia/GK16Df03.html (accessed on 9 January 2014).
48. For more information see Amit Baruah, "Has Nepal been put up by Pakistan?," *The Hindu*, 13 November 2005, at http://www.hindu.com/2005/11/13/stories/2005111312930800.htm (accessed on 25 August 2013).
49. The statement was made by Charge'd Affaires of Pakistan Embassy in Kathmandu, Ahmar Ismail, in a gathering of Nepalese journalists, intellectuals and scholars on 5 February 2012. For details of the speech see "Pakistan will strive for regional peace and prosperity," *The Weekly Mirror*, Kathmandu, Date of publication is not available. Available at http://www.weeklymirror.com.np/index.php?action=news&id=1926 (accessed on 28 April 2014).
50. Yubaraj Ghimire, "Nepal's agony", Seminar, 3 September 2002, at http://www.india-seminar.com/2002/517/517%20yubaraj%20ghimire.htm (accessed on 13 January 2014).
51. Peter Burleigh, "Nepal: Western Views of the Maoist Insurgency and the Royal Takeover", Working Paper, 9 July 2005, Institute of Governmental Studies, University of California, Berkeley, p. 8.
52. "Indo-Nepal border the new den of militants", *The Hindu*, 9 March 2005, at http://www.hindu.com/2005/03/09/stories/2005030906550300.htm (accessed on 13 January 2014).
53. Yubaraj Ghimire, "Nepal's agony", n.50.
54. Following are the joint ventures established under the Nepal-Pakistan JEC: Silver Fibre Textile Mill at Nawalparasi, Vivid Textile Mill at Chitwan, Peacock Textile at Parsa, Himalayan Bank and Hotel Peaceful Palace, Kathmandu. The Nepal government has also approved six more Pakistan-based companies located in Kathmandu.
55. M.R. Josse, *Nepal and the World, Vol. 1*, Published by the author, Kathmandu, 1984, pp. 124-30.

56. Hiranya Lal Shrestha, *Golden Jubilee-Nepal-Pakistan Relations*, n. 7.
57. Ibid.
58. ibid.
59. "Nepal ready to make special bilateral trade arrangements", *Daily Times*, Lahore, 21 June 2012, at http://www.dailytimes.com.pk/default.asp?page=2012%5C06%5C21%5Cstory_21-6-2012_pg5_7 (accessed on 25 August 2013).
60. Ahmad Rashid Malik, "The Emerging Dimensions of Pakistan-Nepal Trade", *IPRI Journal*, Islamabad, 10 (1), Winter 2010, pp. 77-92.

CHAPTER 8

Conclusion

The presence of external powers in the Himalayan region has posed a critical challenge for Nepal's security and political stability. While Nepal has benefited from the flow of aid and economic assistance from these countries, due to their divergent strategic interests, they have acted at cross-purposes. This has had a deleterious impact on the internal political dynamics and hampered the twin processes of reconciliation and democratisation in Nepal. In certain cases, external intervention/involvement has intensified the inherent contradictions within Nepalese society and complicated the process of political transition.

For example, the US support to King Gyanendra against the Maoists had undeniably played its role in intensifying the conflict and affected the process of dialogue and reconciliation during 2001-2005. The US had reportedly discouraged the king from entering into any direct peace talks with the Maoists clearly misjudging the popular opinion in Nepal in favour of cessation of hostilities. Similarly, the role played by Western countries in exacerbating inter-ethnic discord can hardly be overlooked.

In recent years, China has also sought to deepen its relationship with Nepal with a view to countering the influence of India and various Western countries. In the process, it has tried to micro-manage internal politics of Nepal and ensure that the political transition in the post-monarchy period does not hamper its interests. Since 2008, China is seen to be proactively engaged with Nepal and sending several delegations at frequent intervals to understand the evolving political dynamic in Nepal. It is trying its best to strengthen its contacts with the state apparatus to manage its security concerns. With the abolition of the institution of monarchy, with whom China was quite effectively engaged, it has realised the need to build contacts with various political groups who are vying for influence in a democratic setting in Nepal.

As a small landlocked country, for a long time, Nepal spent much of its resources and diplomatic efforts to secure its territorial integrity and maintaining its identity as a sovereign country. Until 1955, Nepal was distinctly uneasy about the Chinese claims of suzerainty over various Himalayan countries. However, after King Mahendra took over, the threat perception to Nepal's security shifted from the north to the south more for political reasons. The king took advantage of the impact of the Cold War in South Asia and the border disputes between India and China. King Birendra, who succeeded Mahendra, followed the same policy with some modifications after taking global and regional developments into account. Despite the introduction of multiparty democracy in 1990, the monarchy continued to play a dominant role in Nepalese politics and foreign policy.

In the post-monarchy period, despite the Chinese worries about the political transformation in Nepal, the first democratically elected Maoist government largely continued the king's policy of maintaining 'equidistance' from India and China. The then Maoist government led by Prachanda sought to set a new trend in Nepal's foreign policy by visiting China before embarking on any other foreign trip in order to seek the support of the Chinese government on ideological grounds. It has been a trend in Nepal that the head of any new government makes his first foreign visit to India given the close relationship between the two countries. The Maoist-led government came to an end with the resignation of Prachanda in May 2009. Until the second Maoist-led government was formed under Baburam Bhattarai in August 2011, the radical elements of the Maoist party undertook several trips to Beijing and other cities of China to garner support for a Maoist-led government in an effort to neutralise India's influence.

As an influencial neighbour, India has been an important factor in Nepalese political dynamics. Some analysts even hold the view that India has been able to determine the course of Nepalese domestic politics for the longest time. They perceive that the fall of the Maoist government led by Prachanda as well as the delay in the Maoists' return to power was occasioned by India's intervention in Nepal's internal politics. This perception regarding India's role has, to some extent, made China to have a relook at its policy towards Nepal. China has, especially since 2008, sought to limit India's influence in Nepal by expanding its influence through developmental activities and cultural exchanges. There are indications that China's engagement with Nepal is not exclusively driven by its obsession with Tibet, but it may be part of its new strategic policy for South Asia, in keeping with its global aspirations. The emergence of the Maoists as a major political force and the declaration of Nepal as a Republic have also led to increasing engagements of the US, the UK, the EU and other European countries in Nepal. These external powers allegedly have their own favourites in Nepalese politics and also the capacity to influence their course of action.

India-Nepal relationship is based on strong historical and cultural ties that were institutionalised by the signing of the India-Nepal Treaty of Peace and Friendship in July 1950. Despite the existence of this Treaty, the relationship between the two neighbours has witnessed some strained phases because of various domestic, regional and global factors. India's traditional influence on Nepal has been adversely affected by the growing interest shown by extra-regional powers in Nepal in recent years. India's neighbours and extra-regional actors are not too mindful of India's genuine strategic interests in Nepal and strong historical, cultural, political and economic linkages between the two countries. Their interventions have contributed to an atmosphere of mistrust and suspicion in which India-Nepal relationship is currently embedded. There have also been some major shortcomings in India's foreign policy initiatives since independence towards the Himalayan States. First, immediately after independence, India largely followed the policy options evolved by the British colonial power towards its Himalayan neighbours. There was no real innovation in its approach. Until the mid-1970s, India's smaller neighbours felt insecure vis-à-vis India about their territorial integrity. Second, India's policy towards these neighbours has been reactive in nature. For example, India's annual development assistance to Nepal has been expanded from infrastructure to social sectors mainly in response to the aid policies of the US and the EU towards Nepal. This trend continues despite the policy-makers in India being aware of the growing Chinese influence in South Asia. Third, India's foreign policy, especially towards its South Asian neighbours in general and Nepal in particular, is overwhelmingly security-centric. Lastly, since foreign policy has not been an election issue at the domestic level and India's neighbourhood policy is dominated by Pakistan and China; Indian leaders have failed to give sufficient attention to smaller neighbours. Moreover, there is also high degree of complacency amongst policy-makers who take India's neighbours for granted even with regard to issues, which they consider sensitive. This has generated a sense of insecurity in these countries vis-à-vis India. Therefore, over a period of time, India's position on various issues perceived by the member of SAARC countries as hegemonic, where India has been continually trying to retain its sphere of influence in the neighbourhood, including in Nepal.

On the other hand, Nepal's excessive dependence on external powers (primarily for aid) and prolonged political instability in the post-monarchy period has made it vulnerable to the agenda of foreign countries. The differences between these external powers on various issues influence the position taken by political parties and civil society groups. This is reflected in the debates on various contentious issues during the Constitution-drafting process. The lack of consensus on the federalism issue, which was the main reason for the dissolution of the first Constituent Assembly, is a prime example. It took four years (from August 2008) to complete the process of integration of the former Maoist combatants into the Nepalese Army. Not only the political parties, but also the external powers remain divided over some of the issues that were debated in the Constituent Assembly. While India suggests an indigenous (Nepalese political party-driven) formula, with minimum influence of external powers to resolve the outstanding issues in Nepal, China and the US are seeking to play a larger role. As S.D. Muni observes, unlike India, China does not have any emotional and close links with Nepal; therefore, it can work with any party and institution, subject to their agreeing to take strong action against Tibetan refugees.[1]

The US argues that the UN should play a major role in the peace process and in the Constitution-drafting process. This is not acceptable to both India and China. Both were, to some extent, uncomfortable with the presence of UNMIN in Nepal, which wrapped up its mission in January 2011. Some Western analysts believe that India played a major role in the withdrawal of UNMIN from Nepal. China believes that the Western presence in Nepal (which includes many INGOs and NGOs backed by Western countries) will embolden the Tibetan rebels.

The developments in Nepal following the dissolution of the CA on 27 May 2012 and subsequent election for CA-II on 19 November 2013, indicate that political forces within Nepal continue to remain divided over many issues which may continue to pose challenges for the Constitution-making process. The prevailing uncertainty has also affected Nepal's economy and infrastructure development. The annual budget has been either delayed or hurriedly prepared, without taking people's interests into consideration. As a result, there has been closure of factories, flight of capital, loss of employment and entrepreneurial opportunities, labour migration, a huge trade deficit, energy crisis and double-digit inflation. The banking and financial sectors were in the throes of a liquidity crisis. FDI inflows into the country have declined; and new joint ventures have been delayed in the absence of a coherent economic policy. Investors felt insecure in Nepal due to the unstable political situation and the absence of a Constitution. The economic survey of Nepal, 2010/11 reported that Nepal's economic growth rate was limited to 3.5 per cent in comparison to 4.5 per cent GDP [Gross Domestic Product] growth achieved in 2009/10.[2] This has forced Nepal to depend on donor countries for funds to manage the development programmes. A depressed economy badly affected by chronic political instability makes Nepal even further vulnerable to political manipulation by external powers.

In the prevailing scenario, both India and China are now competing to invest in Nepal; this could turn out to be positive for Nepal if it is managed properly. China is already pressurising Nepal to give more concessions to its companies and take action against the Tibetan refugees. It may be recalled here that the Chinese Premier initially cancelled his trip to Nepal in December 2011 on the grounds that Nepal was not able to control anti-China activities of Tibetan refugees. Further, despite some improvement in the relations between India and China, the latter's unease over the possible coming together of the US and India against it, could also prompt Chinese proactive engagement in Nepal. Since China feels vulnerable due to the presence of Tibetan refugees in Nepal and India, and Western countries are perceived to be sympathetic to their cause, Beijing has sought repeated assurances from Nepal regarding its adherence to the 'one China policy' and commitment to take strong action against Tibetan rebels. Therefore, the former Chinese Ambassador to Nepal, Zheng Xianglin, declared: "Any foreign intervention in Nepal will not be tolerable for China."[3]

Chinese concern regarding the Tibetan unrest in Nepal was also emphasised when China reportedly discussed possible closure of the joint-military training facilities in Mustang district during the visits of political and military delegations to each other's country in 2013. China has also been suspecting, although baseless, that the Indian Army pension camps in Pokhara are being used to extend support to the anti-China elements (read Tibetan refugees). Therefore, China has been repeatedly demanding opening of a Consulate in Pokhara for monitoring purposes. China had considered India's presence near the Arnnapurna Conservation area as India's forward camp close to the southern Tibetan border. Therefore, China has been trying to counter-balance this by making its presence felt in Pokhara and Lumbini.

Nepal's Options

The diversification of Nepal's foreign policy in the early 1960s was an attempt to ensure regime security and its territorial integrity against perceived threat from its neighbours and also to reduce its dependence on India. The external powers took advantage of it and were motivated partly because of their own interests to have a foothold in this part of the world. While geography has remained a constant and a major determinant of Nepal's foreign policy, there have been occasions when some Nepali leaders misread the developments in the region and beyond, and tried to use external powers against regional actors.

Nepal has used its relationship with the Western countries to meet its developmental needs. In the past, this had also enabled to counter-balance India's influence. Until the early 1970s, the US was the top foreign aid donor to Nepal. In the post-Cold War period, the US influence in Nepal's domestic politics diminished as it shifted its focus to other regions of the world. Nepal again caught US attention due to the rise of India and China and the onset of the Maoist insurgency. The US tried to help the king in his anti-Maoist counter insurgency operations. While the political situation changed in 2005 and favoured the democratic forces, the US gradually came to recognise (reluctantly until 2009) India's efforts towards peace initiatives and political stability in Nepal. Interestingly, the US considered India to be a reliable partner in South Asia in the post-2012 period, when it enunciated its rebalance policy towards Asia. Since the third Indo-US strategic dialogue in 2011 it has more pronouncedly sought to partner with India to address common challenges in the region.

For China, Nepal will remain strategically relevant as long as the Tibet issue remains alive and the Tibetans continue to use Nepal as a transit point between India and Tibet. China has been undertaking large-scale development work in Tibet apart from its rapid 'Hanaisation' efforts to ensure a violence-free Tibet. However, with the changing geopolitical situation—with US and India synchronizing their policies, and with China and India choosing dialogue over confrontation to settle their dispute— Nepal's option of playing the 'US card' against India and its second option of using the 'China card' against India and vice-versa may not prove to be as effective as it was earlier. This is not to deny that Nepal will retain its strategic importance for all these countries. For India, Nepal is too important to be ignored. For China, Nepal is unlikely to lose its relevance. As part of the 'go global' policy, Chinese economic engagements with Nepal are also likely to grow in coming days followed by political engagement to ensure security for Chinese investors and to ward off any kind of threats from external forces by using Tibetan refugees living in Nepal.

Nepal, which was not earlier part of China's list of countries labeled as 'gateways to South Asia', is being reconsidered by China as a vibrant bridge after a proposal from former Nepalese Prime Minister Baburam Bhattarai to this effect. The US policy of rebalance to Asia and growing Indo-US ties are also likely to deepen Chinese interest in Nepal. So far, while strengthening its presence in Nepal, China has been careful about not antagonising India due to its larger geo-economic interests. However, given the existing trust deficit in India-China relations, largely due to unresolved border disputes and the effect of US rebalancing strategy in the region, situation may change rapidly. In such changed circumstances, growing Chinese influence in Nepal may reverse the strategic advantages that India has had in Nepal over the years. So far, various Nepalese rulers were using the 'China card' to extract benefits from India. However, if China increases its clout in Nepal, very soon India may have to contend with an even more unpleasant reality of China playing the 'Nepal card' against India. This could pose a strategic challenge for India.

Since the abolition of monarchy and re-introduction of multi-party democracy in 2008, common people in Nepal talk about the relevance of 'China card' against India. After the dissolution of the first CA, the younger generation and ultra-leftists and ultra-rightist groups are enthusiastic about strengthening their relationship with China, given its economic rise, and the perceived unsuccessful attempts by India since 2008 to bring about political stability in Nepal. There has also been a feeling that Western powers would have limited role in the political transition. The perception in Nepal is that India would have less leverage in Nepal with the improved connectivity between China and Nepal in the next 20 years or so. Industrialisation in Tibet and improvement in border infrastructure will create an alternative market for Nepal. In this context, given the negative public perception of India in Nepal, the new political forces/actors there may attempt to play the China card to balance India.

The changing geopolitical dynamics, both at the regional and international level, demands that instead of adopting a policy of pitting one against the other, Nepal should engage both India and China by taking into account their genuine security concerns. Moreover, it is in Nepal's interest to take advantage of the economic rise of its neighbours rather than depending on countries from other regions.

*

NOTES

1. Deepak Adhikari, "With an Eye to India and Tibet, China Courts Nepal," *Time*, 29 March 2011, at http://www.time.com/time/world/article/0,8599,2061794,00.html# ixzz1rXLzW7 AHACCESSE (accessed on 25 October 2013).
2. *Economic Survey* (fiscal year 2010/11), Vol. I, July 2011, Ministry of Finance, Government of Nepal.
3. "Interview with Zheng Xianglin", *ekantipur*, 12 June 2007. Sudheer Sharma interviewed Zheng Xianglin, Chinese Ambassador to Nepal, at http://www.ekantipur.com/2007/06/12/oped/interview-with-zheng-xianglin/112467.html (accessed on 25 October 2013).

APPENDICES

APPENDIX-I

Road Network of Nepal, Proposed Dry Ports by China, Transit Points at India–Nepal Border

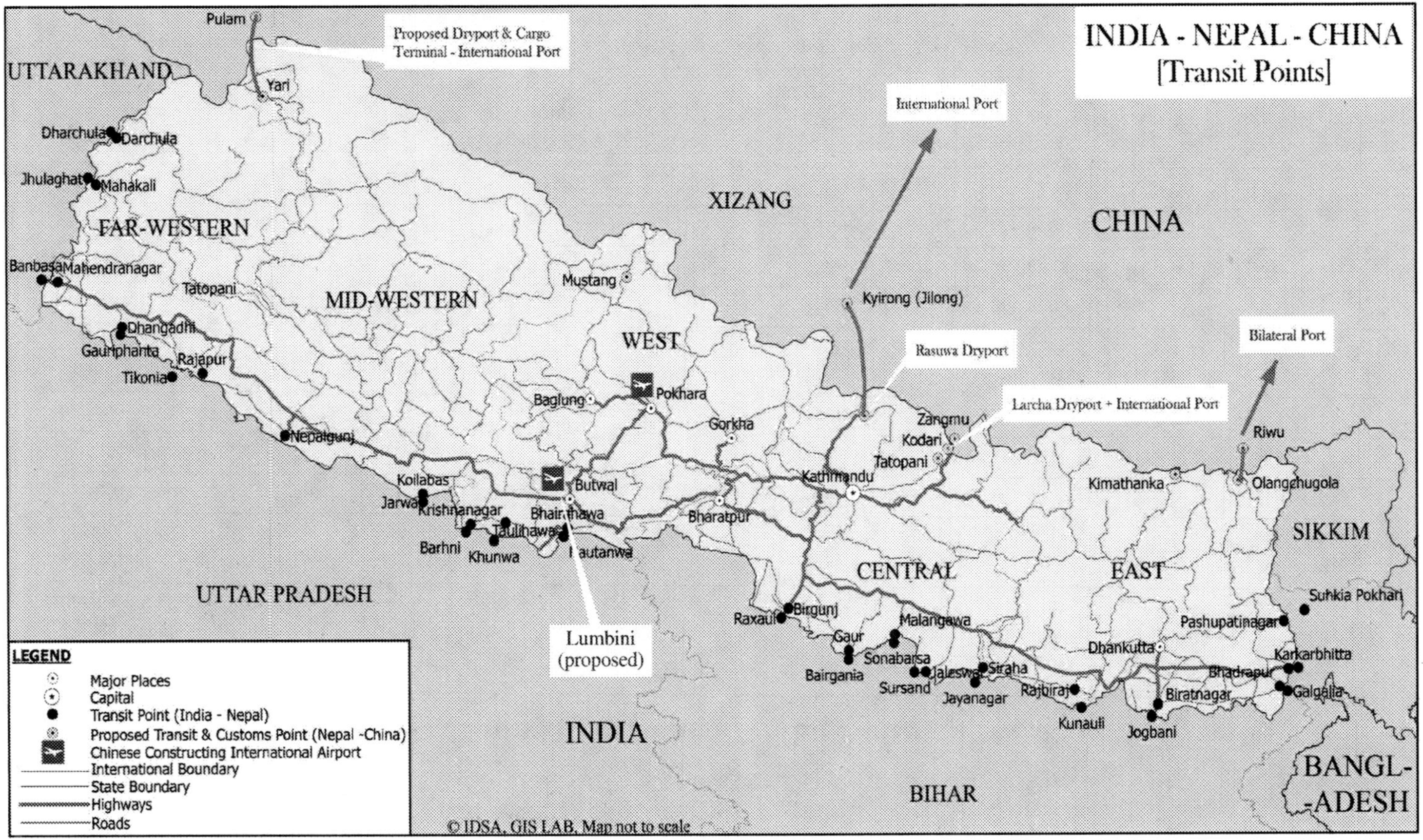

Source: Compiled by author from English media published from Nepal, India and China.

APPENDIX-II

Chinese Engagements in Hydro Projects in Nepal

Project/ River	*Location/District*	*Estimated Cost*	*JV/Direct*	*Capacity*	*Project status*
Upper Marshyangdi Hydro Electricity Project 'A' (UMHEP)	Bhulbhule VDC, Lamjung	$138 million	Sino Hydro Sagarmatha Power Company-JV	50 MW	To be Completed by 2015
Kulekhani III Hydroelectricity Project (KTHEP)-Reservoir type	Bhaise-6 of Makawanpur	NPR 1.08-billion contract in 2008	Sino Hydro got contract from NEA	14 MW	To be completed December 2011
Sunkoshi			grant assistance	10MW	
Trishuli-3A			soft loan	61MW	
Nalsyaugad			Chinese aid	400MW	
Trishuli 2			Hydrochina Corporation on contract for construction	102MW	
UpperTamakoshi			Chinese contractors are involved	456MW	
Chamelia			Chinese contractors are involved	30MW	
Lower Indrawati			Chinese contractors are involved	4.5MW	
Madi			Chinese contractors are involved	20MW	
West Seti Reservoir type	River Seti/South Western region	US$ 1.6b	Joint venture between Three Gorges International Corporation and NEA	750 MW	Yet get Parliament approval

Source: Compiled by author from English media published from Nepal, India and China.

APPENDIX-III

Sino-Nepalese Treaty of Peace and Friendship, Kathmandu, April 1960

THE Chairman of the People's Republic of China and His Majesty the king of Nepal, desiring to maintain and further develop peace and friendship between the People's Republic of China and the Kingdom of Nepal.

CONVINCED that the strengthening of good-neighborly relations and friendly co-operation between the People's Republic of China and the Kingdom of Nepal is in accordance with the fundamental interests of the peoples of the two countries and conducive to the consolidation of peace in Asia and the world,

HAVE decided for this purpose to conclude the present Treaty in accordance with the Five Principles of peaceful co-existence jointly affirmed by the two countries, and have appointed as their respective Plenipotentiaries:

The Chairman of the People's Republic of China:
Premier Chou En-lai of the State Council,

His Majesty the king of Nepal:
Prime Minister Bishweshwar Prasad Koirala.

THE above-mentioned Plenipotentiaries,

HAVING examined each other's credentials and found them in good and due form,

HAVE agreed upon the following:

Article I

The Contracting Parties recognize and respect the independence, sovereignty and territorial integrity of each other.

Article II

The Contracting Parties will maintain and develop peaceful and friendly relations between the People's Republic of China and the Kingdom of Nepal. They undertake to settle all disputes between them by mean of peaceful negotiation.

Article III

The Contracting Parties agree to develop and further strengthen the economic and cultural ties between the two countries in a spirit of friendship and co-operation, in accordance with the principles of equality and mutual benefit and of non-interference in each other's internal affairs.

Article IV

Any difference or dispute arising out of the interpretation or application of the present Treaty shall be settled by negotiation through normal diplomatic channel.

Article V

This present Treaty is subject to ratification and the instruments of ratification will be exchanged in Peking as soon as possible.

The present Treaty will come into force immediately on the exchange of the instruments of ratification1 and will remain in force for a period of ten years.

Unless either of the Contracting Parties gives to the other notice in writing to terminate the Treaty at least one year before the expiration of this period, it will remain in force without any specified time limit, subject to the right of either of the Contracting Parties to terminate it by giving to the other in writing a year's notice of its intention to do so.

DONE in duplicate in Kathmandu on the twenty-eighth day of April 1960, in the Chinese, Nepali and English languages, all texts being equally authentic.

Plenipotentiary of the People's Republic of China

Sd/-

CHOU EN-LAI

Plenipotentiary of the Kingdom of Nepal

Sd/-

B.P.KOIRALA

APPENDIX-IV

Treaty of Peace and Friendship Between the Government of India and the Government of Nepal

Kathmandu, 31 JULY 1950

The Government of India and the Government of Nepal, recognising the ancient ties which have happily existed between the two countries; Desiring still further to strengthen and develop these ties and to perpetuate peace between the two countries; Have resolved therefore to enter into a Treaty of Peace and Friendship with each other, and have, for this purpose, appointed as their plenipotentiaries the following persons, namely,

The Government of India
His Excellency Shri Chandreshwar Prasad Narain Singh,
Ambassador of India in Nepal.

The Government of Nepal
Mohun Shamsher Jang Bahadur Rana,
Maharaja, Prime Minister and Supreme Commander-in-Chief of Nepal,

who having examined each other's credentials and found them good and in due form have agreed as follows:

Article 1

There shall be everlasting peace and friendship between the Government of India and the Government of Nepal. The two Governments agree mutually to acknowledge and respect the complete sovereignty, territorial integrity and independence of each other.

Article 2

The two Governments hereby undertake to inform each other of any serious friction or misunderstanding with any neighbouring State likely to cause any breach in the friendly relations subsisting between the two Governments.

Article 3

In order to establish and maintain the relations referred to in Article 1 the two Governments agree to continue diplomatic relations with each other by means of representatives with such staff as is necessary for the due performance of their functions. The representatives and such of their staff as may be agreed upon shall enjoy such diplomatic privileges and immunities as are customarily granted by international law on a reciprocal basis: Provided that in no case shall these be less than those granted to persons of a similar status of any other State having diplomatic relations with either Government.

Article 4

The two Governments agree to appoint Consuls-General, Consuls, Vice-Consuls and other consular agents, who shall reside in towns, ports and other places in each other's territory as may be agreed to. Consuls-General, Consuls, Vice-Consuls and consular agents shall be provided with exequaturs or other valid authorization of their appointment. Such exequatur or authorization is liable to be withdrawn by the country which issued it, if considered necessary. The reasons for the withdrawal shall be indicated wherever possible. The persons mentioned above shall enjoy on a reciprocal basis all the rights, privileges, exemptions and immunities that are accorded to persons of corresponding status of any other State.

Article 5

The Government of Nepal shall be free to import, from or through the territory of India, arms, ammunition or warlike material and equipment necessary for the security of Nepal. The procedure for giving effect to this arrangement shall be worked out by the two Governments acting in consultation.

Article 6

Each Government undertakes, in token of the neighbourly friendship between India and Nepal, to give to the nationals of the other, in its territory, national treatment with regard to participation in industrial and economic development of such territory and to the grant of concessions and contracts relating to such development.

Article 7

The Governments of India and Nepal agree to grant, on reciprocal basis, to the nationals of one country in the territories of the other the same privileges in the matter of residence, ownership of property, participation in trade and commerce, movement and other privileges of a similar nature.

Article 8

So far as matters dealt with herein are concerned, this Treat: cancels all previous Treaties, agreements, and engagements entered into on behalf of India between the British Government and the Government of Nepal.

Article 9

This Treaty shall come into force from the date of signature by both Governments.

Article 10

This Treaty shall remain in force until it is terminated by either party by giving one year's notice.

DONE in duplicate at Kathmandu this 31st day of July 1950.

Chandreshwar Prasad Narain Singh
For the Government of India.
(Signed)

Mohun Shamsher Jang Bahadur Rana,
For the Government of Nepal
(Signed)

APPENDIX-V

Basic Operating Guidelines agreed to by Undersigned Agencies in Nepal

Based on principles agreed internationally and in Nepal, we the undersigned have adopted the following Basic Operating Guidelines for all development and, if necessary, humanitarian assistance in Nepal.

1. We are in Nepal to contribute to improvements in the quality of life of the people of Nepal. Our assistance focuses on reducing poverty, meeting basic needs and enabling communities to become self-sufficient.
2. We work through the freely expressed wishes of local communities, and we respect the dignity of people, their culture, religion and customs.
3. We provide assistance to the poor and marginalized people of Nepal, regardless of where they live and who they are. Priorities for assistance are based on need alone, and not on any political, ethnic or religious agenda.
4. We ensure that our assistance is transparent and we involve poor people and their communities in the planning, management and implementation of programmes. We are accountable to those whom we seek to assist and to those providing the resources.
5. We seek to ensure that our assistance tackles discrimination and social exclusion, most notably based on gender, ethnicity, caste and religion.
6. We recruit staff on the basis of suitability and qualification for the job, and not on the basis of political or any other considerations.
7. We do not accept our staff and development partners being subjected to violence abduction, harassment or intimidation, or being threatened in any manner.
8. We do not work where staffs are forced to compromise core values or principles.
9. We do not accept our assistance being used for any military, political or sectarian purposes.
10. We do not make contributions to political parties and do not make any forced contributions in cash or kind.

11. Our equipment, supplies and facilities are not used for purposes other than those stated in our programme objectives. Our vehicles are not used to transport persons or goods that have no direct connection with the development programme. Our vehicles do not carry armed or uniformed personnel.
12. We do not tolerate the theft, diversion or misuse of development or humanitarian supplies. Unhindered access of such supplies is essential.
13. We urge all those concerned to allow full access by development and humanitarian personnel to all people in need of assistance, and to make available, as far as possible, all necessary facilities for their operations, and to promote the safety, security and freedom of movement of such personnel.
14. We expect and encourage all actors concerned to comply strictly with international humanitarian principles and human rights law.

ANNEX TO THE BASIC OPERATING GUIDELINES

Promotion of Diversity and Inclusion in Development Activities

The International Community recognises that more is needed to promote the rights and inclusion of indigenous peoples and other disadvantaged groups.

The ILO Convention 169 stresses the *distinctive contributions* of indigenous and tribal peoples to the social harmony of humankind. The convention recognizes consultation, participation, mutual respect and equality as fundamental principles for its implementation and for development in general.

Convention 169 (Article 6(b)) requires governments to establish means by which these peoples can freely participate, to at least the same extent as other sectors of the population, at all levels of decision-making in elective institutions and administrative and other bodies responsible for policies and programmes which concern them.

It also requires governments to adopt special measures to ensure *equal opportunities* and equal treatment in employment for men and women from indigenous and tribal peoples.

The Government has established a task force on the implementation of ILO Convention 169 with the participation of NFDIN and NEFIN, amongst others. This task force has drafted a national action plan. The international community will support the implementation of this plan once it has been approved by the Government of Nepal.

The ILO Convention 169 promotes a peaceful approach. Any resort to violent means, threat or coercion would breach its spirit and impair the rights and freedom of others.

Whereas, ILO convention 169 stipulates that "peoples shall have the right to retain their own customs and institutions, where these are not incompatible with fundamental rights defined by the national legal system and with internationally recognized human rights", it then continues to state that "Procedures shall be established, whenever necessary, to resolve conflicts which may arise in the application of this principle".

The implementation of Human Rights protected by and enshrined in international law cannot be claimed by resorting to violence threats and coercion.

In Nepal, the signatories of the Basic Operating Guidelines (BOGs) are committed to strive for diversity within their organizations and development programmes.

Through the Basic Operating Guidelines these development agencies are committed to Inclusion, Accountability, Transparency and Impartiality.

These development agencies recruit staff on the basis of suitability for the job and are committed to promoting workforce diversity. The signatories of the Basic Operating Guidelines do not recruit staff on the basis of political or other influence.

Furthermore, the UN Country Team of Nepal has signed its own Declaration of Joint Principles of Workforce Diversity and is committed to the inclusion of historically excluded groups and regions to professional opportunities within the UN system.

For further information and reference

For more information on the implementation of ILO 169 in Nepal, the authority to be contacted is: Ministry of Local Development, Government of Nepal.

Select Bibliography

Acharya, Alka, *China & India: Politics of Incremental Engagement*, Har-Anand publications Pvt. Ltd, New Delhi, 2008.

Agrawal, Govind Ram and Rana, Jai P., *Nepal and Non-alignment*, Centre for Economic Development and Administration, Tribhuvan University, Kathmandu, 1982.

Agrawal, Govind Ram, Rajeshwar Acharya and Pustun Pradhan, *Fundamentals of Nepalese Foreign Policy*, Centre for Economic Development and Administration, Tribhuvan University, Kathmandu, 1985.

Ahmed, Ali, Jagannath P. Panda and Prashant K. Singh (eds), *Towards a New Asian Order*, Shipra Publications, New Delhi, 2012.

Aitchison, C. U., (compiler), *Collection of Treaties, Engagements and Sanads relating to India and Neighbouring Countries: Eastern Turkistan, Tibet, Nepal, Bhutan and Siam*, Mittal Publications, Delhi, 1983.

Ali, S. Mahmud, *Cold War in the High Himalayas: The USA, China, and South Asia in the 1950s*, St. Martin's Press, New York, 1999.

Arpi Claude, *India and her Neighbourhood: A French Observer's Views*, Har-Anand Publications Pvt. Ltd, New Delhi, 2005.

Bahadur, Kalim and Mahendra P. Lama (eds), *New Perspectives on India-Nepal Relations*, Har-Anand Publications, New Delhi, 1995.

Baral, Lok Raj (ed.), *Looking to the Future: Indo-Nepal Relations in Perspective*, Anmol Publications, New Delhi, 1996.

____ (ed.), *Nepal: Quest for Participatory Democracy*, Adroit Publishers, New Delhi, 2006.

____, *Nepal: Facets of Maoist Insurgency*, Adroit Publishers, New Delhi, 2006.

____, *The Politics of Balanced Interdependence: Nepal and SAARC*, Sterling Publishers Pvt Ltd., New Delhi, 1988.

____, *The Regional Paradox: Essays in Nepali and South Asian Affairs*, Adroit Publishers, Delhi, 2000.

Barston, R.P. (ed.), *Other Powers: Studies in the Foreign Policies of Small States*, George Allen and Unwin Ltd., London, 1973.

Basnet, Purna, 'China's Success,' *Himal*, Kathmandu, April 2011.

Bauwens, Werner, Armand Clesse, and Olav F. Knudsen, (eds), *Small States and the Security Challenge in the New Europe,* Brassey's, London, 1996.

Bhasin, Avtar Singh (ed.), *Nepal–India, Nepal-China Relations: Documents 1947-2005,* Geetika Publishers, New Delhi, 2005.

____, *Nepal's Relations with India and China: Documents 1947-1992,* Volume 1-2, Siba Exim, Delhi, 1994.

Bhattarai, Rajan and Geja Sharma Wagle (eds), *Emerging Security Challenges of Nepal,* Nepal Institute for Policy Studies (NIPS), Kathmandu, 2010.

Buzan, Barry and Ole Waever, *Regions and Powers: The Structure of International Security,* Cambridge University Press, New York, 2003.

Campbell, Ivan, "China and conflict-affected states: Between Principle and Pragmatism (Nepal)," Saferworld, January 2012.

Chanakya, "China's Policy in Nepal," 21 October 2010, http://www.irgamag.com/analysis/neighborhood-watch/item/773-chinas-policy-in-nepal

Chauhan, R.S., *Nepal's Policy of Neutrality,* University of Rajasthan, Jaipur, 1968.

Chay, John and Thomas E, Ross, (eds), *Buffer States in World Politics,* Westview Press, Boulder, 1986.

Chengappa, Bidanda M., *Islamisation, Army, Foreign Policy,* APH publishing Corporation, New Delhi, 2004.

Chung, Tan (ed.), *Across the Himalayan Gap: An Indian Quest for Understanding China,* Indira Gandhi National Centre for Arts, New Delhi, 1998.

Clarke, Colin and Tony Payne, *Politics, Security and Development in Small States,* Allen & Unwin, London, 1987.

Commonwealth Secretariat, *Vulnerability, Small States in the Global Society,* London, 1999.

Dahiya, Rumel and Behuria, Ashok K. (eds) *India's Neighbourhood: Challenges in the Next Two Decades,* Institute for Defence Studies and Analyses with Pentagon Press, New Delhi, 2012.

Dastidar, Mollica, *Understanding Nepal: Muslims in a Plural Society,* Har-Anand Publications, New Delhi, 2007.

Dharamdasani, M.D. (ed.), *Democratic Nepal,* Shalimar Publishing House, Varanasi, 1992.

Dhungel, Dwarika N. and Santa B. Pun, (eds), *Nepal-India Water Relationship: Challenges,* Springer, New York, 2009.

Einsiedel, Sebastian v., David M. Malone, Suman Pradhan (eds), *Nepal in Transition: From People's War to Fragile Peace,* Cambridge University Press, New York, 2012.

Gaige, Frederick H. *Regionalism and National Unity in Nepal*, Vikas Publishing House, Delhi, 1974.

Ganguly, Sumit, and Thompson, William R., (eds), *Asian Rivalries: Conflict, Escalation, and Limitations on Two-level Games*, Stanford University Press, Stanford, 2011.

Ghoble, T. R., *China-Nepal Relations and India*, Deep and Deep Publications, New Delhi, 1986.

Ghosh, Partha S., *Cooperation and Conflict in South Asia*, Manohar Publishers, New Delhi, 1989.

Gulati, M.N., *Tibetan Wars through Sikkim, Bhutan and Nepal*, Manas Publications, New Delhi, 2003.

Gupta, Virendra, Sumita Kumar, Vishal Chandra, (eds), *India's Neighbourhood: Challenges Ahead*, Institute for Defence Studies and Analyses, 2008.

Hafiz, Abdul M. and Abdur Rob Khan (eds), *Security of Small States*, University Press Limited, Dhaka, 1987.

Handle, Michael, *Weak States in the International System*, Frank Cass & Co. Ltd., London, 1990.

Holslag, Jonathan, *China and India: Prospects for Peace*, Columbia University Press, New York, 2010.

Hutt, Michael (ed.), *Himalayan 'People's War': Nepal's Maoist Rebellion*, Hurst & Co., London, 2004.

Inbar, Efraim and Gabriel Sheffer (eds), *National Security of Small States in a Changing World*, Frank Cass, London, 1997.

Institute of Foreign Affairs, *Nepal's Relations with United States of America*, Kathmandu, 2004.

Jain, Rajendra K. (ed.), *US-South Asian Relations 1947-1982*, Radiant Publishers, New Delhi, 1983.

Jain, Rajendra K., *Soviet-South Asian Relations 1947-1978*, Radiant Publishers, New Delhi, 1978.

Jha, Hari Bansh (ed.), *Duty-Free Border Trade and Special Economic Zone between Nepal and India* Modern Printing Press, Kathmandu, 1995.

____, *Nepal-India Border Relations*, Centre for Economic and Technical Studies, Kathmandu, 1995.

____, *Economy of Terai Region of Nepal: Prospects for its Sustainable Development*, Centre for Economic and Technical Studies, Kathmandu, 2010.

Jha, Shree Krishna, *Uneasy Partners: India and Nepal in the Post-Colonial Era*, Manas Publications, New Delhi, 1975.

Kalegama, Saman (ed.), *Foreign Aid in South Asia: The Emerging Scenario*, Sage Publications, New Delhi, 2012.

Kapur, Ashok, *India and the South Asian Strategic Triangle*, Routledge, Oxon, 2011.

Khadka, Narayan, *Foreign Aid and Foreign Policy: Major Powers and Nepal,* Vikas Publishing House, New Delhi, 1997.

Khanal, Ajaya Bhadra, "Nepal not part of China's strategic gateway", *The Himalayan Times*, 2 September 2012, http://www.thehimalayantimes.com/fullNews.php?headline=Nepal+not+part+of+China's+strategic+gateway&News ID=345852

Khatri, Sridhar K. (ed.), *Regional Security in South Asia*, Centre for Nepal and Asian Studies, Kathmandu, 1987.

Kodikara, Shelton U. (ed.), *External Compulsions of South Asian Politics*, Sage Publications, New Delhi, 1993.

Kondapalli, Srikanth, and Emi Mifune, (eds), *China and its Neighbours*, Pentagon Press, New Delhi, 2010.

Lawoti, Mahendra and Anup K. Pahari, (eds), *Maoist Insurgency in Nepal: Revolution in the Twenty-First Century*, Routledge, London, 2010.

Leo, Rose E. and John T. Scholz, *Nepal: Profile of a Himalayan Kingdom,* Select Book Service Syndicate, New Delhi, 1980.

Leo, Rose E., *Nepal: Strategy for Survival*, University of California Press, Berkeley, 1971.

Malik, Mohan, *China and India: Great Power Rivals*, First Forum Press, Boulder, 2011.

Malone, David M., *Does the Elephant Dance? Contemporary Indian Foreign Policy*, Oxford University Press, New York, 2011.

Manandhar, Vijay Kumar, *A Comprehensive History of Nepal-China Relations Up to 1955 A.D.*, Pinnacle Technology, 2004.

____, *Cultural and Political Aspects of Nepal-China Relations*, Adroit Publishers, Delhi, 2007.

McGarr, Paul M., *The Cold War in South Asia: Britain, the United States and the Indian Subcontinent, 1945-1965*, Cambridge University Press, Cambridge, 2013.

Mehta, Ashok K., *Royal Nepal Army: Meeting the Maoist Challenge*, Rupa and Company, New Delhi, 2005.

Mihaly, Eugene Bramer, *Foreign Aid and Politics in Nepal: A Case Study*, Himal Books, Lalitpur, 2003.

Ministry of Foreign Affairs, Nepal, *Report on Nepal's Foreign Affairs 1990-93*, Kathmandu, 1993.

Mohapatra, Anil Kumar, *Small States in South Asia: A Security Perspective of the Himalayan States,* Panchashila, Bhubaneswar, 2008.

Moller, Bjorn, *Non-Offensive Defence as a Strategy for Small States*, Centre for Peace and Research Conflict, Copenhagen, 1993.
Muni, S.D. (ed.), *Nepal: An Assertive Monarchy*, Chetana Publications, New Delhi, 1977.
Muni, S.D. and Tan Tai Yong (eds), *A Resurgent China: South Asian Perspectives*, Routledge, New Delhi, 2011.
Muni, S.D., *Foreign Policy of Nepal*, National Publication House, Delhi, 1973.
——, *Impact of the King on the Foreign Policy of Nepal*, University of Rajasthan, Jaipur, 1968.
——, *India and Nepal: A Challenging Relationship*, Konark, Delhi, 1992.
——, *India's Foreign Policy: The Democracy Dimension*, Foundation Books, New Delhi, 2009.
Narayan, Shriman, *India and Nepal: An Exercise in Open Diplomacy*, Popular Prakashan, Bombay, 1975.
Neuman, Stephanie G. (ed.), *Small States and Segmented Societies: National Political Integration in a Global Environment*, Praeger, New York, 1976.
Onesto, Li, *Dispatches from the People's War in Nepal*, Pluto Press, London, 2005.
O'Reilly, Brendan P., 'Nepal Claims Strategic Middle Ground', *Asia Times*, 31 July 2013.
Orton, Anna, *India's Borderland Disputes: China, Pakistan, Bangladesh and Nepal*, Epitome Books, New Delhi, 2010.
Pandey, Nishchal Nath (ed.), *Nepal-China Relations*, Institute of Foreign Affairs, Kathmandu, 2005.
——, *Nepal's Maoist Movement and Implications for India and China*, Manohar, New Delhi, 2005.
——, *New Nepal: The Fault Lines*, Sage Publications, New Delhi, 2010.
Pant, Harsh V., *China's Rising Global Profile: The Great Power Tradition*, Sussex Academic Press, Eastbourne, 2011.
Pant, Prem Kumari, and Shanker Thapa, (eds), *Buddhism: The Icon of Cultural Linkage with China*, Nepal China Society, Kathmandu, 2010.
Parajulee, Ramjee P., *The Democratic transition in Nepal*, Rowman & Littlefield publishers, INC, Lanham, 2000.
Pradhan, Bishwa, *Diplomatic Strategy for Nepal*, Durga Devi Pradhan, Kathmandu, 2003.
Prasad, Shashi Bhushan, *China Factor in Indo-Nepalese Relations 1955-72: A Study of Linkage Phenomena*, Commonwealth Publishers, New Delhi, 1989.

Prys, Miriam, *Redefining Regional Power in International Relations: Indian and South African Perspectives*, Routledge, Oxon, 2012.

Prakash, Raj A., *Four Years in Pakistan*, Nabeen Publications, Kathmandu, 2006.

____, *Maoists in the Land of Buddha: An Analytical Study of the Maoist Insurgency in Nepal*, Nirala Publications, Delhi, 2004.

Rajbahak, Ram Prasad, *Nepal-India Open Border: A Bond of Shared Aspirations*, Lancer Publishers, New Delhi, 1992.

Ramakant (ed.), *China and South Asia*, South Asian Publishers, New Delhi, 1988.

Ramakant, *Nepalese Foreign Policy and China*, All-India Seminar on Foreign Policy of South Asian states, University of Rajasthan, Jaipur, February 1-6, 1968.

____, *Nepal-China and India*, Abhinav Publications, New Delhi, 1976.

Ray, Hemen, *China's Strategy in Nepal*, Radiant Publishers, New Delhi, 1983.

Sandhyarani, Sanasam (ed.), *India-Nepal Relations: Historical, Cultural and Political Perspective*, Vij Books India, New Delhi, 2011.

Schou, August and Arne Olav Brundtland (eds), *Small States in International Relations*, John Wiley & Sons, New York, 1971.

Shaha, Rishikesh, *New Directions in Nepal-India Relations*, Nirala Publications, Delhi, 1995.

Shreshtha, Badri Prasad, *SAARC: An Economic Perspective*, Centre for Nepal and Asian Studies, Tribhuvan University, Kathmandu, 1988.

Shrestha, Buddhi Narayan, *Border Management of Nepal*, Bhumichitra Co. P. Ltd., Kathmandu, 2003.

Shrestha, Sita, *Nepal and the United Nations*, Sindhu Publications, New Delhi, 1974.

Sijapati, Megan Adamson, *Islamic Revival in Nepal: Religion and a New Nation,* Routledge, London, 2011.

Singh, Arun Kumar and Avnindra Dutt Mishra, *Indo-Nepal Economic Relations*, Regal Publications, New Delhi, 2008.

Singh, Rajkumar, *Global Dimension of Indo-Nepal Political Relations, Post Independence,* Gyan Publishing House, New Delhi, 2009.

Singh, Rohit (ed.), *China and India in Asia Power Politics*, Vij Books India, New Delhi, 2011.

Singh, Swaran, *China-South Asia: Issues, Equations and Policies*, Lancer, New Delhi, 2003.

Subedi, Surya P., *Dynamics of Foreign Policy and Law: A Study of Indo-Nepal Relations*, Oxford University Press, Oxford, 2005.

Thapa, Deepak and Bandita Sijapati, *Kingdom Under Siege: Nepal's Maoist Insurgency, 1996-2003*, Zed Books, London, 2005.

Thapa, Manjushree, *Forget Kathmandu: An Elegy for Democracy*, Viking, New Delhi, 2005.

Thapliyal, Sangeeta, *Mutual Security: The Case of India-Nepal,* Lancer Publishers, New Delhi 1998.

Trivedi, Ramesh (ed.), *India's Relations with her Neighbours,* Isha Books, New Delhi, 2008.

Upadhya, Sanjay, *Nepal and the Geo-Strategic Rivalry Between China and India*, Routledge, London, 2012.

Upreti, B.C. and Ramakant (eds), *India and Nepal: Aspects of Interdependent Relations*, Kalinga Publications, Delhi, 2001.

Upreti, Bishnu Raj, *Armed Conflict and Peace Process in Nepal: The Maoist Insurgency, Past Negotiations, and Opportunities for Conflict Transformation,* Adroit Publishers, New Delhi, 2006.

Uprety, Prem R., *Nepal-Tibet Relations 1850-1930: Years of Hopes, Challenges and Frustrations,* Ratna Pustak Bhandar, Kathmandu,1998.

Vishwakarma, R.K. (ed.), *People's Power in Nepal,* Manak Publications, New Delhi, 2006.

Vital, David, *Survival of Small States: Studies in Small Power-Great Power Conflict*, Oxford University Press, London, 1971.

Warikoo, K. (ed.), *Himalayan Frontiers of India: Historical, Geo-political and Strategic Perspectives,* Routledge, Oxon, 2009.

Zhao, Suisheng, (ed.), *Chinese Foreign Policy: Pragmatism and Strategic Behaviour*, M.E. Sharpe Inc., New York, 1976.

*

Index

*